Politics of Citizenship and Migration

Series Editor
Leila Simona Talani
Department of European and International Studies
King's College London
London, UK

The *Politics of Citizenship and Migration* series publishes exciting new research in all areas of migration and citizenship studies. Open to multiple approaches, the series considers interdisciplinary as well political, economic, legal, comparative, empirical, historical, methodological, and theoretical works. Broad in its coverage, the series promotes research on the politics and economics of migration, globalization and migration, citizenship and migration laws and policies, voluntary and forced migration, rights and obligations, demographic change, diasporas, political membership or behavior, public policy, minorities, border and security studies, statelessness, naturalization, integration and citizen-making, and subnational, supranational, global, corporate, or multilevel citizenship. Versatile, the series publishes single and multi-authored monographs, short-form Pivot books, and edited volumes.

For an informal discussion for a book in the series, please contact the series editor Leila Simona Talani (leila.talani@kcl.ac.uk), or Palgrave editor Isobel Cowper-Coles (isobel.cowpercoles@palgrave.com).

This series is indexed in Scopus.

Kanishka Chowdhury

Border Rules

An Abolitionist Refusal

Kanishka Chowdhury
University of St. Thomas
Saint Paul, MN, USA

ISSN 2520-8896 ISSN 2520-890X (electronic)
Politics of Citizenship and Migration
ISBN 978-3-031-26218-0 ISBN 978-3-031-26216-6 (eBook)
https://doi.org/10.1007/978-3-031-26216-6

© The Editor(s) (if applicable) and The Author(s), under exclusive licence to Springer Nature Switzerland AG 2023

This work is subject to copyright. All rights are solely and exclusively licensed by the Publisher, whether the whole or part of the material is concerned, specifically the rights of translation, reprinting, reuse of illustrations, recitation, broadcasting, reproduction on microfilms or in any other physical way, and transmission or information storage and retrieval, electronic adaptation, computer software, or by similar or dissimilar methodology now known or hereafter developed.

The use of general descriptive names, registered names, trademarks, service marks, etc. in this publication does not imply, even in the absence of a specific statement, that such names are exempt from the relevant protective laws and regulations and therefore free for general use.

The publisher, the authors, and the editors are safe to assume that the advice and information in this book are believed to be true and accurate at the date of publication. Neither the publisher nor the authors or the editors give a warranty, expressed or implied, with respect to the material contained herein or for any errors or omissions that may have been made. The publisher remains neutral with regard to jurisdictional claims in published maps and institutional affiliations.

Cover illustration: enviromantic\gettyimages

This Palgrave Macmillan imprint is published by the registered company Springer Nature Switzerland AG.
The registered company address is: Gewerbestrasse 11, 6330 Cham, Switzerland

For Behula—sister, friend, inspiration

ACKNOWLEDGMENTS

I want to begin by acknowledging all of those who have suffered and continue to suffer the brutalities of border rules. Their struggle and their resistance inspired this book, and are—I hope—honored throughout its pages.

A significant portion of this book was written during the two-year period at the height of the coronavirus pandemic, when people across the globe were coping with its many—and sometimes overwhelming—challenges. I recognize the enormous privilege I had during this time to be in good health and to read and write and teach and work from home even as millions around the world suffered from the virus and lockdowns in various ways, including being forced to toil in unsafe conditions.

A book does not get written without institutional and financial support. Thanks to the University of St. Thomas for a sabbatical leave and a sabbatical assistance grant for the 2021–2022 academic year. Many thanks to Roxanne Kendle from the Center for Faculty Development for her immense help navigating and managing the challenges of travel during the years 2021–2022.

My work on this book has been informed by the valuable scholarship of many "border" scholars and activists. Harsha Walia's work, especially, has been formative in my thinking about borders. I have also been inspired by the work of too many others to name; however, I will mention here Justin Akers Chacón, Nicholas De Genova, Nick Estes, Greg Grandin, Daniel Immerwahr, Reece Jones, Todd Miller, and Vijay Prashad. Of course, the foundational work of many scholars—Gloria Anzaldúa, Angela Davis,

viii ACKNOWLEDGMENTS

W.E.B. Du Bois, Frantz Fanon, Stuart Hall, and Walter Rodney, to name a few—continues to inspire and inform my scholarship.

To the artists Yorch (Jorge Pérez Mendoza) and LxsDos (Christian and Ramon Cardenas) and the many others in Ciudad Juárez/El Paso whose murals are so inspiring, and to the many activists and organizations who continue to fight to resist the oppressive border rules that do so much damage to the lives of millions across the globe: I have learned much from your work, and I hope that my effort honors your courageous and imaginative attempts to create a more just world. Thanks to both Yorch and Ramon for speaking to me about their work. Finally, a big thank you to Richard Wright for introducing me to many of the murals in Ciudad Juárez, to Omar and Cristela Ríos for providing the context for Yorch's mural, and to Alex Fath of Las Americas, El Paso, for educating me about the challenges of seeking asylum.

I also want to express gratitude to my outstanding graduate research assistants, Morgan Coleman, Christine Decleene, and Cali Mellin, for their excellent research and editing skills. I benefited a great deal from their research questions and suggestions, and this book would be much weaker without their efforts and contributions. I am particularly grateful for all of Morgan's efforts in the final weeks before submission—her helping with the citations and endnotes and compiling the index at a very busy time. I also want to thank the graduate students in my "Borders" class and the students in two sections of my undergraduate class on "Refugee Writers, Refugee Lives" for their questions, insights, and spirited discussions. Their willingness to engage in complex and thought-provoking conversations in these classes gave me ample food for thought. A Master's essay project with Cali Mellin on mural art in Ciudad Juárez also offered important opportunities to discuss and reflect on that particular subject.

I am very grateful for the friendship and insights of my *Belly of the Beast* podcast comrades, Amy Finnegan, Todd Lawrence, and Ry Siggelkow. Their encouragement and intellectual comradeship have sustained me during these last few years.

To the reviewers of my sample chapters and book proposal, much gratitude for your encouraging and helpful feedback. Thank you for all the time and effort that you devoted to my project. The book is much better for your comments and scrupulous attention to theoretical questions.

Many thanks to Sarah Roughley and Isobel Cowper Cowles, my editors at Palgrave, for their wisdom, expertise, and advice during the process of publication. I also want to express my gratitude to Ruby Panigrahi, Project

ACKNOWLEDGMENTS ix

Coordinator and NirmalKumar GnanaPrakasam, Project Manager for Springer Nature for their help in making the process of delivery a smooth one and for always being so willing to answer my many questions.

I am enormously grateful also to my comrades Ericka Beckman, Beverly Best, Ariane Fischer, Peter Gardner, John Maerhofer, Courtney Maloney, Carl Martin, Henry Schwarz, and Paul Stasi for friendship and intellectual solidarity and inspiration. A special thanks to Bret Benjamin and Barbara Foley for being such fantastic friends and mentors. I have learned so much from the two of you. Also, thanks to my *Black Reconstruction* reading group, Kamika Bennett, Kristin Bergen, Curtis Browne, Paola Del Toro, Reuben Kadushin, Tahseen Kazi, Pat Keeton, Jules Kerman, Anthony O'Brien, and Joe Ramsey for some marvelous discussions about Marx, Du Bois, and abolition democracy.

A huge thank you to some special folks for their support over many years: much gratitude to Amy, Doug, Sarah, Nik, Emily, James, Arthur, Akshar, Jenny, Lucy, Olga, Cathy, Fernando, Heather, Carmela, Jonelle, Padmaja, UB, Dina, Jennifer, Irene, Pao, Sonia, and Juli for continuing friendship; to Alexis and Brett, for inspiration and warmth; to Sal and Theresa for companionship, kindness, and generosity—especially during the pandemic; to Andy, Mary Lou, Young, Ray, Joan, and Parvati for always being there for intellectual and emotional sustenance; to Pratap, Rakesh, Ronny, and Shanu for camaraderie, laughs, and memories; to Todd and Lucia for sustaining warmth, reassuring comradeship, and stimulating discussions; and to John, Erika, Lucien, and Elias for unfailing support, enduring affection, and inspiring optimism.

My family continues to be the greatest source of comfort and warmth to me, and all that I do is sustained by their love. It's been many years since the death of my father, but he continues to inspire me with his intellectual rigor and political wisdom and commitment. Although my mother passed away in January 2021, she remains in my heart, guiding me and inspiring me with her love of history, politics, and literature. I hear her voice gently challenging me when I think I have all the answers. Many thanks also to Clarence—I so appreciate your continuing encouragement and support, wholeheartedly given even while your health has been declining. To my niece, Inaya, thanks for being such an optimistic presence in my life. I'm grateful for your friendship and affection. An immense debt of gratitude to my sister, Behula, to whom this book is dedicated with much love and thankfulness. You continue to inspire me with, your persistence and courage in the face of adversity; your lifelong pursuit of knowledge;

X   ACKNOWLEDGMENTS

your unflagging enthusiasm for travel and adventure; and your ability to balance discipline and integrity with your *joie de vivre*. Writing this book would not have been possible without your steadfast support—including through the most difficult of times.

To Susan, my companion and comrade, mere words on the page cannot mark my immense gratitude for your loving presence in my life. I cannot thank you enough for your constant encouragement—or for your astute critical appraisal of my work, especially your thoughtful insights on Yorch's mural. Thanks for the unconditional support and love. I benefit every day from your brilliance, your creative gifts, your love for learning, your curiosity about the world, your sense of adventure, your endless efforts to address the many injustices confronting us, your sense of humor, and your infinite generosity and kindness.

CONTENTS

1   Border Rules and Oppositional Currents   1

2   Border Rules: Imperialism, Race, and the Politics of Development   25

3   Theorizing Borders in the Shadow of Imperial Violence   69

4   Narrating the Border: Fluidity, Gender, and Resistance in Rabih Alemmedine's *The Wrong End of the Telescope* and Yuri Herrera's *Signs Preceding the End of the World*   105

5   Documenting the Migrant Journey in Ai Weiwei's *Human Flow* and Diego Quemada-Díez's *La Jaula de Oro*   139

6   Visualizing Borders: M.I.A.'s "Borders" and Mural Art in Ciudad Juárez and El Paso   177

7   A Borderless World: Abolition Democracy and the Politics of Refusal   223

Index   249

LIST OF FIGURES

Fig. 6.1 Yorch, Under the Bridge/Bajo el Puente, View from the
Bridge, 1 May, 2022   202

Fig. 6.2 LxsDos, "Sister Cities/Ciudades Hermanas," 3 May 2022   211

Fig. 6.3 LxsDos, "Sister Cities/Ciudades Hermanas," Lattice Detail,
3 May 2002   212

CHAPTER 1

Border Rules and Oppositional Currents

Description of the Project

This book, *Border Rules: An Abolitionist Refusal,* examines both border policies and oppositional narratives of "the border," demonstrating that it is not merely a line of territorial control but also a set of social relations shaped by persistent, racially differentiated colonial structures and, more recently, by neoliberal modes of accumulation. Marx's comment about capital offers a helpful analogy: "*capital is not a thing, it is a definite social relation of production* pertaining to a particular historical social formation, which simply takes the form of a thing and gives this thing a specific social character" (*Capital Vol. III,* 953, my emphasis).[1] Perhaps it is not too much of a stretch to claim the same for a border: that it, too, is *not a thing, but a set of social relations.*

This book explores these social relations in two ways: initially (and briefly) in analyses of the official border policies and dominant representations of migrants and the border in the present, informed, of course, by the long history of these policies and representations, and secondly, in

---

[1] Marx goes on to emphasize the dialectical force of these relations: "Like all its forerunners, the capitalist production process proceeds under specific material conditions, which are, however, also the bearers of specific social relations which the individuals enter into in the process of reproducing their life. Those conditions, like these social relations, are on the one hand the presuppositions of the capitalist production process, on the other its results and creations; they are both produced by it and reproduced by it" (957).

© The Author(s), under exclusive license to Springer Nature Switzerland AG 2023
K. Chowdhury, *Border Rules,* Politics of Citizenship and Migration, https://doi.org/10.1007/978-3-031-26216-6_1

more detail, in analyses of oppositional accounts and narratives in a variety of cultural forms in response to two specific border zones, US–Mexico and the EU–Southern Mediterranean, in a specific time period, 2011–2021.

In Chaps. 2 and 3, which explore official policies and dominant representations, I argue that the trajectories and complexities of these social relations are fundamental and enforced through the dialectic of border rules. These rules comprise not only actual state policies and forms of governance but also a range of representations, all of which create bordered subjects.[2] Some of these border rules are produced in concrete ways through the passage of xenophobic immigration laws, the construction of walls, fences, and detention centers, and the imposition of working and living conditions that are designed to keep populations in positions of subservience.[3] Other rules operate in less overt forms through the production and circulation of dominant representations of bordered subjects, labeled as "migrants," "refugees," "asylum seekers," "detainees," and/or "deportees." These representations attempt to position subjects as, say, criminals or trafficking victims, or in specific racialized or gendered ways. A dialectic operates: such representations, created by official policies, in turn influence official policies—reproduce, enhance, and amend existing

[2] For one account of the ways in which these subjects are produced, please see Sandro Mezzadra and Brett Neilson's *Border as Method, or, the Multiplication of Labor.*

[3] In 2003, shortly after the invasion of Iraq, and in the aftermath of the catastrophic refugee crisis of the Balkan wars, the Asian Dub Foundation put out their single "Fortress Europe." Their vision of the future (2022) has come to be:
"2022, a new European order /
Robot guards patrolling the border
/ Cybernetic dogs are getting closer and closer /
Armored cars and immigration officers /
A burning village in Kosovo /
You bombed it out, now you're telling us go home
/ Machine guns strut on the cliffs of Dover /
Heads down, people look out, we're going over."

The uncanny precision with which the group some two decades back imagines the militarization of the border in our times and forecasts the rise of the technology of surveillance is uncanny. The "burning village" in Kosovo has now been replaced by burnt out cities and villages from Yemen and Iraq to Syria and Afghanistan. And the millions of asylum seekers who have been turned away from European shores may well utter these words: "You bombed it out, now you're telling us go home." The "new European order" now includes walls and fences, detention centers and camps, and boats and planes to turn away and imprison those who seek refuge from the bombings. The borderless new Europe is characterized by its opposite: a Europe defined by its borders.

border rules, at times creating even more coercive policies or ways of regulating populations in a more effective manner, materially restricting, surveilling, and dispossessing specific social groups. These representations also reinforce existing ideas about citizenship, legality, and sovereignty—and create new ones. Moreover, in this back-and-forth dialectical process, the bordered subject may be reproduced or reconstructed as well. The fluidity of this process certainly makes border rules particularly effective; however, as I will argue at the end of this book, it also leaves the idea of the border open to reinvention—and even to abolition.

Early in the book, I not only explore the dialectic of these border rules and situate my work amid other studies of the border; I also attempt to lay bare an essential element of these rules: how they perform certain practices of invisibility. What might appear on the surface to be an ordinary enactment of a law, or an innocuous image of an individual migrant, effectively obscures the constitutive social relations that extract value from people and authorize forms of racial hierarchy and exclusion. These harmful relations are obfuscated by practices that work at two levels: One practice normalizes these rules within the juridical language of sovereign states, thus using existing discourses of rights and justice to frame border matters while obscuring the real mechanisms of repression and state violence, the oppressive demands of the commodity market, the financialization of everyday life, and the enforcement of labor discipline. A second practice positions migrants in particular ways, as, say, victims or disruptors of sovereign space, eliding the migrants' connections to their role within the transnational circuits of capital, either as potentially productive workers, as contingent movable units of labor, or as disposable surplus labor. In this early section of this book, then, I attempt to demystify these relations and make visible the politics of capital accumulation and the racialized social arrangements that inform and produce border subjects and the space of the border.[4]

---

[4] It goes without saying that intrinsic to the ideology and the political economy of racialized rule as a mode of governance are the dynamics of gender and sexual violence. I will discuss this subject in greater detail in Chaps. 4, 5, and 6. Also, please see Rana M. Jaleel's *The Work of Rape*, Kerry F. Crawford's *Wartime Sexual Violence: From Silence to Condemnation of a Weapon of War*, Sara Meger's "The Fetishization of Sexual Violence in International Security," or Michelle Téllez's "Border Crossings and Sexual Conquest in the Age of Neoliberalism in the Sonoran Desert" for specific details on these intersections.

In the process of making visible the regimes of capital accumulation and the ways in which relations of dominance are forged, I highlight the forms of "development" politics imposed on countries of the Global South, which, in turn, fuel the attendant project of continuing primitive accumulation.[5] I also pinpoint how and why border relations allow capital to benefit from both the movement of labor and its entrapment in particular economic zones. I then attempt to distinguish my analysis of the border from different strains of contemporary border scholarship, highlighting the centrality of my study's attention to the politics of global capital accumulation, as well as my skepticism toward many of the scholars of border studies who view the potential for border liberation within the existing confines of the nation state.

Throughout the book, I argue for the necessity of moving away from a nation-centered analysis, stressing instead the importance of rethinking both the conceptual and the political space of the nation state. This move is especially useful since the nation state, because of perceived economic and political pressures, is endlessly capable of adapting and changing, particularly in its border rules (which relate to trade, currency regulations, foreign policy, and so on). Thus, part of what I will demonstrate in this book is that not only is the border a social relation; it also acquires force from constantly being made and remade by those in power. Consequently, whether it is a sovereign state, such as Hungary, implementing a system of closed borders within a so-called open European community in order to block the entry of "migrants," or Myanmar's deciding how and why the Rohingya people must be eliminated from within the borders of their nation, or countries around the world locking indigenous groups into zones of containment, borders can be reconfigured by the state both as political and as representational spaces.

After examining damaging social relations, I turn to an analysis of a range of cultural texts that offer oppositional accounts of the border. Culture, of course, is a highly contested battleground in which ideas about the border are shaped, and many powerful texts have resisted dominant

---

[5] It is worth mentioning, as Robert Nichols reminds us, that while Marx's original formulation of primitive accumulation, "the classic form," attempts to "explain the strange alchemy of capital's emergence out of noncapital, subsequent focus shifts to the subsumption of noncapital by already existing capital" (69). Nichols suggests a "disaggregation of the component elements of primitive accumulation in favor of an analysis that contemplates alternative possible relations between these elements" (70). It is in the spirit of this suggestion that I allude to "continuing primitive accumulation."

narratives and representations of both borders and border subjects. Limiting my exploration to the US–Mexico and the EU–Southern Mediterranean border zones from 2011 to 2021, I analyze several of these oppositional texts, including two novels, two films, and two murals alongside a music video. While lauding the efforts of these artists to contest hegemonic representations of borders and border subjects, I also identify problems in the ways that their texts navigate complex aesthetic and political contexts. Moreover, I consider the extent of the artists' investment in the politics of border abolition. I suggest that their positions on borders, which variously include reform, refusal, and revolution, are sometimes compromised by their imbrication in the state's foundational narratives of justice, rights, and sovereignty.

If, as I argue throughout the book, borders constitute social relations—relations anchored in systems of state power and forms of resource extraction and labor exploitation—hopes for a future free from exploitation cannot be contained in the abstract notions of justice and equality, or the language of citizens' or migrants' rights, embedded as these ideas are in Western epistemic logic. In my final chapter, then, I make a case for an abolitionist refusal of borders. Even as I call for a "refusal," I insist on the necessity of abolition: refusal is not enough.[6]

[6] It is important to acknowledge the groundbreaking work of Audra Simpson and her consideration of "refusal" within the context of settler colonialism. Simpson contrasts refusal to the concept of recognition. The former, she argues, is a "political and ethical stance that stands in stark contrast to the desire to have one's distinctiveness as a culture, as a people, recognized. Refusal comes with the requirement of having one's *political* sovereignty acknowledged and raises the question of legitimacy for those who are usually in the position of recognizing. What is their authority to do so? Where does it come from? Who are they to do so?" (11). Furthermore, despite the colonialist designation of sovereignty, Simpson concludes that "sovereignty matters, and such mattering also engenders other ethnographic forms; in this case, one of refusal." She affirms, to "think and write about sovereignty is to think very seriously about needs and that, basically, it involves an ethnographic calculus of what you need to know and what I refuse to write" (105). Refusal, for Simpson, is an affirmative political stance, one that contests "conditions of settlement—this structural condition of ongoing Indigenous dispossession and disavowal of that dispossession and structure" (105).

Why Cultural Representations Matter

Any discussion about borders, of course, will have to consider the current situation of the migrant population, and the many ways in which they are produced as particular subjects. In Chap. 4, I will consider how even the simple matter of labeling a person a "migrant "or a "refugee" has life-and-death implications. As I have stated above, because the state and other international institutions reproduce the migrant not merely through juridical dictates, but also through a range of dominant representations, a significant critical task in this book is to analyze a variety of cultural texts in order to discern how these subjects are being produced, and how those representations, in turn, are being contested in oppositional accounts of the border. Although one may think a specific law or a public policy has a greater impact on migrants than any representation, for instance, in the form of a media report or the home page of the International Rescue Committee (https://www.rescue.org), it is important to affirm that representations of the border exist, as I have suggested, in a dialectical relationship with real-world policies.

An attention to representations is also helpful in framing a politics of liberation: because borders produce subjects, certainly in a real sense of creating citizens and non-citizens, "legal" and "illegal" migrants, "good" and "bad" refugees, and myriad other categories, artists opposing borders often attempt not merely to contest these formations, but also to unsettle, forever, their insidious logic. Thus, understanding how these subjectivities are negotiated and contested is an important part of countering border regimes themselves.[7] Ultimately, as in any cultural analysis that investigates the representation of others, my critical goal is not only to point to the cruelties of the present bordered system but also to seek out and illuminate the work of activists and artists who are offering us alternatives to the existing structures of domination, as well as—when necessary—to point out the limitations of their work.

The artists I focus on are themselves border dwellers, migrants on the move, refugees and asylum seekers and thus are best suited to speak about the violence that they encounter. As potential border crossers, they also are able to imagine what transnational solidarities might look like, and what challenges and possibilities are contained in confronting existing

---

[7] For a discussion of these constructed subjectivities, see Dina Nayeri's *The Ungrateful Refugee: What Immigrants Never Tell You.*

border rules. Because the humanity of millions is being degraded in order to fulfill the demands of capital and the state, and because the migrants' need for movement is often thrust upon them as a result of planned abandonment and relentless acts of military aggression that have decimated their lives, an attention to cultural texts is never just an aesthetic pursuit, and I aim in this analysis to make visible the multifarious ways in which aesthetics, politics, ethics, and economics intersect.

Chapters 4, 5, and 6 of this book, particularly, focus on the work of artists and activists, and their interrogation of border regimes. Examining artistic representations of the border offer us a way to consider how hegemonic and prescriptive uses of the border, which reaffirm imperial dictates, may be challenged. These representations arguably have a stronger hold on the public imagination than discussions at international conferences since they circulate more widely and are subject to instant debate and discussion through social media platforms. Relations of power, forms of identity, and notions of sovereignty are all on trial as these representations attempt to question and challenge existing tropes of the border. Since a form of representational orthodoxy—performing nationalism through ideological, military, and surveillance rituals such as the large-scale construction of walls, fences, and detention centers—has attained more prominence in the last decade, it is vital that counter representations offer the possibility of imagining a world that bypasses and abolishes the restrictive impositions of border ideologies.[8]

Thus, I approach the subject of border politics with the understanding that contesting the border as a reified space of knowledge is as much a charge for an oppositional politics, as is the actual political battle to undermine a world built around border rules. Indeed, it is part of that battle. Culture is an important site for contesting the narrative of the "natural" that underlines dominant border rituals, shedding light precisely on those antagonistic social relations that rulers try to obscure.

---

[8] For information on the increase in detention centers, please see Emily Kassie's "Detained: How the U.S. Built the World's Largest Immigrant Detention System." For information on the increase in walls and fences, please see Kim Hjelmgaard's "Trump Isn't the Only One Who Wants to Build a Wall. These European Nations Already Did."

Scope of the Work: Analyzing the EU-Mediterranean and the US–Mexico Borders, 2011–2021

Quite clearly, a book on borders can be vast in scope, even—ironically—all encompassing. I therefore limit my discussion of this subject to selected texts produced within the last decade, 2011–2021, from two of the primary border zones in the world. The reasons for my selection of these geopolitical spaces and temporal contexts are several. A few words first about the geographic locations: in my study, I examine the border zone of the southern Mediterranean, primarily Greece and Italy's borders with North Africa and West Asia, and the one between the United States and Mexico. Clearly, these are the two border zones from which many of the debates about borders and many of the reports about migration emerge, whether they be from academic circles, western media outlets, or non-governmental organizations. This is partly the case because the imperial centers have the political and economic power to produce this discourse and to determine how it circulates and takes shape. And, of course, as Todd Miller and others have pointed out, the European Union and the United States have been instrumental in enlisting other countries to support their border policies. Miller calls this arrangement an emerging "global border system" where the imperial center is involved in "sorting, classifying, and repelling or incarcerating people from the Global South, while employing and deploying countries of the Global South as enforcers" (157–58). These factors allow the imperial center's narratives about borders to gain prominence as the normative mode of border analysis and commentary. Thus, it is crucial that this discourse is challenged since it shapes the destinies of millions across the globe. Contesting the border discourse in these two regions, then, offers significant points of intervention for an oppositional politics of the border. However, even though these two axes of influence will constitute the primary material in this book, I will also refer to other border areas, including, for instance, those between Israel and Palestine, India and Pakistan, and Togo and Ghana. Numerous areas around the world have inherited border conflicts from the colonial and cold war eras, and alluding to the material realities of these border regions offers illuminating links to the two selected border zones.

A second way in which my study is limited is through my focus on the years 2011 through 2021. These two border zones have witnessed a vast movement of people over the last decade.[9] Moreover, this period has seen the increasing militarization of borders across the world, the rise of white nationalism in Europe and the United States, the passing of Brexit, the emergence of Trumpism, and the building of walls on the US–Mexican border and between EU nations. Of course, the starting point of my study, 2011, is also a significant year since it marked the beginning of the war in Syria in March and ignited a movement of people that saw over six and a half million Syrians becoming refugees and asylum seekers, while another six and a half million people became part of an internally displaced population (the total number constitutes over half the Syrian population). However, it is worth noting that even though many of the migrants attempting to reach Europe during the last ten years were from Syria, millions more were from other regions in the Middle East, South Asia, North Africa, and sub-Saharan Africa.[10] At the mid-point of the decade, 2015–2016, over 9000 people had died trying to cross the Mediterranean. Over 25,000 migrants have died/gone missing in the Mediterranean since 2014, and in that same period, over 7000 people have died/gone missing trying to cross the US–Mexico border in journeys from Latin and Central America and the Caribbean.[11] In 2021, over 2000 people lost their lives attempting the same crossings (1350 in the Mediterranean, 650 at the US–Mexico border) ("Missing Migrants Project"). The year ended with the spotlight on the Belarus-Poland border, where thousands were left to

---

[9] According to John Gramlich and Alissa Scheller, there were 1.6 million migrant encounters (i.e., encounters in which US Border Control engaged in either expulsion or apprehension) at the US—Mexico border in 2021. For more information on crossings at the US—Mexico border, please also see Joel Rose's "Border Patrol Apprehensions Hit a Record High. But That's Only Part of the Story." For information about the increase in border crossings in Europe, please see Frey Lindsay's "EU Border Agency Says Irregular Migration Continues to Increase in 2022" or Harry Taylor's "Number of People to Reach UK in Small Boats in 2022 Nears 10,000."

[10] Please also see Renata Brito's "Europe Welcomes Ukrainian Refugees—Others, Less So."

[11] Please see Miranda Cady Hallett and Jamie Longazel's "Murder It Remains" for more details on "the differential exposure to death experienced by global migrants" (1).

freeze in the forests while the two countries played diplomatic roulette with their lives.[12]

Meanwhile, the final months of 2021 at the US–Mexico border saw the brutalization of the Haitian migrants and the continuing implementation of the cruelly named Migrants Protection Protocol (MPP), also known as the "Remain in Mexico" policy, which forced thousands of asylum seekers to stay on the Mexican side of the border, subject to widespread abuse and violence. A recent piece in the *New York Times* (October 2021) reported that in 2021 "A record 1.7 million migrants from around the world, many of them fleeing pandemic-ravaged countries, were encountered trying to enter the United States illegally [*sic*] in the last 12 months." This was the highest number since 1960. These numbers included 147,000 children without parents or guardians. Although a majority of these migrants were from Mexico and many others from Central America (78 percent of the total), over "160 countries in Asia, Africa and Latin America" were represented. A vast majority of over a million migrants—children and adults were expelled by the government (Sullivan and Jordan).

The years 2011–2021 also saw a hardening of migration policies in the United States and Mexico. The Obama administration deported about three million people between 2009 and 2016. Meanwhile, refugee resettlement also reached its lowest number during this decade. By 2020, the ceiling for refugee admission to the United States was cut to 15,000, declining from 85,000 in 2016. Of course, the many cruelties of border policies at the US-Mexico border—the forced separation of families; the imprisonment of children in detention centers; and the increasing incidents of abuse against migrants by border agents and ICE personnel—have been a regular feature of the migrant condition over the last ten years. Accompanying these visible traces of cruelty, as mentioned earlier,

---

[12] In a recent piece, following the flight of Ukrainian refugees to the Polish border, Andrew Higgin reminds us that when refugees tried to enter Poland from Belarus a few months back, "Polish security forces beat them back with batons. At least a dozen died in the forests that straddle the border." Higgin contrasts the reception of White, Christian Ukrainian refugees with the current group of refugees: "Refugees arriving from Ukraine, however, have been greeted with welcoming smiles, hot drinks and transport to the nearest railway station. Police officers handed out fruit, doughnuts and sandwiches to Ukrainians camped out in the waiting room." Poland, it should be mentioned, has just pledged over 350 million Euro to build a wall on its border with Belarus. Meanwhile, Hungary's virulently anti-refugee prime minister Viktor Orban "is now organizing reception centers and temporary housing for Ukrainians." Marcin Ociepa, the deputy minister of defense, commented, "We will accept as many refugees as will be needed."

are the continuing migrant deaths. Finally, the pandemic has seen an increase in border violence, with Western nations dramatically reducing the number of refugees that are granted asylum, as well as exposing migrants to dangers and hazards as they attempt to seek refuge. These nations have resorted to labeling migrants as a "security risk," as potential bearers of the virus, spreading disease to an unsuspecting population, thus posing them as an even more exaggerated form of an external threat.[13] In other words, border as a social relation in the time of Covid reenacts and renews forms of violence, which bear the long shadow of colonial modes of abjection.[14]

The abuses on the EU-Mediterranean border during this period have been no less egregious, and, of course, even though the consequences of crossings are not as lethal on the land borders of the Balkan states, these regions see many acts of violence by the state. Perhaps most tellingly, the annual budget for Frontex, effectively the EU border police, increased from 364 million Euro in 2020 to 535 million Euro in 2021. In 2022, the budget had reached 754 million Euro (Frontex, "Key Facts"). The organization Refugee Rights, Europe has documented multiple

> illegal operations that involve migrants being forcibly removed from European states, notably along the land borders of Croatia, Serbia, and Bosnia & Herzegovina. Pushbacks have also been documented in the

[13] For reports of politicians arguing for this position, please see Andrew Zhang's "Texas Republicans Pushed Biden Administration to Keep Rule That Turns Asylum-Seekers Away at the Border" or Uriel J. García's "Judge Blocks Biden Administration from Lifting Public Health Order Used to Quickly Expel Migrants," or Leonardo Castañeda and Katie Hoeppner's "5 Things to Know About the Title 42 Immigrant Expulsion Policy." It's curious that the $45 billion cruise line industry that played a huge role in spreading the virus has not been called to account as a security risk. For a discussion of cruise lines and the spread of Covid, please see Tanya Snyder's "Coronavirus on the High Seas: Why the U.S. Can't Touch Cruise Lines."

[14] For information on previous instances in the United States when populations of color have been linked to the spread of disease, please see Nayan Shah's *Contagious Divides: Epidemics and Race in San Francisco's Chinatown*, Christian W. Chun's "The Return of the 'Yellow Peril': The Fear of Getting Sick from the Other," Nahia Idoiaga Mondragon's "Understanding an Ebola Outbreak: Social Representations of Emerging Infectious Diseases," Sarah Monson's "Ebola as African: American Media Discourses of Panic and Otherization," Laura Eichelberger's "SARS and New York's Chinatown: The Politics of Risk and Blame During an Epidemic of Fear," or Lok Siu and Claire Chun's "Yellow Peril and Techno-orientalism in the Time of Covid-19: Racialized Contagion, Scientific Espionage, and Techno-Economic Warfare."

Aegean Sea, with the NGO Aegean Boat Report **listing 324 nautical push-backs in 2020 alone**. Since 2017, an estimated 18,200 individuals have experienced violence and other abuses at European borders. As well as beatings and property destruction, refugees have shared stories of psychological abuse and torture-like acts such as electric shocks and cigarette burns. (Jackson, emphasis in original)

One can safely assume that these numbers exclude a vast number of abuses and deaths that never come to light, so the actual figures are, presumably, much higher.

There is, clearly, little doubt that the change in both the form and the content of border rules over the last ten years justify a rigorous examination of border policies, rituals, and representations during this time. However, I want to clarify that I did not choose these border zones and that time period only because of the gravity of these situations or the extreme hardship endured by millions—the deaths, the struggles and the tragic losses suffered by the migrants during these times—even though, undoubtedly, my work will highlight the savage injustices and cruelties of border practices. In addition to shedding additional light on these grim realities, let me reiterate another significance of these regions and this period. As I have indicated earlier, the border as a social relation has an impact stretching far beyond its functions as a territorial line. This social relation, encapsulated most sharply in the politics of race and capital, is clearly delineated in the two border zones I have selected because of the imperial relations that continue to dominate these regions.

Moreover, the contradictions of capital movement and labor (im) mobility are best captured in many of the dynamics of border rules in these areas because of the vast volume of trade and the regulation of labor in these zones.[15] Even as the imperial states bristle at the "crisis" on their doorstep, the business of labor exploitation of undocumented and contingent workers continues in these regions, and the imposition of unequal trade "rules" ensure the subjugations of nations of the Global South.

Also, because the world's wealthiest democracies attempt to justify their border rules, border norms and policies are inevitably caught up in the language of Western liberalism, and questions attached to citizenship, nationality, rights, and identity are constantly being defined, reshaped, and

---

[15] For just one illustration of this point, consider the sheer number of migrant agricultural laborers in the United States and the EU.

contested in the terms determined by that language. Indeed, as I have already argued, one of the reasons that it is necessary to intervene against the border rituals at these points of crossing is because these wealthy countries control and disseminate much of what is considered "legitimate" discourse on borders and migrants' rights.

One of the most obvious examples of this process of legitimization is a phrase that has acquired great ideological weight over the last ten years: the "refugee crisis." This phrase has become ubiquitous and has effectively accomplished a negation of the person who is framed within this signifier of displacement and disruption. One way of putting it is that the subject has disappeared into its objective form as crisis. And, of course, the reason this movement of people is designated as a crisis is because it involves the West. So, the arrival of refugees on the shores of Europe in greater numbers and the presence of accompanied minors at the US border is a crisis not so much for those who are its subjects, but for those who must confront the reality of their presence.[16] Since these moments are accorded a specific narrative appearance, characterized as a disruption of order, and capture the greatest prominence in the media and in international courts and institutions, their effects go far beyond having an impact in their own regions, but transfer over to the adjudication of border disputes in Asia, Latin America, and Africa. Israel, India, or Myanmar, for instance, can resort to the same narrative logic when addressing "crisis" and quelling "disturbances" and "disorder" in the Occupied Territories, Kashmir, or the Rakhine state. What becomes particularly telling in these moments of crisis is the slippage between the outside and the inside. Who belongs within which borders is one of the central questions in these moments. It is no secret, for instance, that the Kurdish people, the Uyghur, or the Maya Q'eqchi' have garnered little leverage in international courts of opinion—despite professed sympathy for their cause—partially because none of the imperial powers want to set a precedent for minority communities to have certain rights, which may then expand from political gains to rights of access to land, water, and mineral resources.

---

[16] Gholam Khiabany offers a pointed analysis of the "crisis," arguing that "[i]t is in fact impossible to comprehend the current crisis without taking into account the increasing social inequalities at national and global levels, the financialisation of global capitalism, the rapid environmental degradation, as well as increased imperialist interventions in the Middle East and Africa, as a major source of forced migration and staggering levels of displacement. 'They' (refugees) are here because 'we' are there" (760).

I have provided the details above to emphasize the point that though my work may be limited by specific temporal and spatial categories, I intend to show the wider implications of both the legal and political policies imposed in these border spaces. Seeing the "crisis," for example, through the lens of capital's reach across borders and its relation to labor regulation offers a radically different perspective on border "norms." Likewise, making visible the Eurocentric terms of a narrative that only locates crisis when migrants arrive at the doors of White-dominated nations is an important departure from the dominant narratives about migrants. Where, one wonders, is the crisis or the Western media's attention when countries such as Jordan, Lebanon, Turkey, or Pakistan, which have "hosted" the majority of the world's refugees for several decades, appeal for international aid in the face of overwhelming need?[17] Finally, even though I focus in this book on two specific spaces, my reflecting on these two border locations makes it possible to consider wider questions: so many people outside, within, and in-between nations are involved in the crossings at these two zones that analyzing these spaces also allows us to contemplate what an oppositional transnational and non-national solidarity movement against borders might look like, and in this effort the work of artists and activists is crucial in articulating an alternative vision of the world—one free of borders.

Summary of the Six Chapters

Chapter 2, "Border Rules: Imperialism, Race, and the Politics of Development," considers the various ways in which the border presents itself in its most violent and explicit form as a territorial limit. However, I contend that this overt, localized instrumentality veils how the border operates in its primary form: as a set of social relations, one that is determined in ways that extend far beyond the immediacy of territorial mapping and control. These relations, or the bordering process, I argue, are produced and intensified by the circuits of capital accumulation, and in the case of the imperial centers, through the regulatory politics of racialized exploitation and exclusion. In turn, these relations enable the work of capital and allow the state to govern through the politics of labor

---

[17] For example, see William Worster's "Customary International Law and the Shifting Patterns of Refugee Migration." According to the UNHCR, "Low- and middle-income countries host 83 per cent of the world's refugees."

regulation and racial differentiation. On the one hand, there are fixed orthodoxies through which the border determines a set of social relations: for instance, those between citizens and non-citizens and those named as legal and those deemed illegal. These designations result in death sentences for some and endless mobility for others, and function through the assignment of juridical rights, the privileges of travel and movement, and the ability to access resources. On the other hand, the border is also a constitutive space, guided by economic and political exigencies of the moment, so these relations are constantly being redrawn and reimagined in their specific contexts. Thus, representations of the border and the ways in which people experience the border collide with, affirm, and contradict actual geographical demarcations and separations. Having illustrated and expanded on these points, I underline how and why imperialist practices—historically and in the present—must be considered when we attempt to understand the continued insistence by the power brokers to maintain borders as a vital way to mark political and national life. Current imperialist practices, masquerading as the "politics of development," I contend, are a vital component in determining border rules. The chapter concludes by examining and complicating the Marxist categories of primitive accumulation and surplus populations in order to explore how, in the realm of political economy, borders are essential for regulating the movement of capital and labor, as well as for managing the ravages caused by the continuing project of "development."

In Chap. 3, "Theorizing Borders in the Shadow of Imperial Violence," having demonstrated how forms of primitive accumulation, the imposition of neoliberal politics of development on the Global South, and methods for regulating surplus populations shape the way borders function as social relations, I examine some of the contributions from the field of border studies over the last 25 years, arguing that while many of the critics expand and complicate this theoretical landscape, extending it to questions beyond territorial geopolitical matters, they often shy away from an analysis grounded in the materiality of political economy, resorting instead to explanatory categories, such as "scapes" and "edges." Consequently, their work often reifies the border as a scape of ambiguity, where meanings are constantly unsettled and contingent. Moreover, some of these critics also seek solutions, such as arguing for the right to migrate, that do little to unsettle the structures of the nation state or the embedded repressions of border rules.

16   K. CHOWDHURY

As I attempt to establish in my analysis of these texts, such explanations of and reactions to border rules limit the scope and possibilities of these critical contributions, moving them away from a more specific focus on the ways in which the historical traces of settler colonialism and imperialism and the contemporary spatial politics of neoliberalism and capital accumulation operate in the construction of borders. The movement of wealth, the circulation of commodities, and the regulation of labor are vital nodes in understanding why borders exist, why they persist, and why they take the forms that they do, even as the work that they do shifts and changes over time. Of course, as I describe in Chap. 2, rigidity and fluidity constitute the lifeline of the border, and the notion of scapes and edges does capture some of the volatility that accompanies a border space, as well as its multiscalar functions. However, scapes are also sites where the production of debt, the circulation of currency, and the regulation of commodities and labor acquire real, material forms, the workings of which are not fully exposed by the notions of scapes and edges. I conclude the chapter by commenting on three materialist readings of border politics by Justin Akers Chacón, Reece Jones, and Harsha Walia, suggesting that these critics offer a more productive analysis of the border as a relation firmly located within the politics of race, empire, and capital accumulation.

Chapter 4, "Narrating the Border: Fluidity, Gender, and Resistance in Rabih Alameddine's *The Wrong End of the Telescope* and Yuri Herrera's *Signs Preceding the End of the World*," begins with an attempt to provide a rationale for analyzing the efficacy of borders through an examination of a range of cultural representations. I reflect on what can be gained from such a focus even as I acknowledge the argument that the border is most starkly manifested at the material level of rules and strictures, exclusions and inclusions, and tariffs and trade. What, then, is to be gained from exploring a mural on a border wall, a music video, or a literary text? One way to address this question is to return to a point I made earlier: that one of the most effective ways in which the border functions is through performance and representations. These performances also produce certain kinds of subjectivity, both when people accede to and navigate the material force of the border and when they oppose the legitimacy of this force.

Specifically, this chapter examines two recent novels: Rabih Alameddine's *The Wrong End of the Telescope* (2021), which focuses on a community of migrants and aid workers on the island Skala Sikamineas, a fishing village in Lesbos, Greece, in the Mediterranean. The other text, Yuri Herrera's

Señales que precederán al fin del mundo, translated by Lisa Dillman into English under the title *Signs Preceding the End of the World* (2015) concentrates on the journey of a woman, Makina, who seeks her brother at, what appears to be, the US–Mexico border. Each writer presents the readers with bordered worlds that must be navigated in multiple ways. In witnessing the creative methods used by the characters in both texts to negotiate these borders, the readers come to an understanding of how they may also begin the process of liberating themselves from these borders. *The Wrong End of the Telescope* is unfailingly critical of many aid workers, charitable organizations, and NGOs, revealing their self-centered approach to the arrival of refugees on their shores. Alameddine does not flinch as he satirizes the "help" offered by groups and individuals as the refugees arrive in Lesbos. The novel interrogates the work of borders at every level. Not only is Lesbos literally a border land between the so-called East and West, but the protagonist, Mina, a surgeon, also has to traverse the strictly bordered gender identities and roles in her life.

Herrera's protagonist, Makina is at the opposite end of the social spectrum. She is a telephone operator in her village and is forced to take a trip across borders. Her journey highlights not only the material act of crossing over and the violence that accompanies that journey but also the surreal elements of existing in a time and space that is made more hallucinatory because of the crossing-over experience. Both novels offer an unflinching look at the violence bred by borders and highlight the way capital, race, gender, and labor get marked, erased and/or renewed in these borderlands. While exploring these elements of crossing over, I also point to the ways in which both novels are sometimes limited by their focus on the individual's ability to sublate and transcend border politics rather than on the possibility or necessity of abolition itself.

Chapter 5, "Documenting the Migrant Journey in Ai Weiwei's *Human Flow* and Diego Quemada-Díez's *La Jaula de Oro*," examines two films about border crossers, Ai Weiwei's *Human Flow* (2017), which has received wide recognition, and a lesser-known film, Diego Quemada-Díez's *La Jaula de Oro* (*The Golden Dream*, 2013). *Human Flow*, at one level, is a showpiece for its creator, Ai Weiwei to engage at a personal level with people and places who constitute the current landscape of migration and to provide commentary on the disastrous response to it by so many states and international organizations. Clearly, as a refugee himself, even if one with a rare set of privileges, Ai is well aware of the vicissitudes of exile and displacement. He is also an appropriate person to question the West's commitment to human rights since he is held up as an example of the West's celebration of an individual's right to freedom of expression and for their promotion of democratic and humanitarian values. As a poster child, then, of Western liberalism and its opposition to Chinese totalitarianism, Ai's riposte to the West in *Human Flow* is apposite. By laying bare Western governments' utter failures to offer refuge to those escaping war and by highlighting Western leaders' moral culpability and silence in the face of human suffering, and indeed their unwillingness to live up to the principles of international law, Ai makes an appropriately relevant intervention in the West's self-congratulatory narrative as a defender of human rights. However, by looking closely at the cinematic techniques used by Ai (iPhone footage, drone shots, narrative insertions) and by examining the narrative layers in the film, I suggest that he replicates the ideological valence of the systems that he sets out to critique, embedding the film within the troubled texts of human rights and "humanitarian" actions, texts that participate in legitimizing borders and the destructive work that they do. Furthermore, the insertion of his own persona into the narrative and the representation of refugees' suffering raise significant questions about the ethical direction of his work.

Diego Quemada-Díez's *La Jaula de Oro* (2013), unlike *Human Flow*, combines fact—replicating, in documentary style, the actual conditions that migrants encounter during their journeys across Mexico—and fiction, incorporating a narrative that imagines one such journey by three teenagers. The aesthetic and political textures of the film are complicated by this ever-present dialectic between fact and fiction. As a viewing experience, I argue, the film, by design undermines the audience's affective identification with the characters: just when we become accustomed to the rituals of a traditional fictional narrative (for instance, the predictable conflicts between characters, the emergence of a love triangle, the overcoming of barriers, the striking montages of passing landscapes) and attach ourselves emotionally to the characters, an unsettling reality intrudes upon our equanimity and disrupts this relationship. Indeed, one could argue that these disruptions in the trajectory of the migration narrative produces a distancing or estrangement effect (Brecht's notion of *Verfremdungseffek*), interrupting an aesthetic experience rooted in an implicit pact between viewer and filmmaker regarding the familiar practices of storytelling. In this sense, then, *La Jaula de Oro*, although lacking the visceral real-life images of *Human Flow*, with its bombed-out buildings and refugees traveling on dinghies, may require an even more radical accounting with the realities of the violence engendered by border rules.

Chapter 6, "Visualizing Borders, Visualizing Abolition: M.I.A.'s 'Borders' and Mural Art in Ciudad Juárez and El Paso," explores the work of the British musician, Maya Arulpragasam, better known as M.I.A., and three border muralists, who practice their art in the border cities of Ciudad Juárez and El Paso. Although I consider the trajectory of M.I.A.'s 20-year career as a refugee artist, I primarily focus on the video "Borders," which was released during the peak moment of migrant deaths in the Mediterranean in 2015. In this discussion, I point to the many ways in which she has been targeted by the Western media for her position as a celebrity spokesperson for refugees' rights. However, rather than focus on these narrow and self-fulfilling critiques of M.I.A.'s music and politics, I explore questions about representation, identity, and resistance in her video, and consider how those questions may add to our understanding of the border as both a destructive, violent means of surveillance and control and a generative space for resistance and struggle. This, I hope, offers a more productive line of inquiry. In the video, M.I.A. moves the listener to encounter the reality of migrants' lives, eviscerating, at the same time, the superficiality of Western self-empowerment mantras and offering, instead, hope for the prospect of transnational solidarity in the face of border rules. Her representation of borders adds an important element to our understanding of the ways in which borders are viewed and seen in the popular imagination. The success of the song/video makes us consider how effectively one can use dominant perceptions of borders and migrants, working on and against them to create a resistance narrative that will disrupt these very same perceptions. In this chapter, I question whether M.I.A. can resolve the contradictions in two forms of representation—speaking for displaced people and presenting a homogenized image of them—as well as overcome the challenges in both cases of addressing a primarily Western audience. How might the aestheticization of the migrants in the video compromise the action of "speaking for" this embattled group of people? Is this tension heightened by M.I.A.'s position as the only one who speaks in the video, implicating her as yet another Western voice participating in the silencing of those who already have no voice?

Contrasting the global reach of a music video and M.I.A.'s contradictory embeddedness in global capitalist culture are the necessarily place-bound murals created by artists in Ciudad Juárez and El Paso (formerly called Paso del Norte), sister cities that are tied together through familial, social, economic, and political histories. Both cities have also experienced the impact of being a major hub of labor exploitation and commercial traffic over the last several decades. In this section of the chapter, I focus on two sets of murals on different sides of the US–Mexico border. Just as a music video operates within particular aesthetic and political registers, allowing for certain kinds of visibility and distribution, so, too, in the case of murals, their actual locations are an essential element of how they function and how they are read and "seen" within their specific contexts. This is particularly true for art forms that are part of the fabric of everyday life, located among people and places that give them a special significance.

The two murals I examine are a 65-foot mural "Under the Bridge/Bajo el Puente," designed by Jorge Perez Mendoza, also known as Yorch, of the Colectivo Rezizte located in Ciudad Juárez and "Sister Cities/ Ciudades Hermanas," a creation of LxsDos in the El Segundo Barrio in El Paso. LxsDos is a duo that consists of partners Ramon and Christian Cardenas. These murals mark historical and contemporary traces of border life, and I attempt to make some of those traces more visible while juxtaposing my own viewing encounters with the murals. The first mural depicts a farmworker, a bracero, tilling a field; to his right is a woman in a *maquiladora* uniform, juxtaposed against the gears of industrial machines. Uniting these two figures is a bridge which transforms into two arms, gripping each other. The "two" sides of the bridge are indistinguishable from each other; indeed, the mural highlights the fact that there is no "otro lado." This same spirit animates the, "Sister Cities/Ciudades Hermanas" mural: the two women, representing the two cities, are embodied as one, announcing the fact that the two cities are inseparable. Their hair fuses, as do their bodies. Their eyes are directly facing the artificial boundary erected by the states, one that the sisters' presence clearly contradicts. The lattice work that clothes them conveys both realities of the border. On the one hand, it resembles the fences that separate many families, and yet, on the other hand, the lattice work also serves to unify the composition and, thematically, to unify the cities. It is both enclosure and link, a chain that imprisons, and a chain that binds. The lattice work is dotted with images of cacti, flowers, and faces. The cruelties of border rules and the possibilities of solidarity are captured by both murals.

Creating art in the shadow of the militaristic state, I argue, has a special significance since it not only directly confronts the many barriers and walls that loom over these adjoining neighborhoods, but also affirms unapologetically that these neighbors will not be separated by a state that cares little about their lives other than capturing the surplus that can be extracted from them. This spirit of resistance is alive not just because the artists want to affirm it but also because they see it in the textures of peoples' everyday lives. There is a refusal in these communities of the borderlands to accede to the artificial separations imposed upon them. Through their everyday actions, their art, and their crossings, their lives enact an opposition to border rules.

Although the muralists and MIA may seem to occupy different artistic terrains, their creations reflect their spirit of solidarity with those who are on the receiving end of border rules. Of course, as I have already mentioned, MIA is embedded in the world of capitalist commodity relations, problematizing her acts of solidarity with the dispossessed and oppressed. The muralists, meanwhile, are very much of the community, and their work emerges from and is dedicated to that same community. Despite these differences, however, the artists in both cases make use of visually charged, accessible art forms, challenge the norms of border rules, and point the way toward abolition.

Chapter 7, "A Borderless World: Abolition Democracy and the Politics of Refusal," the concluding chapter, takes on the particular challenge of framing an abolitionist refusal of border rules, using lessons from Abolition Democracy, a political philosophy and movement that spans over 150 years. I am careful to include in my call for a "refusal" an insistence on the necessity for abolition. As I discuss in this chapter, refusal in itself is not enough since that suggests a rejection rather than an abolition of "the present state of things," and early in the book, I complicate the concept of "refusal," drawing on the work of Audra Simpson. Locating my discussion of a borderless future both in the foundational abolitionist work of W.E.B. Du Bois and in current calls to action by scholars such as Angela Davis and Ruth Wilson Gilmore, I argue for an abolition of borders and thus a transformation of existing social relations.

One of the principal points to take from abolition movements is that the battle against borders must be, at the core, an anti-capitalist one. I have emphasized throughout the book that a borderless world will remain a Utopian horizon, one never to be reached, if the current economic system stays in place. In short, a transformation of the capitalist racist patriarchy is a necessary accompaniment for a borderless future. In my concluding comments, I will not suggest that such a future has a clearly delineated, marked path, beginning with a set of actions, culminating in a predetermined moment, and reaching a specific end. Indeed, reforms, collective acts of resistance, and a growing commitment to class solidarities across borders will all be part of the process of transformation. However, what can be made clear is what a borderless world must encompass. Based on my analysis of borders as a social relation, the vision of a borderless society is not one defined by the absence of the negative: the removal of the inability to migrate or the lifting of oppressive limitations of territorial boundaries. These changes to our current bordered world represent only one element of a borderless society. Nor is such a society characterized merely by the seamless flow of goods and labor, or by refusing to criminalize people for desiring to move. Nor, ultimately, is it about the reformation of the nation state. While these are laudable goals for mitigating the cruelties and injustices of the current system, these changes in themselves clearly do not constitute a transformation in social relations. After all, the eradication of territorial boundaries does not signal the end of class rule. Nor is a society rooted in the commons automatically free from gender hierarchies.

This book will end with the suggestion that a borderless world is one where the social relations of production based on those who own capital and those who are forced to sell their labor power are permanently disrupted. This revolutionary process will, of course, involve a dialectical motion, which is to say that the actors of the revolutionary movement will not proceed with preconceived notions about change and transformation, but that their actions will be shaped by the course of the events themselves. In other words, rather than see the elimination of borders as the intended goal, it may well become apparent during the "real movement that abolishes the present state of things" that any significant forward movement is untenable without their removal.

Works Cited

Asian Dub Foundation. "Fortress Europe." *Enemy of the Enemy*, X-Ray Production, 2003.

Brito, Renata. "Europe Welcomes Ukrainian Refugees—Others, Less So." *AP News*, 28 Feb. 2022, https://apnews.com/article/russia-ukraine-war-refugees-diversity-230b0cc790820b9bf8883f918fc8e313.

Cady Hallett, Miranda, and Jamie Longazel. "Introduction: Murder It Remains." *Migration and Mortality: Social Death, Dispossession, and Survival in the Americas,* edited by Miranda Cady Hallett and Jamie Longazel, Temple University Press, 2021, pp. 1—20.

Castañeda, Leonardo, and Katie Hoeppner. "5 Things to Know About the Title 42 Immigrant Expulsion Policy." *ACLU*, 22 Mar. 2022, https://www.aclu.org/news/immigrants-rights/five-things-to-know-about-the-title-42-immigrant-expulsion-policy.

Chun, Christian W. "The Return of the 'Yellow Peril': The Fear of Getting Sick from the Other." *Language, Culture, and Society*, vol. 2, no. 2, 2020, pp. 252–259.

Crawford, Kerry F. *Wartime Sexual Violence: From Silence to Condemnation of a Weapon of War.* Georgetown University Press, 2017.

Eichelberger, Laura. "SARS and New York's Chinatown: The Politics of Risk and Blame During an Epidemic of Fear." *Social Science & Medicine*, vol. 65, no. 6, 2007, pp. 1284–95.

"Five Ways Disney's 'Encanto' Celebrates Refugees." *International Rescue Committee*, 7 Feb. 2022, https://www.rescue.org/article/five-ways-disneys-encanto-celebrates-refugees.

García, Uriel J. "Judge Blocks Biden Administration from Lifting Public Health Order Used to Quickly Expel Migrants." *Texas Tribune*, 20 May 2022, https://www.texastribune.org/2022/05/20/title-42-border-judge-ruling-migrants/.

Gauditz, Leslie. "The Noborder Movement: Interpersonal Struggle with Political Ideals." *Social Inclusion*, vol. 5, no. 3, 2017, pp. 49–57.

———. "Opportunity of Encounter: Negotiating Difference in the No Borders Movement in Athens." *Social Identities: Journal for the Study of Race, Nation, and Culture*, vol. 28, no. 1, 2022, pp. 19–40.

"Global Trends Report 2021." *UNHCR*, https://www.unhcr.org/en-us/publications/brochures/62a9d1494/global-trends-report-2021.html?query=2021%20global%20report.

Gramlich, John, and Alissa Scheller. "What's Happening at the U.S.—Mexico Border in 7 Charts." *Pew Research Center*, 9 Nov. 2021, https://www.pewresearch.org/fact-tank/2021/11/09/whats-happening-at-the-u-s-mexico-border-in-7-charts/.

Higgin, Andrew. "At the Polish Border, Tens of Thousands of Ukrainian Refugees." *New York Times*, 25 Feb. 2022, https://www.nytimes.com/2022/02/25/world/europe/ukrainian-refugees-poland.html.

Hjelmgaard, Kim. "Trump Isn't the Only One Who Wants to Build a Wall. These European Nations Already Did." *USA Today*, 24 May 2018, https://www.usatoday.com/story/news/world/2018/05/24/donald-trump-europe-border-walls-migrants/532572002/.

Jackson, Theo. "The Violent Abuse of Migrants at Europe's Borders." *Refugee Rights Europe*, 2 July 2021, https://refugee-rights.eu/2021/07/02/the-violent-abuse-of-migrants-at-europes-borders/.

Jaleel, Rana M. *The Work of Rape*, Duke University Press, 2021.

Kassie, Emily. "Detained: How the U.S. Built the World's Largest Immigrant Detention System." *The Guardian*, 24 Sept. 2019, https://www.theguardian.com/usnews/2019/sep/24/detained-us-largest-immigrant-detention-trump.

"Key Facts." *Frontex*, https://frontex.europa.eu/about-frontex/faq/key-facts/.

Khiabany, Gholam. "Refugee Crisis, Imperialism and the Pitiless Wars on the Poor." *Media, Culture & Society*, vol. 38, no. 5, 2016, pp. 755–762.

Lindsay, Frey. "EU Border Agency Says Irregular Migration Continues to Increase in 2022." *Forbes*, 17 Feb. 2022, https://www.forbes.com/sites/freylindsay/2022/02/17/eu-border-agency-says-irregular-migration-continues-to-increase-in-2022/?sh=5886ca355b85.

Marx, Karl. *Capital: A Critique of Political Economy, Vol. 1.* 1867. Translated by Ben Fowkes, Penguin, 1983.

Meger, Sara. "The Fetishization of Sexual Violence in International Security." *International Studies Quarterly*, vol. 60, 2016, pp. 149–159.

Mezzadra, Sandro and Brett Neilson. *Border as Method, or, the Multiplication of Labor.* Duke University Press, 2013.

Miller, Todd. *Empire of Borders: The Expansion of the U.S. Border around the World.* Verso, 2019.

"Migration Within the Mediterranean." *Missing Migrants Project*, 14 July 2022, https://missingmigrants.iom.int/region/mediterranean. Accessed 21 July 2022.

Mondragon, Nahia Idoiaga. "Understanding an Ebola Outbreak: Social Representations of Emerging Infectious Diseases." *Journal of Health Psychology*, vol. 22. no. 7, 2017, pp. 951–960.

Monson, Sarah. "Ebola as African: American Media Discourses of Panic and Otherization." *Africa Today*, vol. 63, no. 3, 2017, pp. 3–27.

Nayeri, Dina. *The Ungrateful Refugee: What Immigrants Never Tell You.* Catapult, 2019.

Nichols, Robert. *Theft is Property: Dispossession and Critical Theory.* Duke University Press, 2020.

Rose, Joel. "Border Patrol Apprehensions Hit a Record High. But That's Only Part of the Story." *NPR*, 23 Oct. 2021, https://www.npr.org/2021/10/23/1048522086/border-patrol-apprehensions-hit-a-record-high-but-thats-only-part-of-the-story.

Shah, Nayan. *Contagious Divides: Epidemics and Race in San Francisco's Chinatown.* University of California Press, 2001.

Sharma, Nandita. *Home Rule: National Sovereignty and the Separation of Natives and Migrants.* Duke University Press, 2020.

Simpson, Audra. *Mohawk Interruptus: Political Life Across the Borders of Settler States.* Duke University Press, 2014.

Siu, Lok, and Claire Chun. "Yellow Peril and Techno-orientalism in the Time of Covid-19: Racialized Contagion, Scientific Espionage, and Techno-Economic Warfare." *Journal of Asian American Studies*, vol. 23, no. 3, 2020, pp. 421–440.

Snyder, Tanya. "Coronavirus on the High Seas: Why the U.S. Can't Touch Cruise Lines." *Politico*, 11 Mar. 2020, https://www.politico.com/news/2020/03/11/coronavirus-cruises-126426.

Sullivan, Eileen and Mariam Jordan. "Illegal Border Crossings, Driven by Pandemic and Natural Disasters, Soar to Record Highs." *New York Times*, 22 Oct. 2021, https://www.nytimes.com/2021/10/22/us/politics/border-crossings-immigration-record-high.html.

Taylor, Harry. "Number of People to Reach UK in Small Boats in 2022 Nears 10,000." *The Guardian*, 4 June 2022, https://www.theguardian.com/uk-news/2022/jun/04/number-of-people-to-reach-uk-in-small-boats-in-2022-nears-10000.

Téllez, Michelle, et al. "Border Crossings and Sexual Conquest in the Age of Neoliberalism in the Sonoran Desert." *International Feminist Journal of Politics*, vol. 20, no. 4, 2018, pp. 524–541.

Worster, William Thomas. "Customary International Law and the Shifting Patterns of Refugee Migration." *Fordham International Law Journal*, vol. 45, no. 5, 2022, pp. 853–872, https://doi.org/10.2139/ssrn.4074725.

Zhang, Andrew. "Texas Republicans Pushed Biden Administration to Keep Rule That Turns Asylum-Seekers Away at the Border." *Texas Tribune*, 30 Mar. 2022, https://www.texastribune.org/2022/03/30/biden-immigration-asylum-title-42/.

CHAPTER 2

Border Rules: Imperialism, Race, and the Politics of Development

To write about borders at a time when 100 million displaced people have been forced to flee is, undeniably, an urgent task; however, to do so in any meaningful way, it is necessary to place that discussion within a global context of circulating capital, surplus extraction, climate crisis, and both gender and racial violence.[1] These contexts, in turn, intersect with concerns connecting the role of the state and its attempts to manage and control populations on the move. My analysis in this chapter—and in the book as a whole—attends to these concerns and takes these contexts into account. I begin by highlighting what may appear to be two somewhat unrelated media events from the summer of 2021—Vice-President Kamala Harris's speech in Guatemala and Richard Branson's test flight into space—events that reveal different ways of viewing borders and offer a useful entry point for an analysis of the border as both constitutive space and material force. Beginnings, by their very nature, signal a specific mode of analysis. What my analyses of these two events will demonstrate, I hope, is how border rules and border discourse are both startlingly visible and partially repressed in the national imagination.

---

[1] According to the UNHCR, "as of May 2022, 100 million individuals were forcibly displaced worldwide. This accounts for an increase of 10.7 million people displaced from the end of the previous year, propelled by the war in Ukraine and other deadly conflicts" ("Refugee Statistics").

© The Author(s), under exclusive license to Springer Nature Switzerland AG 2023
K. Chowdhury, *Border Rules*, Politics of Citizenship and Migration, https://doi.org/10.1007/978-3-031-26216-6_2

Borders: Fluidity and Rigidity, Mobility and Statis

On a visit to Guatemala in June 2021, the poster child for the immigrant success story in the United States, Vice-President Kamala Harris, made the following announcement: "I want to be clear to folks in the region who are thinking about making that dangerous trek to the United States-Mexico border ... Do not come. Do not come. The United States will continue to enforce our laws and secure our borders" (Naylor and Keith). Representative Alexandria Ocasio-Cortez, in response, correctly pointed out that "seeking asylum at the US border is a 100% legal method of arrival," and that "the US spent decades contributing to regime change and destabilization in Latin America. We can't help set someone's house on fire and then blame them for fleeing" (qtd. in Roche). The latter point is true for a large majority of asylum seekers who arrive at the US border, whether they be from other Central American countries or from Haiti, Afghanistan, or Iraq. Indeed, if the proposals for reparations for Native nations and African Americans in this country were to be extended on a global scale, then the United States would be morally and materially obliged to grant refuge to the millions whose lives they have directly or indirectly overturned through their military policies.

Take, for instance, Haiti. Arguably, migrants from this country, which has been at the receiving end of 200 years of US hostility and interference, merit the highest moral claim for refuge. Instead of a policy of reparations and refuge, however, a threat similar to the admonition directed to Guatemalan citizens by Vice-President Harris, was given to Haitians on March 24, 2021, when the US embassy in Port-au-Prince tweeted a message from Biden in Creole, saying "*Mwen ka di sa byen klé: pa vini*"; "I can say quite clearly, don't come over" (@USEmbassyHaiti). According to *The Invisible Wall* position statement, published in March 2021 by the Haitian Bridge Alliance, The Quixote Center, and The UndocuBlack Network, "More Haitians have been removed per the Title 42 policy in the weeks since President Joe Biden and Vice-President Kamala Harris took office than during all of Fiscal Year 2020" (Phillips and Ricker 7).[2] Despite the many promises to implement a more "humane" immigration policy than his predecessor, Biden's position on Haitian migration should not surprise

---

[2] According to Phillips and Ricker, 895 individuals were deported to Haiti during 2020. However, 1200 individuals were deported during the first two months of the Biden administration (between January 20, 2021 and March 22, 2021).

anyone. Policies excluding Haitian refugees have been pursued by every US administration over the last 40 years, even as presidents stretching back to Eisenhower have provided undying support to the brutal Duvalier regimes for three decades and undermined any attempt to establish democratic rule in the country.[3] I mention Haiti here to point to my claim that current border pronouncements and policies often arrive carrying the traces of a long lineage of imperial violence. The contemporary migrant, whether she be from El Salvador, Eritrea, the Democratic Republic of Congo, or Bangladesh, bears on her back the scars of this Western imperial violence. These scars in the present, after the end of formal occupation and colonization, have not healed; instead, more wounds have been inflicted by the neoliberal holy trinity of privatization, financialization, and extraction. The economic and political landscapes of these nations leave very few options for ordinary citizens other than escape, especially given the power of a collusive elite, whose military machinery has been strengthened by the former colonizers. When all the resources in a country are possessed by the few, mostly secured in the Global North, citizens are pushed in the direction that offers hope for survival. Thus, any talk about migration, borders, and migrant journeys—including Kamala Harris's speech—must be read keeping this fact and such imperial contexts in mind.

The second event that I want to reference—actually two "events" and related news coverage—took place on July 12, 2021. On that date, Virgin Galactic owner Richard Branson completed a test flight to "space." (Defined by the US Air Force, "space" is 50 miles above the Earth's surface/approximately 80 km.)[4] Branson's "accomplishment" received global media coverage and pushed Covid reporting and the many global crises off the mediascape as star-struck reporters gushed over Branson's "flight to the future" (Wattles). Enough has been said about this "event," but my interest in it and its widespread coverage extends to include another story involving occurrences in the same region as Branson's launching site that received only passing mention in the media. On the same day as Branson's

---

[3] For analyses of US involvement in Haitian politics, please see Yveline Alexis's *Haiti Fights Back: The Life and Legacy of Charlemagne Péralte,* Patrick Bellegarde-Smith's *In the Shadow of the Powers: Dantès Bellegarde in Haitian Social Thought,* and Robert Fatton Jr.'s *The Guise of Exceptionalism: Unmasking the National Narratives in Haiti and the United States.*

[4] This is not the only definition of "space." According to the National Oceanic and Atmospheric Administration (NOAA), the so-called Kármán Line, the most common demarcation of the "edge of space" has this point beginning at 60 miles or 100 kilometers above earth.

flight, AP reported that "the bodies of an unusually large number of migrants who died in Arizona's borderlands are being recovered this summer amid record temperatures in the sun-scorched desert and rugged mountains" (Snow). Interestingly enough, Branson's launch pad for his space flight was in southeast New Mexico, not far from the deserts of Arizona, where many of the bodies were recovered. The geographical proximity of these two sites, in a glaring irony, lays bare the reality of these contrasting worlds. In one world, Branson bursts forth, traveling through planetary constraints, quite literally calling attention to his capacity to reach beyond earth's confines. In the other world, migrants who died in the desert did so because borders and state actions—the closing of border crossings not least among them—made it impossible for them to seek refuge, to break through the barriers that had been deliberately placed in their path.[5] Refusing to be confined to a life of violence and exploitation, they chose the path of mobility, but unlike Branson, they were unable to overcome the limits placed upon their movements.

It is important to note that this flight to space did not merely serve to demonstrate Branson's penchant for performative excess. There are real material gains to be acquired through such displays of narcissistic bravado. Branson's flight, by all accounts, raised the value of Virgin shares by $841 million, boosting the company's plan to debut tourism trips next year (i.e., in 2022), which will cost each passenger at least $450,000 (Bachman and Bloomberg). On the other side, not merely of the US–Mexico border but of a global divide between the North and the Global South, the migrants, even if they are so fortunate as to cross over successfully, face an uncertain future. If they are lucky enough to secure back breaking, hazardous employment, the possibility of incarceration, deportation, and wage exploitation are the everyday realities that will make up the texture of their lives. It might also be added that in between this

---

[5] For more information about how crossings have been made more difficult by deliberately closing certain routes, please see Geoffrey Alan Boyce et al. "Bodily Inertia and the Weaponization of the Sonoran Desert in US Boundary Enforcement: A GIS Modeling of Migration Routes through Arizona's Altar Valley;" Samuel Norton Chambers et al. "Mortality, Surveillance and the Tertiary 'Funnel Effect' on the U.S.-Mexico Border: A Geospatial Modeling of the Geography of Deterrence;" Thomas E. Sheridan and Randall H. McGuire's edited collection *The Border and Its Bodies: The Embodiment of Risk Along the U.S.-Mexico Line*, Vicki Squire's "Governing Migration through Death in Europe and the US: Identification, Burial, and the Crisis of Modern Humanism;" and Wendy Vogt's *Lives in Transit: Violence and Intimacy on the Migrant Journey*.

exploitative chain separating, for example, the Bransons from the nameless migrants are others—here, the residents of New Mexico, one of the poorest states in the union, who paid $220 million to build Spaceport America, the site for the space launch. Moreover, alongside the drain of this public wealth lies the grim fact that the town which hosted Branson's space flight had an unemployment rate of 11 percent in 2018, while a third of its residents live in poverty (Schlitz).

Mobility and immobility; confinement and the freedom to move; borders and transcendence; media saturation and media silence; state help to enable the accumulation of private wealth and state intervention to deny human beings the basic right to make a living—these are a few of the oppositional axes around which the two stories about Branson and the migrants develop. Distinguishing one story, the freedom to occupy and conquer, and exemplifying the other, a series of barriers constructed to suppress and limit. The barriers that suppress and limit also underlie Harris's speech. That speech and the two New Mexico- and Arizona-based stories not only highlight that there are different rules for different people but also reveal quite different ways of thinking about borders: for the state, borders are something to be enforced; for Branson, something to be transcended.

Based on the examples provided above, I want to begin with a claim that will be substantiated throughout this study: The border is not just a site defined by geography and geopolitics, a measure of territorial limits, but a social relation that in its contemporary manifestation is marked by the long shadow of historical violence. It is a relation that determines access to wealth and resources and enables the management of labor, the extraction of surplus, and the accumulation of capital. In short, it is a determinant in creating, maintaining, and reproducing a specific set of political and economic relations. Border rules, the operative framework for enforcing and regulating these relations, consist of material state and inter-state policies, as well as performative rituals such as the representation of bordered subjects that enact and reproduce these exploitative and oppressive relations. As Mezzadra and Neilson put it: "Borders, on one hand, are becoming finely tuned instruments for managing, calibrating, and governing global passages of people, money, and things. On the other hand, they are spaces in which the transformations of sovereign power and the ambivalent nexus of politics and violence are never far from view" (3–4). While I agree with them that borders play a vital role in managing the "global passage" of people and commodities, I part ways with these authors when they suggest borders are "finely tuned"; this description suggests a seamless, ordered, regulatory process. The unstable nature of border politics belies that claim. Even if we view the social relations generated by borders over the last ten years—a time that has included Brexit and the building of countless walls—it is apparent that they are relation characterized by disorder and volatility, relations that exact an even more terrible toll precisely because of this volatility.

It is specifically because of this instability that the border is also a place to produce a performance, a performance that is intended to demonstrate the iron will of the state. Detention centers, walls, and gates, of course, are meant to physically obstruct movement and immobilize populations, but they also serve to perform an aesthetics of expulsion and containment.[6] The visible presence of borders—in the form of barbed wire and check posts, walls and gates, documents and stamps, and a biometric attention to fingerprints and faces—is there for all to see. In this material form, it constitutes a very real space of entry and denial, belonging and nonbelonging. In some senses, the more spectacular this space—armed guards accompanied by large dogs, signs warning of severe penalties at the very hint of an infraction, grim-faced immigration officers scouring passports and papers for any irregularity—the more clearly is the announcement that this is where power is absolute, where one's fate rests entirely on the whims of an individual or on the idiosyncrasies of immigration "law." Yet, this materiality is accompanied by a co-constitutive imaginary, one where the border comes to be an ever-expanding space for negotiating a variety of contradictory political antagonisms. In the Global North, for instance, the border is a site where the exclusionary ideologies of race and empire intersect with the material needs of transnational labor, both of which then determine questions about legality, citizenship, and nationality. Caught between these volatile symbolic and material markers are the actual lives of those who are forced to traverse these contradictory spaces. What for them are hostile spaces where mere survival sometimes seems impossible is for the "native born" a sign of an unsettled present; the migrants' real and spectral presence marks the return of those who are the castoffs of empire, eliciting nativist anxieties in the heart of empire. At the root of this anxiety is the recognition of the other as racialized, as the abject to a nation that has determined itself to be formed as the space of exclusionary whiteness.

---

[6] See, for example, Wendy Brown's *Walled States, Waning Sovereignty*.

Certainly, if Brexit and the election of Donald Trump quite convincingly demonstrated that borders are a way to mark difference in racial and national terms, it is important not to forget that the border is also an essential mechanism for ensuring the extraction of surplus and the management and reproduction of living labor. In other words, if capital is value in motion, then borders are essential conduits for circulating and reproducing that value. This is not to suggest that the politics of race and the business of surplus extractions and management are separate issues; clearly, there are many intersecting political and economic factors that meet at the point of the border. One way to characterize this relationship between racial politics and surplus extraction is to affirm that the border brings together international policies around trade, commerce, and immigration and internal policies around employment, welfare, housing, and education and collapses any apparent distinctions between the two. All these apparently distinctive factors are imbricated in the politics of race and nation, and these, in turn, determine how and in what ways labor and capital are regulated. So, for example, the supply chains for products, whether for individual clothing items such as T-shirts or a vital commodity such as oil, are entirely dependent on the mechanism of the border. It is as necessary for a labor pool to be stagnant at the point of origin (say, in Thailand, for producing garments at low cost for Disney), as it is for certain labor to move from the Philippines, Sri Lanka, and India to Saudi Arabia or Qatar to keep the oil- producing Gulf states economically active. The mechanism of the border not only regulates this movement, but also maintains and reproduces a racialized global hierarchy of value, as I will demonstrate in more detail later in the chapter.

The exploitation of labor is intimately connected to the politics of movement, and this regulation and racialization of labor must be accompanied by forms of surveillance, and control. I will illustrate this point by briefly sketching two instances where the dialectical relationship between racialization and regulation of labor is startlingly apparent: one from a specific historical moment and one in its contemporary incarnation, both of which also highlight the intersection of racial politics with the movement of labor. Right after the Civil War in the United States, one of the first Black Codes to be imposed in the United States was related to "vagrancy," and severe penalties were imposed on the movement of the newly free black population. Punishment for those who broke the law included imprisonment with hard labor, as well as forcible hiring out to white employers for free labor. An important goal of these laws was to keep the "free" population captive so that their labor could be exploited.[7] While some of these restrictions were lifted during Reconstruction, new laws re-imposing the limitation of movement and criminalizing "vagrancy" were put in place once Reconstruction ended.

A contemporary instance of this racialized regulation of movement, as mentioned at the beginning of this chapter, is the criminalization, detention, and deportation of those from the Global South who, in compliance with international refugee laws, seek asylum and protection from war and human rights violations. Instead of nations meeting their international obligations to give careful attention to claims and, meanwhile, protect those requesting asylum, these migrants are stopped at sea and shipped back or detained on land to confront barbed wire, guns, and tear gas. While in the case of the post-Civil War South, the laws were devised to capture labor at the point of origin, in the contemporary example, the attempt is to expel, what is, potentially, excess labor. In both cases, however, the border is a containment zone (vagrancy laws, detention camps, holding cells, and so on), a place that is meant to impede movement; a place from which the return journey of deportation or servitude commences. Borders, whether they are constructed through internal policies or at the nation's edges, will let in or lock in those whose labor is required by the state, but eliminate the surplus that can be momentarily held back until it becomes necessary. In other words, borders perform the task required of them by the owners of capital: they regulate a mobile labor force that is easily accessible to fulfill the owners' needs, but one that also must be strictly maintained and controlled. As Marx puts it: "Capital can only create surplus labour by setting necessary labour in motion … It is its tendency, therefore, to create as much labour as possible; just as it is equally its tendency to reduce labour to a minimum. It is therefore equally

---

[7] It's worth noting that even the much-celebrated occasion of Juneteenth, which was recently declared a federal holiday, marked such a restriction. When General Gordon Granger arrived in Galveston, Texas in June 1865, he announced General Order No. 3 on June 19: "The people of Texas are informed that, in accordance with a Proclamation from the Executive of the United States, all slaves are free. This involves an absolute equality of personal rights and rights of property between former masters and slaves, and *the connection heretofore existing between them, becomes that between employer and hired labor. The Freedmen are advised to remain at their present homes, and work for wages. They are informed that they will not be allowed to collect at military posts; and that they will not be supported in idleness either there or elsewhere*" (my emphasis). At this moment of liberation, the forces of liberation delineate exactly how this "freedom" is meant to be translated into a meaningful reality, a condition that ensures a banning of movement and mobility.

2 BORDER RULES: IMPERIALISM, RACE, AND THE POLITICS OF DEVELOPMENT 35

a tendency of capital to increase the laboring population, as well as constantly posit a part of it as surplus population" (*Grundrisse* 399). Of course, as I mentioned earlier in this chapter, it is precisely such contradictions that unsettle the idea of a border politics that is "finely tuned."

It would be an oversimplification to suggest that the vast majority of border rules are constructed only in the service of capital or that these rules are merely an extension of racialized ideologies. Clearly, there are local political exigencies that determine how and why certain border policies come to be, even if these "exigencies" are often imbricated in economic and racial factors. These exigencies, however, are often both antagonistic and contradictory. So, for instance, there may be occasions where a racially motivated denial of entry has little to do with actual economic realities on the ground. Consider the fact that even during a time of labor needs, a political emergency, such as the post-9/11 moment, may result in hyperracialized border policies. Likewise, there are times when capital fulfills certain immanent tendencies irrespective of racialized hysteria, such as the regulation and supply of a consistent population of undocumented workers originating from the Global South, since they constitute vital low-paid labor sources for agricultural and construction work. In short, the relation between race and capital as determining factors for border policies is not a consistent one. An unbroken chain of causation cannot be established for all border policies. Undoubtedly, the regulation of labor plays a vital role in determining how borders function (as Marx's point from the *Grundrisse* establishes, capital regulates surplus labor in both ways—expels it or redirects it and draws on it when necessary—and I will address this point in greater detail later in the chapter). It is also true that the technology of border surveillance and its accompanying carceral methods generate large amounts of revenue for private corporations, and that the racial, religious, and economic anxieties of majority populations are appeased by the imposition of draconian border policies. However, there are too many contradictions in place for this relationship to be construed as a "finely tuned" one.

So far, I have concentrated on highlighting how the border functions as a social relation; however, as the examples of Branson's flight and Harris's admonitions demonstrate, there are ways in which the border is also a constitutive space, one which is made and remade through an elaborate mode of representations. Stuart Hall's comments on representation help clarify the implications of this claim: "representation is *constitutive* of the event. It enters into the constitution of the object that we are talking about. It is part of the object itself; it is constitutive of it. It is one of its conditions of existence, and therefore representation is not *outside* the event, not *after* the event, but *within* the event itself; it is constitutive of it" (117). In other words, it is not just the material fact of the border that makes it real; representations of events at the border or crossings there are as much a part of the border and how it comes to be. Branson bursting through the boundary between earth's atmosphere and space demonstrates one kind of border imaginary: that the wonders of technology, and the power of individual entrepreneurial spirit and capital can tear asunder any human limitations; meanwhile, Vice-President Harris's call to "enforce" laws and "secure" borders conjure a contrasting imaginary: securitization of borders, maintained through "enforcement," is necessary to provide safety for US citizens. In these examples, then, borders are not just lines signifying the limits and extensions of territorial sovereignty; they also become part of the national imaginary. They simultaneously signify spaces that enable containment and enclosure, as well as limits that must be transcended. Fluidity and rigidity, mobility and statis reign side by side.

Let me elaborate on this point in the light of Hall's statement: the border exists as a physical space, a line drawn on a map, and there are real material, rigid ways in which the border marks the beginning and end of territories. This spatial reality, however, is only one part of the border's significance in national life. Because of its ideological life and reach, the border also constantly forms and reforms itself according to the ways it gets represented and used in the national imaginary. This, in turn, allows the border valuable purchase in the process of making and unmaking subjects. So, although we think of the border primarily as a regulatory apparatus, a dividing line that marks the limits of movement, this movement or the prohibition of this movement is also a vital element of the border, as it is central in the construction of subjectivity. An individual's encounter with the border makes the border real, just as that encounter constructs a subject in a particular way, and asserts, with brutal force, if necessary, the subject's race, gender, national, and religious identity. I would like to demonstrate this dialectical relationship by reflecting for a moment on this border/subject relation in general, and how these border encounters are translated in actual terms through particular experiences.

Experiences of the border, of course, differ depending on the structural mode that interpellates us into its space. For millions, migrants' journeys to the border and encounters with it are life-and-death experiences, and a successful border crossing often remains a distant dream, forever deferred, despite multiple attempts. Borders are approached, encountered, and crossed in myriad forms, but even the most ordinary form of border crossing, in my view, constructs the subject in specific ways. Consider the international airplane journey, one to which those of us with privilege have access (It is worth noting one related fact: only about 5 percent of people in the world take international flights every year). People create protective personas when approaching the space of the border. A certain set of rituals begin long before arrival and departure at the place of the border. Depending on one's citizenship status and on one's race or class position, it is a preparation process fraught with anxiety. Needless to say, an English-speaking white male carrying a US or a European Union passport navigates borders quite differently from a non-European-language speaking woman of color from the Global South, arriving at the border of a Western nation on a visitor's visa.

Imagine for a moment, this latter arrival, from the perspective of a woman from the Global South, one who has been marked as the "Other" and is about to enter an unfamiliar national space. The moments of anxiety begin to increase a few hours before arrival as flight attendants start passing out landing cards, inquiring about passengers' citizenship status. The flight attendant has already made some assumptions about passengers' citizenship status and has paused when they reach her, expecting a request for a landing card. She has already been hailed as an alien approaching a still invisible border, even though she has not indicated that she desires a landing card. A quick survey of the questions on the card increases her anxiety as she considers whether she can accurately fill in the required information. Is the day of her departure included in the number of days or weeks of her stay? Will filling in inaccurate information result in a refusal to grant entry? As the plane begins its descent, she makes sure, once again, that her passport is secured. She seeks out pieces of paper that contain important pieces of financial information or invitation letters from organizations, or switches on her phone to remind herself of contact numbers and names. After arrival, as she moves through the cordoned off spaces of the airport, a moment of sudden panic seizes her when she is unable to locate her passport. She breathes a sigh of relief when she feels its presence in the inside pocket of her jacket. As she maneuvers through the airport, the presence of uniformed authority figures reminds her that she is marked as a subject who is approaching the space of the border. An even more acute consciousness of her subject position is demanded. It appears that the signs and instructions are directed at her. She is now a person who the state can hinder and harm, if necessary, or confer upon her the privilege of entry. Following the signs directing her to immigration, she is aware that she has reached a place where she must be on alert. The border requires her to recognize that she is marked as a potential threat unless she can prove otherwise. As she arrives at the point where a long row of booths awaits her, she hopes she has chosen the correct line. She hesitates to ask for help, fearing that she will not be understood, and thus ridiculed or singled out for unwelcome attention. She notices that the line for citizens and residents moves rapidly, while her line barely inches along. When it is her turn to be inspected for entry, she steps forward, a knot of anxiety in her stomach. She studies the features of the immigration officer, imagining whether their demeanor indicates that a standard set of questions will follow. How much significance should be given to their race, her gender? Does the South Asian name on the badge reassure her or make her imagine that a more rigorous interrogation will follow? Is it significant that the officer does not smile? Should she smile and greet the officer? Should she keep her eyes lowered or meet their gaze?[8]

The description I have provided for a presumptive border encounter imagines one experience; these encounters of course differ, depending on the particular border being crossed or on the subject position of the border-crosser; some readers may find this description an exaggeration of the anxieties prospective visitors may experience as they encounter a border at the point of arrival (after all, such readers might argue, these are visitors who have the legal right to enter); others, though, may think this description downplays the very specific anxieties experienced by visitors from certain national origins, or particular religious groups, for example. Indeed, these readers might claim, the "legal" right to enter remains in abeyance even past the moment at the immigration booth. It can be rescinded at the Customs crossing. My goal, however, is not to attempt to represent every distinct kind of position occupied by a border crosser or to describe every potential barrier they might face, but to make the larger point that an encounter with a border positions people in particular ways, creating (hyper)awareness of specific identity markers—even forcing border-crossers to occupy particular identities. This moment of relationality contributes to the affirmation of the border's authoritative status, a status that acquires its legitimacy as a means of control and regulation by

---

[8] For an excellent personal account of border performance, see Shahram Khosravi's *The "Illegal" Traveler: An Auto-Ethnography of Borders.*

2 BORDER RULES: IMPERIALISM, RACE, AND THE POLITICS OF DEVELOPMENT   39

our interaction with it. Echoing Hall, one would say that the subject is not "outside" any meaning that makes up the border but is "within" it. And, just as the border-crosser is subject to the mechanisms of the state, the border comes to be because of this ability to create subjects who can be controlled by these mechanisms.

More significantly, as I will demonstrate throughout this study, this moment of interpellation by the state, by Customs and Immigration authorities, although hyper-visible at the designated space of "the border," does not just happen merely at the marked line of entry. The border exists well beyond spatial and temporal boundaries. The current US Immigration and Customs Enforcement (ICE) raids carried out throughout the country are an obvious manifestation of this point.[9] Moreover, as a short anecdote will demonstrate, the border exists both in material and psychic forms far from the "real" line of the border, even for those who have a legal right to be in a country. Let me cite a personal experience.

In the mid-1980s, shortly after arriving in the United States, a South Asian friend and I decided to drive across the country to California in a battered Ford Dodge Charger. While traveling across Arizona on Interstate 40, just west of Flagstaff—thus, several hundred miles from the border—we were pulled over by the state's highway patrol for no apparent reason other than for appearing to be from "elsewhere" and for being in a car that had seen better days. We were told to accompany the officers to a border station where we were asked to prove that we were in the country legally. Since when setting off on this road trip, we had no intention of leaving the country, neither of us was carrying our passports. My friend and I spent some uncomfortable moments squirming in the presence of white authority figures while they checked on our port of entry and our visa status on the computer to verify our account of our legal status. We were finally allowed to leave with a stern warning that we were never to travel without our passports. The officers did not find it necessary to explain to us why we were pulled over; it was obvious to us, however, that our visual "difference" quite clearly played a role. At the time, I, of course, knew nothing about Public Law 613. Passed in 1946, this law granted Border Control agents "unfettered authority to conduct stops and searches within a 'reasonable distance from any external boundary of the United States'" ("How US Border Patrol"). A year after the law passed, the agency specified this "reasonable

---

[9] For a discussion of raids in cities far from the border, please see Jessie Higgins's "ICE Raid Devastated Tiny Midwest Town; 10 Years Later, It's Still Recovering."

40   K. CHOWDHURY

distance" as 100 miles.[10] Apparently, fourth amendment protections against unreasonable search and seizure did not exist when we were apprehended in Arizona. This experience was a rude awakening, the time when I realized the border is not just a designated place of arrival and departure, a point of crossing over, but a social relation where one is marked as "other," where predetermined power relations are always in place.

Imperialism and the Border at Home and Abroad

Although the encounters described above are all too common for the millions who are harassed, surveilled, and deported across the globe—as well as for others—there are reasons that these everyday manifestations of the border are often underrepresented in the popular imagination. Instead, the lines where territorial boundaries begin and end are overdetermined and spectacularized, such as Checkpoint Charlie in Berlin during the Cold War or the Line of Control in Kashmir or the gates out of occupation zones in Palestine. At other times, so-called natural boundaries like the Rio Bravo are seen as the endings and beginnings of nations. However, even though hypermilitarized spaces are among the most recognizable manifestations of borders, borders are characterized by their fluidity: not only do they stretch far from the territorial lines *within* the nation and *between* nations, but dominant powers also extend them wider and wider in the name of "security." This kind of fluidity is dependent on a nation's military and economic strength. For example, the US reach around the world is clearly the most visible extension of borders (it maintains nearly 800 military bases in more than 70 countries and territories abroad).[11] Meanwhile, countries with little economic or political clout—the Central African Republic, Nepal, Niger, or Yemen—experience a different kind of border fluidity; they have no firm borders to speak of, and their sovereignty and territorial integrity can be breached by other countries or transnational organizations with little difficulty.

The United States is not the only country that continues to extend its borders. NATO's tentacles have also spread out, in one case, across North Africa into the Middle East. Since its destruction of the Libyan state in 2011, it has moved more overtly into African political life. France, for

---

[10] For an analysis of Public Law 613, please see S. Deborah Kang, *The INS on the Line: Making Immigration Law on the US-Mexico Border, 1917–195.*

[11] For a discussion of this statistic, please see John Glaser's "Why We Should Close America's Overseas Military Bases." Additional analysis can be found in Todd Miller's *Empire of Borders: The Expansion of the US Border Around the World.*

2 BORDER RULES: IMPERIALISM, RACE, AND THE POLITICS OF DEVELOPMENT 41

instance, continues to determine the financial destinies of its former colonies on the continent.[12] In 2014, for example, France pressured five African countries (Burkina Faso, Chad, Mali, Mauritania, and Niger) to create the G5 Sahel initiative. Ostensibly designed to fight terrorism and to promote "development," this initiative has not only extended France's political and economic control in the region, but also moved France's border further south of the Mediterranean Sea.[13] Meanwhile, the United States runs a multimillion drone base in Agadez (Niger Airbase 201), which conducts bombing operations across the region.[14] It is important, however, not to view these extensions of borders merely as indicators of imperial control, though, of course, they are that. My point is that border policies, much as the actual lines themselves, are not confined to one set of practices, and they do not exist in isolation. So, for instance, the imperial policies of Western nations that are implemented "elsewhere" in turn influence border policies at "home." Likewise, practices from "home" find their way in nations elsewhere. Consider that Charles Graner, who was convicted of abusing prisoners of war in Abu Ghraib, Iraq, was a prison guard in the notorious State Corrections Institution in Greene County, PA, where he was accused of the racial abuse of prisoners in that facility.[15]

[12] For an illuminating account of "the French state's continuous meddling in Africa—a master class in in capitalist villainy, victim-blaming, and versatility," see Ndongo Samba Sylla's interview with Fanny Pigeaud.

[13] For more information on France's interventionist approach, please see Michele Barbero's "France Bids Adieu to Its Military Mission in West Africa."

[14] For a discussion of the role of the Niger Airbase, please see Olayinka Ajala's "US Drone Base in Agadez." Additional discussion can be found in Eric Schmitt and Christoph Koetti's "Remote C.I.A. Base in the Sahara Steadily Grows."

[15] Of course, the brutalization of prisoners is not merely about the actual violence that happens in situ. Incarceration practices are linked to the ways in which housing or health rights are denied or made unavailable to particularly vulnerable portions of the population. Sometimes these connections are apparent, such as when a person who has had any connection to the prison system is denied housing or health benefits upon their return to the community—the "New Jim Crow," as Michelle Alexander has described it. Other connections are structurally normalized and thus harder to discern. Imprisonment, health benefits, and access to housing are part of a continuum of carceral capitalism, which is system that is built on the surveillance, management, and regulation of bodies. This is not merely a biopolitical regime of control, but one that is essential to capital's need to have available or make disposable laboring bodies. Thus, the size of the prison population has little to do with crime, but much more with how a specific group of people—racialized, of course (a third of the prison population consists of black inmates, and almost a quarter, Hispanic) and classed ("49 percent of incarcerated men were employed in the three years prior to incarceration and their median annual earnings were $6250; just 13 percent earned more than $15,000," From "Incarceration and Poverty in the United States")—are controlled and confined.

This interrelationship between the "outside" and the "inside" is a vital one for our understanding of the border and the ways in which it both embeds itself into our consciousness and everyday lives and becomes part of the state apparatus in its relentless task of disciplining populations. As dominant states go about their business of resource-grabbing and territorial control in "foreign" lands, the social cost on their "home" populations continues unabated. An example of this phenomenon can be seen in the many costs of Israel's ruthless 11-day pounding of Gaza in May 2021. Not only is this a manifestation of extreme border enforcement, with a military superpower raining down bombs on one of the poorest regions of the world and killing over 250 people (including 67 children) in the process; the consequences of this bombardment are also evident in Israel's domestic policies that include a clampdown on dissent and anti-war sentiments.[16] Further, in the economic realm, Israel's already existing doctrine of austerity, which has resulted in one of the highest inequality rates in the world, continues unabated. A country that dedicates $2508 per capita of government spending to the military (more than even the United States) must, by necessity, cut back on public programs and social spending.[17]

Meanwhile, here in the United States, enough has been said about the connections between US imperial policing, its migrant policies, and the disastrous inattention to the needs of its own vulnerable population—a point further affirmed by the costs of the pandemic, which have been visited most sharply upon "economically disadvantaged minorities" (Qureshi). What Dr. Martin Luther King, Jr. had pointed to in his groundbreaking speech at the Riverside Church on April 4, 1967, during the height of the Vietnam War, remains true today. In that speech, Dr. King had categorically condemned the US war but also made the damning connection between racism and classism at home and imperial war abroad: "I knew that America would never invest the necessary funds or energies in rehabilitation of its poor so long as adventures like Vietnam continued to draw men and skills and money like some demonic destructive suction tube. So, I was increasingly compelled to see the war as an enemy of the poor and to attack it as such" (143). Let us reflect on that statement not

---

[16] Please see the *Al Jazeera* article "Israel's Killing of Palestinian Children."

[17] For information on Israel's military spending, please see Usaid Siddiqui's "Infographic: What You Need to Know About Israel's Military." For information on US military aid to Israel, please see Jake Horton's "Israel-Gaza: How Much Money Does Israel Get from US?" or Catie Edmondson's "House Approves $1 Billion for the Iron Dome as Democrats Feud Over Israel."

2 BORDER RULES: IMPERIALISM, RACE, AND THE POLITICS OF DEVELOPMENT 43

just for its accurate rendering of a particular moment in US history, but also because it captures where we are almost five and half decades later. The United States continues to wage war across the world, targeting populations in the Global South, whether directly, and most recently, as in Afghanistan, Iraq, or Syria or by proxy in Gaza, Libya, and Yemen. Globally, the United States accounts for almost 40 percent of all military spending, holding the top position at $778 billion (McCarthy). Meanwhile, with the recent expiration of the monthly Child Tax Credit in January 2022, child poverty rates increased from 12.1 percent in December 2021 to 17 percent in the next month ("3.7 Million").

King's point was that the war in Vietnam was not an isolated, disparate moment in the way the ruling class conducted their business. What binds together military violence, the dearth of a health infrastructure, or the persecution of working-class African Americans are the forces of global capital—what King called the "giant triplets of racism, extreme materialism, and militarism." King saw the connections between class war and white supremacist policies at home, and imperial actions abroad. White supremacy and its attendant principles are not just manifest in and flowing from the afterlife of slavery; they have always intersected with the imperial policies of a settler and imperial nation that used many of the same techniques of repression in Wounded Knee, as it did in the Philippines.

These unsettling parallels between ruinations and violence at home and abroad continue in the present. Consider the infrastructural failures in cities such as Flint, Michigan, and Jackson, Mississippi, and other predominantly African American neighborhoods and the fact that the "vast majority of deaths [after the first Gulf War in Iraq] were caused not by the direct impact of bombs but by the destruction of the electric power grid and the ensuing collapse of the public health, water and sanitation systems, leading to outbreaks of dysentery, cholera, and other water-borne diseases" ("Water Under Siege in Iraq"). More recently, the H.R.4437 law (Border Protection, Antiterrorism, and Illegal Immigration Control Act of 2005), which implemented stringent border policies severely limiting the rights of those who could seek refuge in the United States, came to pass at the time when it became apparent to the George W. Bush administration that the wars in Iraq and Afghanistan were going to lead to the displacement of millions, many of whom would seek refuge in the country which had contributed, in great measure, to the destruction of their homelands. In this instance, it is apparent how the racialized internal policies of the United

States are explicitly connected to racialization on a global level.[18] Borders, I suggest, are a vital element in these interrelated structures and moments, and play, in the current conjuncture, even a more explicit role—than they did in Dr. King's day—in a global landscape dominated by the politics of nationalism.

Vijay Prashad's description of recent set of events confirms these increasingly apparent interrelations. In May of 2021, Brazilian President, Bolsonaro backed Israel's use of brutal force against the residents of Gaza a few days after the "police operation against the people of Jacarezinho [the favela with the largest Afro-Brazilian population] in Rio de Janeiro, which resulted in the massacre of twenty-five people" (Prashad). This latter action barely made it to the international spotlight, but one might consider the similarities between these lethal assaults by the state against dispossessed, racialized others. Bolsonaro's support for Israel establishes the fact that borders are not just constructed to demarcate nations, but to establish other boundaries as well; they mark the line between those whose lives the state preserves and those considered expendable and threatening. Indeed, Bolsonaro's approval of Israel's actions in the Occupied Territories is often echoed by the approach of Indian Prime Minister, Narender Modi, who can replicate the same logic when dealing with the perceived threats posed by those he deems "anti-national." Meanwhile, Xi Jinping carries out a war against the Uighur people and the Burmese junta persecute and murder the Rohingya. Borders, according to these regimes, enable the rulers to distinguish between those who justly belong to the nation and those who do not, and thus marked for persecution and destruction.

The persecution of these minority populations is often met with token condemnatory declarations in the West since many of the offending regimes have embraced the dictates of multinational capital and offer full access to their resources and their labor force. Thus, as long as Myanmar, for instance, provides low-cost labor for Western firms, the regime's oppression of the Rohingya will be tolerated. Ironically, then, even as the borders of the Burmese nation are being affirmed against their own people, their national sovereignty is sold out to the constrictive and extractive logic of global banking, debt, and trade infrastructures that ensure the

---

[18] For a look at "both the immersive global trajectories of race and racism, and the international variation in contemporary configurations of racialized experience" see the recent collection, *Global Raciality: Empire, Postcoloniality, Decoloniality (2019)*.

long-term bondage of all the workers in the nation.[19] Borders function to enable both of these seemingly contradictory processes. Most of the national borders in the Global South, which are defended with such ferocity by nation states, including Myanmar's were determined by the departing colonial powers during the process of decolonization. The drawing of these artificial borders has contributed to costly and deadly wars from West Africa and the Middle East to South Asia and the Latin American continent. Also, in the so-called postcolonial age, these borders still serve the interests of global capital, along with, of course, those of the national bourgeoisie.

Neoliberal mystification obscures the fact that narratives upholding territorial sovereignty and the sacredness of borders are built on the wreckage of colonial rule. (The border narratives of India and Pakistan are among the most pervasive constructs that illustrate this irony.) Walter Rodney's *How Europe Underdeveloped Africa* remains a primer about how a continent can be systematically prepared for expropriation and exploitation, and how post-decolonization borders continue to enable accumulation. Rodney describes how, long before the Scramble for Africa and the Berlin Treaty of 1885 divided up the continent between the leading Western European powers, the ground had been prepared for imperial conquest. The so-called pre-colonial period was characterized, of course, by the massive disorder and devastation caused by the slave trade but also by the concomitant disruption of age-old methods of farming and trading and tribal relationships that had been crafted over centuries—a disruption that lay the structural groundwork for the Berlin Treaty. Rodney also points out that capitalist Europe had benefited from its imperialist pillage, which had allowed it to build up and develop armaments for which African nations had no defense. Indeed, in the circular motion of capital, the accumulated wealth from the colonies made the further and continuing subjugation of the colonies more realizable.

Rodney's description of African subjection to European capital, formulated in 1972, remains true today: "So long as foreigners own land, mines,

---

[19] A region in Thailand known as Mae Sot, which is close to Thailand's border with Mynamar, is known for its exploitative treatment of factory workers. After garment workers migrated into Thailand in order to make money to send home to their families, their exploitative working conditions resulted in a lawsuit and collective settlement of $111,000 which Starbucks, Disney, NBC Universal, and Tesco initially refused to pay. For more on exploitation as an integral role in the way that many major brands function, please see Ilana Winterstein's "Global Brands, Global Exploitation."

factories, banks, insurance companies, means of transportation, newspapers, power stations, then for so long will the wealth of Africa flow outward into the hands of those elements. In other words, in the absence of direct political control, foreign investment insures that the natural resources and the labor of Africa produce economic value that is lost to the continent" (27). Of course, even Rodney could not have estimated the extent to which the structure of debt and the collaboration of the postcolonial elite with the forces of global capital would place manacles on the hands of the African people. Nor could he predict how much the requirement for certain minerals, hastened by the demands of the tech industries, would result in catastrophic civil wars fueled by the arms merchants and governments of the West.[20] Nonetheless, the relevance today of his central point regarding the "economic value that is lost to the continent" is evident in a significant statistic, one which is particularly striking during a time of an international health crisis: 64 low-income countries (many of which are in Africa) spend more on debt payments than they do on health care. In fact, many African countries are paying up to five times their health budgets on debt repayments.[21]

Borders, then, function in dramatically different ways within the imperialist network, depending on where those borders are drawn and who benefits from them. Territorial and economic sovereignty only operate for the countries at the top of the imperial pyramid. Middle level countries, such as the BRIC (Brazil, Russia, India, and China) nations have some leverage, but they are also subject to the dictates of the G7, which controls much of the global economy and most of the financial organizations.[22] Meanwhile, the countries at the bottom of the imperial pyramid must allow capital to pass unhindered, attached as these countries are at all levels to the infrastructure of debt, labor, and resource extraction. This infra-

[20] For more information on the relationship between conflict minerals and violence, please see Eichstaedt's *Consuming the Congo: War and Conflict Minerals in the World's Deadliest Place.* Please also see Musamba's and Vogel's "The Problem with Conflict Materials."

[21] Please see "Sixty-Four Countries Spend More on Debt Payments Than Health." To view a debt counter that depicts (in real time) the debt that some of the world's most impoverished countries have repaid to the world's richest countries since the beginning of the Covid-19 pandemic, please see OxFam International's "No Country Should Be Forced to Choose Between Paying Back Debts or Providing Health Care."

[22] For discussion of China's increasing influence, which raises hackles in the West, please see Daniel S. Markey's *China's Western Horizon: Beijing and the New Geopolitics of Eurasia,* Jonathan E. Hillman's *The Emperor's New Road: China and the Project of the Century,* and Joanna Chiu's *China Unbound: A New World Disorder.*

structure is directly connected to border politics, which is to say that borders make it possible for this financial extraction to occur in an efficient manner wherever they operate, at actual sites of production, such as the maquiladoras at the US–Mexico border, which are positioned at the border to enable maximum exploitation, or in restrictions imposed, for instance, by the provisions of an International Monetary Fund loan ensuring that a low-income nation has to cut public sector jobs, curtail various social programs, or enable a greater proportion of foreign ownership and investment.

In the next section, I will focus exclusively on one element of this infrastructure, the exploitation of labor designed to extract value, offering an analysis that will make it evident how the border functions as social relation, constructing and cementing the supply of labor across different sites of accumulation. I will suggest that even though this regulation of movement allows for maximum exploitation, it also opens avenues for cross-border actions of solidarity, which can potentially disrupt the smooth functioning of capital's logic of accumulation.

Borders, Primitive Accumulation, and Surplus Populations

Current imperial practices determine that it is no coincidence that the largest groups of refugees are from those regions of the planet that have been disrupted by imperial violence. Afghanistan, Palestine, and Syria are notable examples. These countries are then further controlled by Western powers and their local allies to keep their populations corralled in place—unable to escape the chaos and violence let loose by the attacks on their countries. The United States has long extended its border controls into Central America and the Caribbean in order to regulate the movement of people, and in recent years, the EU has made deals with countries such as Turkey and Libya to exclude and turn back those seeking refuge. Population movement controls have been militarized with navy gunboats on seas "protecting" the territories of Western nations. What was famously termed as a refugee "crisis" in Europe during the years 2014–2015, primarily came to be because of the West's incitement and prolongation of violence in the countries that the refugees were fleeing. The promotion and extension of this violence came both through direct military interference and through military sales to the far reaches of the earth. The inevitable movement of people displaced by these conflicts was followed by the Western nations' refusal to follow international refugee laws and offer refuge and protection for those who arrived at their shores fleeing that very same violence. The principal of non-refoulment was violated then and continues to be flouted, as is evident from the recent treatment of Haitian refugees at the US–Mexico border.

How, then, do these practices of expulsion and rejection balance with capital's need to have a continuous and consistent army of surplus labor? So far, I have tried to explain the many ways in which border rules extend the reach and domination of capital. Regulating the movement of people constitutes an essential element of this relation. Labor discipline—containing workers within a specific place and absorbing and expelling them when necessary—is a key to maintaining the capital relation. Certainly, there are instances of depopulation or the movement of people that capital cannot entirely control, such as the emptying out of a rural community or a large inflow of people into metropolitan areas, but even in these instances the movement of people offers potential opportunities for capital to appropriate land and resources or to bring down wages. Moreover, we must keep in mind that the "setting free" of "a part of the working class" and "the production of a relative surplus population—*i.e.*, a population surplus in relation to capital's average requirements for valorization— is a necessary condition for modern industry" (*Capital, Volume 1*, 786). Let us recall Marx's exact words linking the accumulation process and the production of this surplus population:

> Capitalistic accumulation itself ... constantly produces, and produces in the direct ratio of its own energy and extent, a relatively redundant population of workers, i.e., a population of greater extent than suffices for the average needs of the valorisation of capital, and therefore a surplus-population .... It is the absolute interest of every capitalist to press a given quantity of labour out of a smaller, rather than a greater number of labourers, if the cost is about the same .... The more extended the scale of production, the stronger this motive. Its force increases with the accumulation of capital. (*Capital, Volume 1*, 782–84)

It is equally important to note, however, as Marx always reminds us, that the "*absolute general law of capitalist accumulation* ... is modified in its workings by many circumstances" (798), that the constitution of this relative surplus population is based on the labor needs of a given moment. So, for instance, the post-war boom and the reduction in labor supply in Europe and the United States saw the direct recruitment of "overseas" workers, such as when the British government enlisted workers to migrate from the Caribbean islands "to assist with labour shortages," particularly in "jobs paying so badly that few whites wanted them" ("The Windrush Generation"). Likewise, after World War II, migration to Europe from African countries (mainly Mali, Senegal, and Mauritania) increased, with small groups of refugees being "readily assimilated into the labor force" (Fassin). And the Bracero Program (1942–1964), brought more than four million Mexican laborers to the United States. Contrarily, in the post-1970s period of long-stagnation, when industrial production was "off-shored," more labor was expelled from Europe and the United States than was absorbed.[23]

One way to reflect on the connections between migration and labor regulation is to consider how the labor needs of capital are dispersed around the globe. Certainly, it may seem a contradiction that the centers of capital that have the most to gain from the exploitation of low-wage refugee labor admit the fewest refugees. However, surplus extraction is most intense and profitable at the point of production, so it is no coincidence that the maximum movement of labor is often located in the less developed regions of the world, where wages are at rock bottom. Consider Nepalese and Bangladeshi migrant laborers in India, Afghan laborers in Iran and Pakistan, Palestinian workers in Lebanon or Turkey, or South Asian laborers in the Gulf states. Each of these "home" economies are heavily reliant on these labor pools. These workers, many of whom are undocumented, have few rights, are paid meager wages, and are subject to frequent abuse; additionally, they almost always work in an "informal" economy, which means they can be "expelled" whenever necessary. Without these laborers, construction industries, transportation networks, and agricultural outlets in these countries would collapse or be seriously compromised. Thus, imperial centers could not successfully depend on their low-cost supply chains without the mobility of these workers within the global South. The proxy exploitation of this labor pool is essential for

---

[23] John Smith in *Imperialism in the Twenty-First Century: Globalization, Super-Exploitation, and Capitalism's Final Crisis* provides some startling figures to support this point: "in 2010, 79 percent, or 541 million, of the world's industrial workers lived in 'less developed regions,' up from 34 percent in 1950 and 53 percent in 1980, compared to the 145 million industrial workers, or 21 percent of the total, who in 2010 lived in the imperialist countries" (101).

the smooth functioning of Western economies. In many ways, the configuration of the global labor pool at the present moment is the best-case scenario for global capital. Keeping a large labor force outside their borders but available so that value can be extracted, Western countries do not have to bear the political costs of admitting those who are seen as economic competitors to their "native" workers, nor offer them any of the benefits of an incorporation into the formal economy, and yet these countries can profit when they need workers from a mobile pool of super-exploited labor.[24] Meanwhile, the elite in the Global South also reap their rewards, serving as intermediaries in this process.

Of course, migration of workers does not merely happen between nations. In fact, for the many millions who can no longer survive on agricultural work, there are very few resources available to seek what is increasingly a very costly attempt to migrate to other countries. In these instances, the borders they cross are internal ones.[25] Indeed, according to the UNHCR (United Nations High Commissioner for Refugees), by the end of 2021, there were 53.2 million Internally Displaced Persons (IDP) ("Internally Displaced People," UNHCR). The UNHCR defines IDPs as those who are forced to move because of "armed conflict, generalized violence or human rights violations." Unless "human rights violations" here include the vast dispossession of rural residents across the globe or the over 700 million people who are forced to face hunger ("The State of Food Security and Nutrition"), these cited causes do not account for the many millions across the world who leave their place of birth because there are simply no resources or means available for their survival. Recently, the scale of these migrations became amply evident in India when millions of workers were forced to return to their home villages in March–April 2020 after the government declared a Covid-related lockdown at very short

---

[24] Drawing from Brazilian Marxist Ruy Mauro Marini's work, Jaime Osorio defines "super-exploitation" as "the processes of violating the value of labor power, whether in its daily aspects, or in its overall dimension" (Osorio 96). While super-exploitation can be a generalized form of exploitation in the capitalist system, easily visible in the imperial centers, where undocumented workers, for example, are paid well below the value of their labor power, or when capitalism, as Osorio puts it, "resorts to superexploitation to counteract the falling rate of profit," what remains distinctive about super-exploitation, Osorio clarifies, is that it exists in "'normal' periods of reproduction," and that it "affects the processes of reproduction of capital" (Osorio 97–98).

[25] The most striking example of this form of migration is in contemporary China, where internal migrants constitute about 20 percent of its population.

notice. While it may appear that this particular movement of labor was defined by a return from urban to rural areas, in many cases, migrant workers have moved within their states and districts, simply because the costs of long-distance moves are prohibitive or act as burdens on family members.

How then do we connect the dots between the creation of pools of surplus labor, diverse migration patterns, and the border practices that make the movement of labor beneficial for capital? One way to begin to understand these relationships is to recognize that capital is forever engaged in a battle to change existing social conditions both because of external needs and because of political instability. So, for instance, the revolutionary movements in Central and East India have been met with a brutal counterattack since they directly impinge on the extraction process.[26] As the demand for global resources grows and the needs of the external economy change, capital is less willing to tolerate existing relations of production. Also in India, the recent move to attempt to "integrate" the agricultural sector into the global commodities market is one such example. In this case, the state is no longer willing to extract in its usual form but must accede to the requirements of the international commodities market.[27] Thus, there is always a back and forth between relations of production and the mode of accumulation; this dialectic is, of course, sharpened by existing political contexts.

As my example from central India makes clear, displacing populations in order to extract minerals and other resources remain a determining factor in the movement of workers and the shaping of internal and external borders. While it is tempting to ascribe this phenomenon to the mechanisms of primitive accumulation, a few supplementary comments are necessary here, not just to affirm some important aspects of Marx's reading, but also to show how that reading illuminates the role of the state—and the work of borders—in determining how and why primitive accumulation may be seen by some as a continuous process that is necessary to meet

---

[26] For a discussion of the impact of mining on indigenous people in India, please see Devleena Ghosh's "The Bones of Our Mothers: Adivasi Dispossession in an Indian State." Please also see Elizabeth Puranam's "The Mine That Displaced India's Indigenous People."

[27] For an excellent analysis of the Modi government's attempts (through the passage of three farm bills in 2020) to weaken existing regulations in the agricultural sphere and hand over complete control to the corporate sector, see "The Farmers' Revolt in India."

52   K. CHOWDHURY

the unending demands of global capital.[28] Before offering further discussion, however, I must make an important qualification about *continuing* primitive accumulation. Although the process of violent proletarianization and expropriation we see in Central India is similar to the process Marx identifies as primitive accumulation, this process, as I indicated in the previous chapter, takes place in our time within the context of a fully capitalist world market. Once capital accumulation has become the dominant, determining force of the world market, that violence is no longer "primitive" or "original" or working to create the conditions for accumulation. It now serves the full-time interests of capital.[29]

Having made this qualification, I will attempt to retain the vital, still relevant elements from Marx's description of primitive accumulation, which may help us comprehend how it enables a disruption of populations, results in the inevitable movement of people, and ultimately is connected to our study of border rules. It may be worth remembering why Marx turns his attention to primitive accumulation at the end of Volume One of *Capital*, rather than at its beginning. If primitive accumulation was the launching point for the capitalist mode of accumulation, why not begin an analysis of capital with the process that made this epoch changing shift possible? Why begin instead with an analysis of the commodity form? To answer this question, we must remember that a primary goal in *Capital* is to demystify the explanatory rationalizations of bourgeois political economists and refute their claims that capitalism is the result of the "eternal laws of Nature" (*Capital, Volume I* 925). It is within that context that we can consider the significance of what Marx argues at the end of Volume One of *Capital*.

In these blistering final chapters, Marx puts to rest any illusion that capitalism came out of a "natural" process. Not just focusing on England and Scotland—especially the sections on the "clearing" of the Scottish Highlands—but also highlighting the barbaric violence in the colonies, Marx makes evident how and why "capital comes dripping from head to foot, from every pore, with blood and dirt" (874). Not only does he shatter any illusion that expropriation rather than "eternal laws" was what provided the wealth necessary for a mode of production to be inaugurated; he also notes that "conquest, enslavement, robbery, murder, in

---

[28] For critiques of primitive accumulation, please see Sylvia Federici, David Harvey, Glen Coulthard, or Massimo De Angelis.

[29] I am indebted to one of my anonymous readers for providing this qualification.

2 BORDER RULES: IMPERIALISM, RACE, AND THE POLITICS OF DEVELOPMENT   53

short, force play[ed] the greatest part" in this process (874). Furthermore, he makes it abundantly clear how millions were displaced and dispossessed from their land, how their ways of making a living were destroyed, how self-earned private property became capitalist private property, how communal cooperation was shattered, and—finally—how all these catastrophes forced all of these people to be trapped within the manacles of wage slavery.

What Marx demonstrates, with razor sharp directness, is that the "origin" story of capital is a very different one from the "nursery tale" proposed by bourgeois political economists (874). Marx, however, was not prepared to leave it at that. As a revolutionary, he also explained that capital had set itself up for its own demise. The "expropriation of the mass of the people by a few usurpers" created the conditions for the "expropriation of a few usurpers by the mass of the people" (930). However, this should not be read as mere historical inevitably, as so many have done—as simply an inevitable negation of a negation. It was necessary that this overturning had to accomplished by a "mass of people" since on the other side were the all-powerful armies of the state, forces that knew they were doomed if the accumulation process was hindered in any way. Indeed, as Michael Heinrich has argued in reference to modern capitalism, "the material foundation of the state is ... directly connected to the accumulation of capital; no government can get past this dependency" (212). The state's dependence on this process ensures that this reverse expropriation is not an inevitability. It will fight to the death to prevent this overturning. One way that the state protects itself is through the imposition of borders, which play a key role in regulating the flow of people and capital, a regulatory process that constitutes the core of its being.

And the soil of the accumulation process must be constantly enriched with the fruits of primitive accumulation. Even though Marx alludes to primitive accumulation—"the expropriation of the agricultural producer, of the peasant,"—as forming the "pre-history" of capital, he is clear that the "history of this expropriation assumes different aspects in different countries, and runs through its various phases in different orders of succession, and at different epochs" (876). "Only in England," Marx affirms, "which we therefore take as our example, has its classic form" (875–76). Marx is not unaware that this process is rampant elsewhere. A few chapters later, he refers to the bloodshed in the Americas, in Africa and India as the "chief moments of primitive accumulation" (915). These "different moments" of primitive accumulation, aided and abetted by the "power of the state," continued to his own time, charting a path of destruction, as with the "Opium Wars against China" (915) and the "famine of 1866, which cost the lives of more than a million Hindus in the district of Orissa" (650). What we see in these concluding chapters, then, is not just an origin story or the description of a uniform world historical process. Marx understood this process of expropriation was continuing, perpetually oiling the gears for capital accumulation.

Arguably, in our times, this process—of dispossession and displacement, the destruction of agricultural occupations and the small producers' livelihoods, the violent shuttling of people all over the Global South into the shackles of wage labor—continues unabated. Marx described the "expropriation of the agricultural producer, of the peasant, from the soil, [as] the basis of the whole process" (876). As we consider the lives of those who have been forced to migrate in our times, from Colombia and Guatemala to the Democratic Republic of Congo and Mozambique to Bangladesh and Thailand, we see that this process of uprooting the tillers of the soil from the land extends into every corner of the globe.[30]

Moreover, Marx's analysis of the role of international credit and the banking system enabling the extraction of wealth from the colonies is no less relevant now. Add in the rapacity of the international debt regime whereby wealth is drained from the South and you have an accumulation process that proceeds at a relentless pace and creates an ever-increasing surplus population that has been uprooted from their lands. Rampant dispossession enables the generation of a population that must sell their labor power in order to survive, so it is also important to affirm that the reserve

---

[30] Saskia Sassen's *Expulsions* reveals the full scope and devastating consequences of land acquisitions in the Global South. It is perhaps well known that many countries (from Gabon and Guatemala to Indonesia and India) are subject to these acquisitions by private companies around the world, but what is less well established is that these companies—because of the products they are harvesting—are responsible for large-scale deforestation. Follow the dots. First, farmers and others are forced off the land so that it can be sold to the highest bidder; second, the land is stripped off all its resources so that after the lease expires there is nothing left to sustain life; third, the displaced farmers and producers have to find other sources of livelihood, fleeing, most probably to the nearest point of production, where they are brutally exploited or find a means of informal employment that barely provides enough for sustenance; finally, the wealth extracted from this land makes its way to a small local elite, and the bulk of it leaves the country. This is Colonialism 101 without the troops or the expense. Acquire real estate, exploit it to the core, and then leave when all the timber, palm oil, or precious minerals are gone. Meanwhile, those expelled from those lands are left to find a means of survival.

army is not just the supplement that is created by the accumulation process and its shedding of labor. This designation also applies to the dispossessed and the displaced, those who are not fully integrated into the production process.

Kalyan Sanyal provides some critical nuance here, affirming a significant distinction between the "being" and the "becoming" of capital. The reserve army, he claims, is part of the *being* of capital since it is very much an extension of the active labor force and is always available when it is necessary to draw upon them. Those many millions in the Global South who are cast asunder from their lands and possessions, on the other hand, do not necessarily become part of the proletariat; they are not constitutive of capital but rather aid in its *becoming*. They may be forced to engage in vast processes of informal labor, and they may also then aid in the reproduction process, but they are not essential to the being of capital. While I am persuaded by Sanyal's attempt to distinguish between the two processes, I disagree with the following point he makes about the dispossessed: that this population cannot be allowed to perish or to be left rootless (even though they are not essential) because "the discourses of democracy and human rights have emerged and consolidated themselves to form an inescapable and integral part of the political and social order" (60). This population, Sanyal argues, must therefore be subjected to developmental governmentality as part of the "environment within which capital has to reproduce itself" (60). I would argue the claim that this population cannot be left rootless becomes contestable when we attach it to the reality of migrant labor and ways in which the border creates deliberate forms of dislocation and disjuncture rather than incorporation.

What remains persuasive in Sanyal's analysis, however, is his assessment of development as synonymous with the process of accumulation. In this formulation, the ideology of development further reproduces capital, while at same time obscuring the rapacity of capital within a narrative of rights or "progress." Since development politics in the Global South has been historically tied to nation-building, it is easy to see how ideas about sovereignty and borders can then legitimize accumulation via regimes of development. An unresolved question, however, is whether, within the modern development framework, capital has any interest in letting a population perish. Achille Mbembe offers an alternative reading of managing populations in his imagining of "war machines," which function to produce an

> unprecedented form of governmentality that consists in the *management of the multitudes.* The extraction and looting of natural resources by war machines goes hand in hand with brutal attempts to immobilize and spatially fix whole categories of people or, paradoxically, to unleash them, to force them to scatter over broad areas no longer contained by the boundaries of a territorial state. As a political category, populations are then disaggregated into rebels, child soldiers, victims or refugees, or civilians incapacitated by mutilation or simply massacred on the model of ancient sacrifices, while the "survivors," after a horrific exodus, are confined in camps and zones of exception. ("Necropolitics" 34)

As Mbembe correctly points out, war machines confine certain populations to specific spaces; whether these populations live or die become irrelevant. Refugee camps, for instance, from Kenya and Turkey to Jordan and Pakistan would be one of these fixed spaces. According to Mbembe, "weapons are deployed in the interest of maximum destruction of persons and the creation of *death-worlds,* new and unique forms of social existence in which vast populations are subjugated to conditions of life conferring upon them the status of *living-dead*" ("Necropolitics" 39–40). Mbembe would argue that these populations are no longer useful to capital; in short, they are not even necessary for exploitation. Certainly, we have seen this to be true in the history of capitalism. Entire populations have been exterminated, if not through direct killings, then through famines and diseases. Indeed, consider the many millions of workers who are bearing the highest cost of the Covid pandemic. Our current labor practices, after all, emerge from the history of colonialism and imperialism and represent continuations of those policies. However, the important question for us in the context of migrant populations is whether a surplus population is ever completely disposable, or, in Mbembe's words, subject to the rituals of "ancient sacrifices"?

As I have argued, a surplus population is a vital necessity for an extractive, exploitative economy that, in the end, serves capital. So, even if this population cannot be exploited directly, they serve a particular purpose. They allow the exploitation of the population who are not confined to "death-worlds" to continue to serve the interests of capital. As Mbembe would say, "the calculus of life passes through the death of the other." Thus, populations may be disposable and necessary at the same time. Kalyan Sanyal adds another layer about the surplus population's use in creating a subsistence economy: "this subsistence economy outside the

2 BORDER RULES: IMPERIALISM, RACE, AND THE POLITICS OF DEVELOPMENT   57

sphere of capital where the surplus population is being rehabilitated is created in order to provide legitimation to capital. But at the same time, capital is also seeking to expand and hence tearing down the subsistence economies. What we have therefore is a process of simultaneous creation and destruction" (104). Once again, capital proceeds onward through the familiar dialectic of creation and destruction, one which exacts the greatest cost from those who are set violently adrift by the motions of capital.

Let us then attempt to bring together these theoretical strands, posing some questions about the ever-fluid politics of the border in managing populations. Is there a way in which the work of the war machines can accomplish both ends for capital—that is, not only put a population in limbo and shed disposable labor, but also create conditions within which elements of that population are always available? What possible ends are accomplished by creating death-worlds, if they do not provide any value? If one of the functions of the state is to enable the continuing process of dispossession, then it will always produce potentially disposable populations. Might there be conditions under which a surplus population, from the state's point of view, be a danger—threaten to destabilize the state? Might borders continue to be a way for the state to manage these seeming contradictions between capital's endless need for expansion and the shedding or freezing of labor?

One way to begin addressing these questions is to pose the possibilities that in the Global South the surplus population can be "outside" capital and that complete transition to a full-fledged capitalism is not necessary.[31] Real subsumption, in short, does not have to assert itself in every form. Indeed, informal economic modes can be tolerated if goods can be brought to market and value realized. If these modes, however, form a significant barrier, then they will frequently be eliminated. Sanyal, for instance, rejects the notion of transition to full capitalism as a necessity and argues that the space of non-capital is not meant to be overcome, finally, by capital; instead, both may exist simultaneously within the postcolonial

---

[31] If we see transition in terms of the inevitability of the historical materialist model, then ultimately primitive accumulation will lead to full-fledged capitalism, to be followed by revolution. Another angle is the Neo-Gramscian one, which poses the idea of passive revolution whereby capital integrates, uses and tolerates non-capital for its own uses. A famous line from Giuseppe Tomasi di Lampedusa's novel, *Il Gattopardo* (*The Leopard*) sums up this arrangement: "Everything must change so that everything can remain the same."

58 K. CHOWDHURY

state.[32] He argues that "the characterization of the post-colonial economic as a complex of capital and non-capital, with the latter emerging in a space produced by and of the internal logic of the former, totally dispenses with the notion of transition" (40). This heterogeneous form of capitalism, according to Sanyal, is what exists in many postcolonial nations. In Sanyal's view, this is not merely an economic configuration, but one forged in the sphere of hegemony via accommodations negotiated among classes in civil society and in the context of the nation state. This is not to say that the non-capital can remain outside the commodity economy or that the non-capital does not aid in the reproduction of labor. What it means is that this space of surplus labor and the ravages suffered by primitive accumulation do not necessarily lead to exclusion or social death.

What are the implications of making such a claim, contra Mmembe? After all, one could argue that this claim is unsustainable when one sees how many millions are being cast into destitution by capitalist predation. Let us take Sanyal's argument forward a few more steps. He claims that the so-called excluded, even if they do not join the ranks of wage labor in the classical sense, become part of a "need economy": "while the products of [this sort of economy] are sold in the market, the purpose of production is to acquire money that will enable the producers to have access through the market to a bundle of goods and services that will satisfy their needs" (69). In this instance, goods are not immediately consumed for their use value; the consumption process must be mediated by the commodity market. This explanation accounts for the many millions in the Global South who are engaged in informal labor and are thus both inside and outside the market. Perhaps the latent reserve army is the closest we

---

[32] Sanyal's position is aligned with, but not identical to Rosa Luxemburg's well-known claim, described with analytical precision in her monumental work, *The Accumulation of Capital*. Of course, there have been many rejoinders to Rosa Luxemburg's analysis regarding the modes of accumulation, in the end, bringing about the "conditions for the decline of capitalism," and to her arguments about capital's dependence on the space of the non-capitalized world; however, her awareness of this dialectic between capital and its others still bears some relevance for our discussion here. In her analysis of "militarism as the province of accumulation," Luxemburg states: "Capitalism is the first mode of economy with the weapon of propaganda, a mode which tends to engulf the entire globe and to stamp out all other economies, tolerating no rival at its side. Yet at the same time it is also the first mode of economy which is unable to exist by itself, which needs other economic systems as a medium and soil. Although it strives to become universal, and, indeed, on account of this its tendency, it must break down because it is immanently incapable of becoming a universal form of production. In its living history it is a contradiction in itself, and its movement of accumulation provides a solution to the conflict and aggravates it at the same time" (447).

2 BORDER RULES: IMPERIALISM, RACE, AND THE POLITICS OF DEVELOPMENT   59

can get to naming those who exist within this category, but, according to Sanyal, it is unlikely that capital needs to pull these laborers into formal wage labor, something that was historically accurate and necessary for the latent army in mid-nineteenth-century England. While agreeing with Sanyal regarding the role of informal labor in the Global South, I would again contest the idea that the space of non-capital is the preserve of "development" politics. I believe that capital is quite content to expel and exclude and to condemn to death millions who are unnecessary for its reproduction. I would thus hold on to Marx's "sphere of pauperism," as one way to describe this category of surplus, which is the "hospital of the active labour-army and the dead weight of the industrial labour army .... It forms the *faux frais* of capitalist production" (797).

Even though many of the mobile labor force may not be moving only to flee the sphere of pauperism, it is true that a significant number constitute the "*faux frais* of capitalist production." As I have already argued, capital relies simultaneously on this movement of labor and on the strict keeping of labor in place. One can only imagine the consequences if workers from the low-wage paying countries such as the DRC, Bangladesh, and Haiti were freely allowed to enter high-wage countries. What would happen to the Western firms whose profits depend on the presence of those low-cost laborers in their home countries? Imagine the political unrest that would be generated by "native" workers who would resent the entry of new workers. Contrarily, however, consider if ill-paid workers from the Global South, engaged in hazardous work, were not part of these wealthy economies, whether in Qatar, the United Kingdom, or Spain. These countries' health systems would collapse; the agricultural and construction sectors would stop functioning; and all sorts of "essential" work would remain undone. Thus, capital will never completely stop the flow of labor. Indeed, as we have seen from its history, from the Transatlantic Slave Trade and the export of indentured labor to the current dispersal of nurses and seasonal fruit pickers, it is vital that this movement continues.[33]

---

[33] It bears mentioning that the migration doors for "skilled" workers operate in different ways from those for other workers. In this situation, not only do Western countries benefit from workers whose education costs they have not had to bear; these low-resource countries also lose out on their own skilled graduates. John Smith provides an astonishing illustration of this point: "among African nations and small island nations in 2010, for example, 46 percent of skilled Jamaicans lived in OECD [Organisation for Economic Co-operation and Development] countries, 43 percent of skilled Zimbabweans, and 41 percent of those born in Mauritius. Guyana topped the list, with close to 90 percent of its graduates living in OECD countries" (111).

60 K. CHOWDHURY

Likewise, it is equally important that some workers remain exactly where they are so they can be exploited at the sites of low-cost production.

Supplementing this view, Nicholas De Genova in "Anonymous Brown Bodies" makes a compelling case that borders enact a "strategy of capture" rather than "functioning as mere technologies of exclusion" (93). The border, he argues, "simply tends to *trap* the great majority of those who succeed in getting across, now caught—indefinitely—*inside* the space of the U.S. nation-state as a very prized kind of highly vulnerable migrant labor" (93). Consequently, there is a direct link between the "multiplication of anonymous migrant and refugee corpses that is a direct effect of border militarization and fortification and other enforcement tactics" and the "systematic relegation of the lives of those who survive the border's lethal perils to a racialized condition of permanent disposability" (93). In a sense, "historically specific productions of migrant 'illegality' must continue to be produced through ongoing practices of bordering and re-bordering. This is because they are sites of ongoing and unresolved struggle" (94). De Genova's position allows us to see the ways in which disposability and functionality are part of the same circuit of exploitation. Because the pool of available labor resources is large, even if many potential workers are "unused," there are enough "trapped" workers available to more than make up for the systematic expulsion and killing of others. It is also important to remember that when the fruits of exploitation are shared across borders—say, a deported worker is forced to work in a *maquiladora*—the value produced by a worker crosses borders even when she herself is trapped.

It would appear that one of the primary elements concerning migration and the movement of migrants is for capital to manage the tension between confining a population at one site in order to extract maximum labor and also to "set it free," so it can travel to the sites of production that require it. Both these functions of "population control" are essential for maximizing surplus extraction. If we see migrant issues and border policies from the perspective of labor management, then it becomes evident that efficient surplus extraction requires borders to constantly "fix" the level of exploitation. Some of these imperatives are made apparent in the frequent talk about "protecting jobs," and keeping out competitors, but what is less evident in the public discourse is how essential the letting in of workers is to national economies. In some cases, such as the Gulf states, entire nations would come to a grinding half if not for the workers who are let in. Moreover, the large pool of undocumented laborers across the globe

2 BORDER RULES: IMPERIALISM, RACE, AND THE POLITICS OF DEVELOPMENT   61

allows for the highest rate of exploitation: the combination of low wages, negligible social cost, and collection of tax revenues is an attractive prospect for the state.

Of course, economic "needs" are always already political projects. Referring to refugees who seek asylum in Britain, Tom Vickers makes a credible claim that these refugees, most of whom are from the Global South, are part of the international army of labor, but because they are "out of place" and have "broken discipline with the reserve army of labor and have contradicted the neoliberal terms for international mobility," they must be cast out. Thus, the British state's asylum policies, much as in the rest of the Western world, are in some measure designed to "re-discipline [refugees] into the reserve army" (110) by rejecting their claims for asylum. This element of "redisciplining," as well as the tension between disposability and exploitability in the West, I have suggested earlier in this chapter, is always a racialized one.

In the case of imperial centers, policies for disciplining refugees are also designed to send a message to a nation's own minority population. When refugees are expelled, it may appear that to dispose of a potential source of value is mere irrationality; however, violent control and regulation are central to the normal functioning of capital. Consider that hundreds of black men are murdered by the police every year in the United States, and one may say that by "disposing" of them, the state is losing out of exploitable labor, as well as a source of expropriation in the form of rents, fines, fees, penalties, and debt payments. However, it is essential to understand that racial violence and the punishment of black citizens are a vital part of the accumulation process. There is a continuity between public whippings and murders of runaway slaves, the lynching during the Jim Crow years, and the executions by police in our times. These public spectacles are meant to strike terror into the hearts of a working population; they are meant to discipline a potentially rebellious force. Without these public spectacles, the ruling class would have to deal with more resistance and uprisings and would have to lock up millions of people, even more than the extraordinary number that are currently incarcerated, an alternative that would be far more harmful for the accumulation of wealth. This spectacular enactment of internal discipline and external border control are not separate elements of state rule but act in conjunction with each other. Police departments across the country and Immigration and Customs Enforcement (ICE) are a dyad rather than discrete departments of control.

Are refugees and asylum seekers, then, part of the surplus and within the bounds of capital? Or can they remain outside of capital, not even necessary for exploitation? Do we then place them in the same category as those Sanyal refers to as the subeconomy—those who are parallel to the accumulation economy and lend legitimation to that economy: "together, the accumulation economy of capital will be legitimized, made acceptable" (107). After all, refugees, as in the case of many non-refugees who labor in the informal economy, are also absorbed into the ethos of development talk, and many of them toil in the informal economy and are, in fact, denied entry into the wage market. Thus, they do aid in accumulation, and are necessary for capitalist reproduction. Recalling Mmembe's description of death-worlds, I am not convinced by the notion that refugees or migrant workers are outside of capital. When and how are a group of workers determined to be outside the frame of exploitation? Even the static population of a refugee camp is a potential site for exploitation. Consider the Dadaab refugee camp in Nairobi, which has a quarter of a million people, none of whom are outside capital in the sense that they are subject to its motions and open to the worst form of exploitation.[34]

Likewise, a refused asylum seeker who is not immediately deported to another country or their country of origin can either eke out a living engaging in informal labor, such as selling wares on the streets, or, in some cases, join the rank of the super-exploited wage workers. They are often confined to intensive labor and restricted to a few occupations, such as restaurant work, delivery and catering work, construction work, and sex work. These jobs are characterized by low pay, long hours, hazardous conditions, lack of bargaining rights, and, often, abuse and wage theft by employers. Workers move across these parallel fields of labor, seldom transitioning to any form of secure labor. Someone might spend the morning

---

[34] Antony Loewenstein describes other ways in which companies and individuals profit from the refugee economy: One Swiss company that runs immigrant reception centers made $99 million in 2014; refugees are overcharged at private housing firms; and some European citizens have even "seen an opportunity to turn a profit and are asking new arrivals for far too much money for water and to charge their smartphones." Nicholas De Genova et al. also point to the intersections between financial exploitation and surveillance: "Electronic vouchers for refugees' services or humanitarian credit cards for refugees (e.g., the Humanity Ventures initiative for Syrian refugees, developed by Mastercard and George Soros [Fortune 2017]) are examples of financial products used in hosting centers across Europe as well as in refugee camps in the Middle East region, which produce databases on refugees' consumption behaviors while also mapping their movements" (253).

carrying bricks at a construction site, the afternoon washing dishes at a restaurant, and the evening delivering food. Since their status is precarious, these workers have little access to health care or other care that is available within official channels. Indeed, there is a whole informal network of care on which many are reliant, and, as became evident especially early in the pandemic, the depth of their vulnerability was revealed by two significant constraints accompanying their precarious status: the terms of their employment meant that they were constantly exposed to the virus; and their lack of access to health care meant that they were far more likely to suffer serious consequences when they did get sick.

In a recent collection, *New Keywords: Migration and Borders*, published in 2015, during the peak of the so-called refugee crisis, the editors describe migrant labor as "the encounter of migrants with a complex set of power technologies that adapt to the need for creating labour power as a commodity, organizing production, opening new ways of accumulation and valorisation, turning ungovernable flows into mobile governable subjects, and negotiating the multiple concrete conditions of the postcolonial world" (78). While there are certainly ways in which migrant labor power has opened up "new ways of accumulation and valorisation" (*maquiladoras* and SEZs, for instance), the Foucauldian calling up of "power technologies" elides the specific social relations that are set in motion by the continuing practices of planned dispossession and abandonment and their attendant ideology of development. Also, the suggestion by the editors that migrant laborers can be managed, made into "governable subjects" echoes the statement I cited earlier: that borders are "finely tuned instruments." What may appear to be stable, governable instruments, enabling the work of empire may in time turn out to be the forces that undermine its logic.

Indeed, it is a critical task in this book to demonstrate that even though it is the work of capital to dehumanize people and arrange them within categories of productive/nonproductive labor or to turn them into "mobile governable subjects," migrants will always resist such categorizations. Yes, refugees and migrants have been dispossessed, exploited, and expelled, but, as this work will demonstrate, they cannot be pigeon-holed as an abstract, disembodied category of the "excluded" or the "surplus. Economic structures depend on their presence or on the promise of their exclusion or the threat of their inclusion. To isolate refugees into a category of workers outside of capital or outside of the realm of the employed is to accede to capital's attempt to assert appearance over essence. Indeed, as Jameson would point out, we cannot isolate the "excluded" from the "structural necessity for capitalism to create a reserve army of the unemployed and to exclude whole sections of society (or here, in globalization, whole sections of the world population)" (*Valences* 576). Yet, they are not merely units of labor or disposable bodies or members of a reserve army; they are also potential agents of change. What if migrant laborers refuse to be merely "governable subjects"? What if Mmembe's death worlds contain the seeds of rebellion? What if the categories of the migrant worker, the refugee were not divorced from the overall laws of accumulation or from their fellow (native) workers? The Salvadorean worker, for instance, who must work in a *maquiladora* in Ciudad Juárez may find affinities with workers across the border.

Even if the presence of a mobile work force can be detrimental to the sort of organizing that is possible within a relatively stable working population, it also allows for unconventional alliances. Moreover, the internal, contradictory logic of capital always remains a factor in its own overcoming. When does capital destroy and move beyond its own logic? How might its (in)ability to regulate populations while extracting surplus become an inevitable spiraling crisis? Borders, even as they attempt to freeze the movement of people, are constantly being breached. How long can they endure as forms of social control? After all, if the last decade has shown us anything, it is that people will migrate, even under the most terrifying conditions, especially when there remain few safety mechanisms that can sustain life. If we take just the official count of displaced people, hundred million people on the move can generate a lot of instability and possibility in a world that requires order to enable endless accumulation.

Works Cited

Ajala, Olayinka. "US Drone Base in Agadez." *The RUSI Journal,* vol. 163, no. 5, 2018, pp. 20–27.

Alexander, Michelle. *The New Jim Crow: Mass Incarceration in the Age of Colorblindness.* The New Press, 2012.

Alexis, Yveline. *Haiti Fights Back: The Life and Legacy of Charlemagne Péralte.* Rutgers University Press, 2021.

Bacchetta, Paola, et al., editors. *Global Raciality: Empire, PostColoniality, DeColoniality.* Routledge, 2018.

Bachman, Justin and Bloomberg. "Richard Branson's Historic Flight into Space was Worth $841 Million for Virgin Galactic." *Fortune,* 12 July 2021, https://fortune.com/2021/07/12/richard-branson-flight-space-virgin-galactic-share-price/.

Barbero, Michele. "France Bids Adieu to Its Military Mission in West Africa." *Foreign Policy*, 7 July 2021, https://foreignpolicy.com/2021/07/07/france-military-leaving-west-africa-colonialism-macron/.

Bellegarde-Smith, Patrick. *In the Shadow of the Powers: Dantès Bellegarde in Haitian Social Thought*. Vanderbilt University Press, 2019.

Boyce, Geoffrey Alan, et al. "Bodily Inertia and the Weaponization of the Sonoran Desert in US Boundary Enforcement: A GIS Modeling of Migration Routes through Arizona's Altar Valley." *Journal on Migration and Human Security*, vol. 7, no. 1, 2019, pp. 22–35.

Brown, Wendy. *Walled States, Waning Sovereignty*. Zone Books, 2010.

Casas-Cortes, Maribel, et al. "New Keywords: Migration and Borders." *Cultural Studies*, vol. 29, no. 1, 2014, pp. 55–87.

Chambers, Samuel Norton, et al. "Mortality, Surveillance and the Tertiary 'Funnel Effect' on the U.S.-Mexico Border: A Geospatial Modeling of the Geography of Deterrence." *Journal of Borderlands Studies*, vol. 36, no. 3, 2021, pp. 443–468.

Chiu, Joanna. *China Unbound: A New World Disorder*. House of Anansi Press, 2021.

Coulthard, Glen Sean. *Red Skin, White Masks: Rejecting the Colonial Politics of Recognition*. University of Minnesota Press, 2014.

De Angelis, Massimo. *Marx's Theory of Primitive Accumulation: A Suggested Reinterpretation*. University of East London, 2000.

De Genova, Nicholas. "Anonymous Brown Bodies: The Productive Power of the Deadly U.S.-Mexico Border." *Migration and Mortality: Social Death, Dispossession, and Survival in the Americas*, edited by Jamie Longazel and Miranda Cady Hallett. Temple University Press, 2021, pp. 83–100.

Di Lampedusa, Giuseppe Tomasi. *Il Gattopardo [The Leopard]*. Feltrinelli, 1958.

Edmondson, Catie. "House Approves $1 Billion for the Iron Dome as Democrats Feud Over Israel." *New York Times*, 23 Sept. 2021, https://www.nytimes.com/2021/09/23/us/politics/israel-iron-dome-congress.html?searchResultPosition=1.

Eichstaedt, Peter. *Consuming the Congo: War and Conflict Minerals in the World's Deadliest Place*. Lawrence Hill Books, 2011.

"The Farmers' Revolt in India." *Tricontinental*, 14 June 2021, https://thetricontinental.org/dossier-41-india-agriculture/.

Fassin, D. "Les Migrantes d'Afrique Noir en France: Quelques Elements d'Histoire pour un Debat Actuel" [Migrants from Sub-Saharan Africa in France: Some Elements for the Present Discussion]. *Developpement et Sante: Revue de Perfectionnement Medical et Sanitaire en Pays Tropical*, vol. 64, 1986, pp. 19–21.

Fatton, Robert Jr. *The Guise of Exceptionalism: Unmasking the National Narratives in Haiti and the United States*. Rutgers University Press, 2021.

Federici, Silvia. *Caliban and the Witch: Women, the Body, and Primitive Accumulation.* Autonomedia, 2004.

Glaser, John. "Why We Should Close America's Overseas Military Bases." *Time,* 7 Oct. 2016, https://time.com/4511744/american-military-bases-overseas/.

Ghosh, Devleena. "The Bones of Our Mother: Adivasi Dispossession in an Indian State." *Routledge Companion to Global Indigenous History,* Routledge, 2021.

Hall, Stuart. "Representation and the Media." Edited by Sanjay Talreja, Sut Jhally, & Mary Patierno, Media Education Foundation, 1997.

Harvey, David. *The Anti-Capitalist Chronicles.* Pluto Press, 2020.

———. *Spaces of Global Capitalism: A Theory of Uneven Geographical Development.* Verso, 2006.

Hayes, Tara O'Neill, and Margaret Barnhorst. "Incarceration and Poverty in the United States." *American Action Forum,* 30 June 2020, https://www.americanactionforum.org/research/incarceration-and-poverty-in-the-united-states/.

Heinrich, Michael. *An Introduction to the Three Volumes of Karl Marx's Capital.* Monthly Review Press, 2012.

Higgins, Jessie. "ICE Raid Devastated Tiny Midwest Town; 10 Years Later, It's Still Recovering." *United Press International,* 29 Aug. 2018, https://www.upi.com/Top_News/US/2018/08/29/ICE-raid-devastated-tiny-Midwest-town-10-years-later-its-still-recovering/3461535551297/.

Hillman, Jonathan E. *The Emperor's New Road: China and the Project of the Century.* Yale University Press, 2020.

Horton, Jake. "Israel-Gaza: How Much Money Does Israel Get from US?" *BBC,* 24 May 2021, https://www.bbc.com/news/57170576.

"How US Border Patrol Persuades Congress to Legalize Unfettered Searches in Wide Border Zones." *Scholars Strategy Network,* 7 Nov. 2018, https://scholars.org/contribution/how-us-border-patrol-persuaded-congress-legalize-unfettered-searches-wide-border-zones.

"Internally Displaced People." *The United Nations Refugee Agency,* https://www.unhcr.org/en-us/internally-displaced-people.html.

"Israel's Killing of Palestinian Children." *Al Jazeera,* 24 Aug. 2021, https://www.aljazeera.com/news/2021/8/24/global-outcry-over-israels-targeting-of-palestinian-children.

Jameson, Fredric. *Valences of the Dialectic.* Verso, 2010.

Kang, Deborah S. *The INS on the Line: Making Immigration Law on the US-Mexico Border, 1917–1954.* Oxford University Press, 2017.

Khosravi, Shahram. *"Illegal" Traveler: An Auto-Ethnography of Borders.* Palgrave Macmillan, 2010.

King, Martin Luther, Jr. "Beyond Vietnam." *A Call to Conscience: The Landmark Speeches of Dr. Martin Luther King, Jr.,* edited by Claybourne Darson, Time Warner Books UK, 2001.

Loewenstein, A. "How Private Companies are Exploiting the Refugee Crisis for Profit." *The Independent*, 23 Oct. 2015, https://www.independent.co.uk/voices/how-companies-have-been-exploiting-the-refugee-crisis-for-profit-a6706587.html.

Luxemburg, Rosa. *The Accumulation of Capital*. Translated by Agnes Schwarzchild, Routledge, 1913, 2003.

Markey, Daniel S. *China's Western Horizon: Beijing and the New Geopolitics of Eurasia*. Oxford University Press, 2020.

Marx, Karl. *Capital: A Critique of Political Economy, Vol. 1*. 1867. Translated by Ben Fowkes, Penguin, 1983.

Mbembe, Achille. "Necropolitics." Translated by Libby Meintjes. *Public Culture*, vol. 15, no. 1, Winter 2003, pp. 11–40.

McCarthy, Niall. "The Countries with the Highest Military Expenditure in 2020." *Forbes*, 28 Apr. 2021, https://www.forbes.com/sites/niallmccarthy/2021/04/28/the-countries-with-the-highest-military-expenditure-in-2020-infographic/?sh=480d260a4e80.

Mezzadra, Sandro and Brett Neilson. *Border as Method, or the Multiplication of Labor*. Duke University Press, 2013.

Miller, Todd. *Empire of Borders: The Expansion of the US Border Around the World*. Verso, 2019.

Musamba, Josaphat, and Christoph Vogel. "The Problem with Conflict Minerals." *Dissent Magazine*, 21 Oct. 2021, https://www.dissentmagazine.org/online_articles/the-problem-with-conflict-minerals.

Naylor, Brian and Tamara Keith. "Kamala Harris Tells Guatemalans Not to Migrate to the United States." *NPR*, 7 June 2021, https://www.npr.org/2021/06/07/1004074139/harris-tells-guatemalans-not-to-migrate-to-the-united-states.

"No Country Should Be Forced to Choose Between Paying Back Debts or Providing Health Care." *Oxfam International*, https://www.oxfam.org/en/no-country-should-be-forced-choose-between-paying-back-debts-or-providing-health-care.

Osorio, Jaime. "Dialectics, Superexploitation, and Dependency: Notes on *The Dialectics of Dependency*." Translated by Gregory Shank and Heather Anne Harper. *Social Justice*, vol. 42, no. 1, pp. 93–106.

Phillips, Nicole, and Tom Ricker. *The Invisible Wall: Title 42 and its Impact on Haitian Migrants*. Haitian Bridge Alliance, The Quixote Center and The UndocuBlack Network, n.d., https://www.quixote.org/wp-content/uploads/2021/03/The-Invisible-Wall.pdf.

Prashad, Vijay. "Sleep Now in the Fire: The Twentieth Newsletter." *Tricontinental*, 21 May 2021, https://thetricontinental.org/newsletterissue/20-palestine/.

Puranam, Elizabeth. "The Mine That Displaced India's Indigenous People." *Al Jazeera*, 7 July 2016, https://www.aljazeera.com/features/2016/7/7/the-mine-that-displaced-indias-indigenous-people.

Qureshi, Zia. "Tackling the Inequality Pandemic: Is There a Cure?" *Brookings Institution*, 17 Nov. 2020, https://www.brookings.edu/research/tackling-the-inequality-pandemic-is-there-a-cure/.

"Refugee Statistics." *The United Nations Refugee Agency*, https://www.unrefugees.org/refugee-facts/statistics/.

Roche, Darragh. "AOC Slams U.S. Stance on Migrants, Says Kamala Harris Comments 'Disappointing.'" *Newsweek*, 8 June 2021, https://www.newsweek.com/aoc-slams-us-stance-migrants-says-kamala-harris-comments-disappointing-1598489.

Rodney, Walter. *How Europe Underdeveloped Africa*. Bogle-L'Ouverture Publications, 1972.

Sanyal, Kalyan. *Rethinking Capitalist Development: Primitive Accumulation, Governmentality and Post-Colonial Capitalism*. Routledge India, 2007.

Sassen, Saskia. *Expulsions: Brutality and Complexity in the Global Economy*. Harvard University Press, 2014.

Schlitz, Heather. "Business Owners in a Tiny Desert Town are 'Excited by Apprehensive' to See Whether a $220 Million Bet on Billionaire Richard Branson's Spaceport Will Pay Off." *Business Insider*, 12 July 2021, https://www.businessinsider.com/taxpayers-bet-richard-branson-virgin-galactic-spaceport-america-town-2021-7.

Schmitt, Eric, and Christoph Koetti. "Remote C.I.A. Base in the Sahara Steadily Grows." *New York Times*, 8 Mar. 2021, https://www.nytimes.com/2021/03/08/us/politics/cia-drones-sahara-niger-libya.html.

Sheridan, Thomas E., and Randall H. McGuire, editors. *The Border and Its Bodies: The Embodiment of Risk Along the U.S.-Mexico Line*, University of Arizona Press, 2019.

Siddiqui, Usaid, et al. "Infographic: What You Need to Know About Israel's Military." *Al Jazeera*, 4 June 2021, https://www.aljazeera.com/news/2021/6/4/infographic-what-you-need-to-know-about-israels-military.

"Sixty-Four Countries Spend More on Debt Payments Than Health." *Jubilee Debt Campaign*, 12 Apr. 2021, https://debtjustice.org.uk/press-release/sixty-four-countries-spend-more-on-debt-payments-than-health.

Smith, John. *Imperialism in the Twenty-First Century: Globalization, Super-Exploitation, and Capitalism's Final Crisis*. Monthly Review Press, 2016.

Snow, Anita. "More Migrant Deaths Recorded in Heat Along Arizona Border." *Associated Press*, 12 July 2021, https://apnews.com/article/arizona-1300cd229c566188f912232edadc1dea.

Squire, Vicki. "Governing Migration through Death in Europe and the US: Identification, Burial, and the Crisis of Modern Humanism." *European Journal of International Relations*, vol. 32, no. 3, 2017, pp. 513–532.

2 BORDER RULES: IMPERIALISM, RACE, AND THE POLITICS OF DEVELOPMENT 69

Sylla, Ndongo Sama, and Fanny Pigeaud. "How France Continues to Dominate Its Former Colonies in Africa." *Jacobin*, 29 Mar. 2021, https://jacobin.com/2021/03/africa-colonies-france-cfa-franc-currency.

"The State of Food Security and Nutrition in the World 2021." *Food and Agricultural Organization of the United Nations*, https://www.fao.org/state-of-food-security-nutrition.

"3.7 Million More Children in Poverty in Jan 2022 Without Monthly Child Tax Credit." *Center on Poverty and Social Policy at Columbia University*, 17 Feb. 2022, https://www.povertycenter.columbia.edu/news-internal/monthly-poverty-january-2022.

"The Windrush Generation." *BBC Caribbean*, 20 June 2008, https://www.bbc.co.uk/caribbean/news/story/2008/06/080620_windrush2.shtml.

@USEmbassyHaiti. "'I can say quite clearly, don't come over.'—@POTUS" *Twitter*, 24 Mar. 2021, 11:02 a.m., https://twitter.com/usembassyhaiti/status/1374753568914292736?lang=en.

United States Army Continental Commands, *General Order 3*, issued by Major General Gordon Granger, 19 June 1865, https://catalog.archives.gov/id/182778372, accessed on 27 Mar. 2023.

Vickers, Tom. *Refugees, Capitalism and the British State: Implications for Social Workers, Volunteers and Activists*. Routledge, 2012.

Vogt, Wendy. *Lives in Transit: Violence and Intimacy on the Migrant Journey*. University of California Press, 2018.

"Water Under Siege in Iraq: US/UK Military Forces Risk Committing War Crimes by Depriving Civilians of Safe Water." *ReliefWeb*, United Nations Office for the Coordination of Humanitarian Affairs (OCHA), 8 Apr. 2003, https://reliefweb.int/report/iraq/water-under-siege-iraq-usuk-military-forces-risk-committing-war-crimes-depriving.

Wattles, Kathy. "First to the Future: Virgin Galactic Founder Richard Branson Successfully Rockets to Outer Space." *CNN Business*, 12 July 2021, https://www.cnn.com/2021/07/11/tech/richard-branson-virgin-galactic-space-flight-scn/index.html.

Winterstein, Ilana. "Global Brands, Global Exploitation." *Al Jazeera*, 2 Nov. 2020, https://www.aljazeera.com/opinions/2020/11/2/global-brands-global-exploitation.

CHAPTER 3

Theorizing Borders in the Shadow of Imperial Violence

In the previous chapter, I attempted to analyze border rules as a primary mechanism for regulating labor mobility, as well as a conduit for accommodating and enabling the process of capital accumulation. In this chapter, I will attempt to review some of the prevailing scholarship in critical border studies and position my reading of border rules in relation to these contributions. While I draw from many of these critics and activists, especially those who pursue a materialist analysis of border practices, my own position will be informed by two primary critical frameworks. One, as I have attempted to establish in the first chapter, is to view borders through the lens of Marxist political economy. The other analytical lens will be informed by an understanding of the politics of imperialism and its imbrication in forms of global raciality. All along, in my response to critical studies on border politics, I will insist that while immigration reform, an adherence to international refugee laws, and support for displaced migrants are laudable aspirational goals for nation states and should be pursued vigorously, one of the arguments I will pose in this book is whether the nation state, even with these reforms in place, forecloses any genuine transformation in the lives of native-born and migrants alike. Indeed, in my final chapter, I will suggest that mass resistance to the working of capital is always already bound up in a resistance to border regimes. In short, a revolutionary future that sees people outside the exploitative grip of capital must, by necessity, be a society that is unimpeded by borders.

© The Author(s), under exclusive license to Springer Nature Switzerland AG 2023
K. Chowdhury, *Border Rules*, Politics of Citizenship and Migration, https://doi.org/10.1007/978-3-031-26216-6_3

Imperial Violence, Race, and the Specter of the "Failed State"

Let me then begin by contextualizing my discussion of contemporary border scholarship within the parameters of continuing imperial violence. No discussion of the role of existing borders is possible without taking into consideration the process by which many of these borders were drawn up by imperial powers. These lines and divisions set in place populations and structures to enable a systematic process of labor exploitation and resource extraction long after the end of official independence. Moreover, the borders dividing the Global South into nation states are also related to the internal politics of imperial nations. In other words, the reproduction of imperial rule does not merely see its effects in previously colonized nations, but always interacts and intersects with domestic policies of imperial nations. To reiterate, a discussion of borders is not limited by an attention to the politics of territoriality or geopolitical influence, but more productively, through an understanding of the border as a set of social relations that impacts how power and wealth are delineated across the globe. This thesis is a vital preamble to our review of the scholarship. In order to consider this imperial lineage, however, we cannot assume that it charts predictable paths over a range of geopolitical landscapes. Quite clearly, the manifestations of this imperial past take shape in its specific contexts, for instance, influencing border ideologies and policies that can be captured in both their rigid and fluid forms. What, then, do we do with these varied histories? More crucially, what is the critical task we perform when we study borders? Part of my work in this chapter is to attempt to address these questions, considering some of the notable contributions within the field of border studies.

As in the previous chapter, I will begin with a glance at some contemporary iterations of border politics and consider how development paradigms applied to nation states continue to be a hallmark of imperial rule. Borders are vital elements of this development paradigm. On the one hand, they enable the rigid drawing up of boundaries within which states in the Global South are locked into specific economic zones of influence and control, strictly guided by regulated systems of extraction. Any breach of this system or a spirited resistance to its logic is marked as an indication of its status as a failed or a "rogue" state by the imperial power structure. Countering this fixity of borders for those who seek livelihood and survival elsewhere, on the other hand, is the fluidity of these same borders for the owners of capital, which enables the seamless circulation of capital and wealth, benefiting both the local elite and those at the imperial center. Let me illustrate how this pattern is reproduced in the present, accompanied as it usually is by a healthy dose of historical amnesia on the part of media commentators and Western politicians.

The dramatic seizing of power in Afghanistan by the Taliban in August 2021 was followed by the usual recriminations from all US domestic political parties about the wisdom of "pulling out" US troops. What all these parties, however, agreed on was that Afghanistan was a nation mired in "insoluble," age-old problems, and that the Afghan troops and their leaders had failed to "do their jobs," despite two decades of US support and the sacrifice of thousands of US lives.[1] Little mention was made of the West's contribution to the present crisis, stretching back over the last two centuries, when Afghanistan was part of the "great game" of British imperialism or the fact that since 2001, occupation forces had only succeeded in putting into place puppet governments even as thousands of civilians have been killed in US drone strikes.[2] And, of course, Afghanistan was just one nation that had suffered such losses. Harsha Walia reminds us that Trump's ban against citizens from seven "Muslim" nations were the "same countries the US had already bombed or imposed sanctions on." "Under Nobel Peace Prize winner Obama," Walia comments, "the US dropped 26,171 bombs—an average of three bombs every hour—mostly through strikes and drone warfare on Syria, Iraq, Afghanistan, Libya, Yemen, Somalia, and Pakistan in the year prior to the ban" (60). Ignoring this reality, Western policy "experts" and the media blame existing conditions and the subsequent need to migrate on a self-generated crisis endemic to "those" regions of the world.

This framework of a "crisis" generated by "native" incompetence and corruption as an explanation for what is a systematic attempt to engineer a country's policies for the West's own interests is not limited to media versions of events, stretching further into so-called liberal academic circles and think tanks that deal explicitly with migrant matters. Take, for instance,

---

[1] For commentary on the performance of the Afghan troops, please see Kori Schake's piece in *The Atlantic* entitled "Why the Afghan Army Folded." Please also see Abdul Basit's "Why Did the Afghan Army Disintegrate So Quickly?" and a piece by Thomas Gibbons-Neff, et al. entitled "The Afghan Military was Built Over Twenty Years. How Did it Collapse So Quickly?"

[2] Please see Eric Schmitt's piece in the *New York Times* entitled "Military Can't Find ISIS Safe House That Prompted Kabul Drone Strike."

74   K. CHOWDHURY

the well reputed duo of Alexander Betts, Director of the Refugee Studies Center at Oxford University and Paul Collier, who is Professor of Economics and Public Policy at the Blavatnik School of Government and a Professorial Fellow of St Antony's College. In their recent book, *Refuge: Rethinking Refugee Policy in a Changing World* (2017), they argue that most refugees are victims of internally produced violence, corrupt regimes, and failed states. Without pointing out the obvious biases that underlie such a claim, it is curious to discern how they formulate this explanatory pattern. Part of the origin story is the familiar one about historically unmanageable regions of the world governed by the corrupt, but that hypothesis is further strengthened by an emphasis on the neoliberal claim that "since the 1990s, global inequality has been falling rapidly" (16). If this assertion can be sustained, then, by their logic, poverty engendered by the rapacity of global capitalism isn't to blame for the migrant "crisis." This is an important claim to establish since it not only removes a plausible cause for migration, but also provides a reason to elide the West's role in causing and enhancing inequalities. The alternative that can then be put firmly in place is the specter of the internally imploding failed state.

According to Betts and Collier, the failed state comes to be not because of certain well-known practices of imperialist countries—grabbing resources or aiding in the attempted overthrow of democratically elected governments (most recently, of Venezuela, 2002, Haiti, 2004, and Honduras 2009)—but, they assert, because "high resource countries are more likely to be autocratic" (23). Applying this logic, one can ignore the West's role in the creation of such "failed" states. Let us take the example of two "failed" states: the Central African Republic and Yemen. In the case of the former, the French government has maintained an iron grip on the state, post-independence, which, not coincidentally, has a vast storehouse of natural resources. Yemen, meanwhile, has been subjected to the brutality of bombing raids, financed by the West. One wonders why CAR, like the Democratic Republic of Congo, rich in resources—"high resource countries"—are "autocratic." Perhaps it is because real democracy would see the country's wealth return to its citizens and not end up in the West (27).[3] After all, history shows that any country in the Global South, be it Chile, Guatemala, Indonesia, or Iran that has attempted to take control of

---

[3] For further information on this point, please see *Making Sense of the Central African Republic*, edited by Tatiana Carayannis and Louisa Lombard.

3 THEORIZING BORDERS IN THE SHADOW OF IMPERIAL VIOLENCE 75

its resources has had a Western engineered coup replace its democratic government with an "autocratic" one, allied to the interests of the West. [4]

However, as far as Betts and Collier are concerned, the causes for the present migrant crisis lie in Islamic extremism or in regional differences, such as Saudi Arabia "undertaking a bombing campaign" in Yemen. US and French policies in these regions, apparently, play no role. Betts and Collier are also confident that economic migrants, who are different from refugees, are in search of "honeypot countries," as if the desire to migrate was based merely on a need to acquire a higher standard of living. Migrants are leaving because staying means certain death. It may not be the bullet of an "extremist" or a gang leader who kills you, but the stroke of the pen used in the boardrooms of Western capitals that dispossesses you of your livelihood. Betts and Collier seem unwilling or unable to see that when Western trade policies and extractive industries dispossess and destroy the livelihoods of millions, from Honduras and Haiti to Nepal and Bangladesh, this, too, is violence. The result is the same. To stay is to die. It is also worth emphasizing that it is well-nigh impossible to secure refuge in a "honeypot" state and most migrants who are lucky enough to do so have to take recourse to the most exploitative jobs. If a "honeypot" is meant to imply a place that offers a "substantial source of money" (Merriam-Webster), for most migrants that honeypot is a distant dream. The vast majority never reach a "honeypot" country. Indeed, it is well documented by the UNHCR that "[t]he world's poorest countries continue to shoulder the burden of the global refugee crisis" and that "84% of refugees live in the developing world." [5]

By locating the migration problem as one generated by internal dysfunction and regional conflicts, rather than one positioned within a larger global system of extraction and exploitation, it is little wonder that the next step is to seek a solution that comes out of the neoliberal playbook. Not surprisingly, the remedy for the crisis of migration is to create safe haven "development" zones where these surplus/refugee workers can be

---

[4] For further reading on these coups, please see Vijay Prashad's *Washington Bullets: A History of the CIA, Coups, and Assassinations*, Alexander B. Downes's *Catastrophic Success: Why Foreign-Imposed Regime Change Goes Wrong*, Luis Roniger's edited collection entitled *Exile, Diaspora, and Return: Changing Cultural Landscapes in Argentina, Chile, Paraguay, and Uruguay*, or Lawrence Wu and Michelle Lanz's article in NPR entitled "How the CIA Overthrew Iran's Democracy in 4 Days."

[5] See Charlotte Edmond's article on the *World Economic Forum* entitled "84 Percent of Refugees Live in Developing Countries."

76   K. CHOWDHURY

put to work. The World Bank, NGOs, and the notorious McKinsey Global Institute are held up as exemplary organizations to enable this process (233).[6] Guided by vast cultural generalizations—"Somalis are among the most entrepreneurial and economically successful communities in exile but have a highly dysfunctional society back home" (232)—Betts and Collier operate within the same tired neoliberal paradigms: haven countries "need to open up their markets in order to entice businesses to invest. Business investment has a central role to play" (234); fears of exploitation of workers, according to them, are alarmist because of the "reputational concerns of large corporations" (236). Leaving aside these pieties of economic "logic," it is enough to point to Betts and Collier's questionable use of cultural categories as a measure for economic justice. Consider, for instance, that in Minnesota, where a large Somali immigrant population are residents, 54 percent live below the poverty line, and 65 percent of children live in poverty.[7] Based on this reality, one might question the authors' claims regarding honeypot countries allowing refugees to fulfill their natural "entrepreneurial" talents, as opposed to the reality of the vast majority languishing in low-paying, exploitative positions. Of course, little needs to be said about the even more outlandish claim that multinational companies will somehow correct themselves because they fear for their "reputation" rather than extract maximum value from a disposable work force.[8]

Let me pursue these points in greater detail since the neoliberal development paradigm proposed by Betts and Collier has a direct relationship to border politics and their deployment for the owners of capital. While there are multiple instances that can be highlighted, I will focus on a particularly explicit example of the ways in which these relationships play out in the case of Haiti. In the Western media, Haiti is represented as being in the state of perpetual crisis. The narrative that enumerates the reasons for Haiti's "problems" fits neatly into the familiar paradigm articulated by Betts and Collier and so many other Western "experts": internal

[6] For more information on the McKinsey Global Institute, see Salem Saif's "When Consultants Reign" and Nathan Robinson's "McKinsey and Company is an Elitist Cult. Why is Buttigieg Defending it?".

[7] For a detailed account of the many inequities faced by the Somali community in Minnesota, please see the report "Somali Population" by the Minnesota Compass.

[8] For a recent account of the ways in which many refugee workers are exploited, please see Aisha Gani's piece in *The Guardian* entitled "An Afghan Refugee Commuted Hours for His Uber Job. Then He Was Shot in His Car."

3 THEORIZING BORDERS IN THE SHADOW OF IMPERIAL VIOLENCE   77

mismanagement, authoritarian leaders, rampant corruption, and so on. In September 2021, for instance, the world was witness to the graphic images of Haitian refugees, terrorized by American border guards, at the US–Mexico border without little context for the reasons for their presence. Let us take a few steps back from this moment at the border and consider how the larger politics around borders brought those migrants to that moment. In this case, it is not even necessary to trace the history of slavery and the 200 years of post-independence exploitation of the country by the West.[9] I will, instead, limit myself to development politics just in the last decade, acknowledging, of course, that the long history of Western violence in Haiti enables the present violence as well.

The story of how borders enable multiple forms of exploitation is best exemplified by what happened in Haiti after the catastrophic earthquake of January 2010.[10] I will focus on one aspect of post-earthquake rebuilding to illustrate my claim. In January 2011, a community in Northern Haiti—one of the few left relatively untouched by the earthquake—of over 400 peasant farmers, who were successfully growing many crops (black beans, peas, okra, peanuts, etc.) on fertile soil, were forcibly evicted from their lands to make way for the Caracol Industrial Plant, a brainchild of the Clinton Foundation and the Inter-American Development Bank (IDB). Funded by earthquake relief money and these organizations, this park was leased to Sae-A Trading Co. Ltd., a garment manufacturer based in South Korea (UN Secretary-General Ban Ki-Moon, who had connections to this company, also appointed Bill Clinton as special envoy to Haiti in 2010). Following a global trend of such "parks" built to employ low-paid workers to manufacture goods for Western consumers, this project is yet another example of how global capital respects no borders, while Haitian citizens are locked within borders in order to enable the exploitation of low-wage labor.[11]

---

[9] For more information on this history of imperial violence, please see Raphael Dalleo's *American Imperialism's Undead: The Occupation of Haiti and the Rise of Caribbean Anticolonialism*, Yveline Alexis's *Haiti Fights Back: The Life and Legacy of Charlemagne Péralte*, or Mary A. Renda's *Taking Haiti: Military Occupation and the Culture of U.S. Imperialism, 1915–1940*.

[10] Please see Keir Forgie's "US Imperialism and Disaster Capitalism in Haiti" for further details.

[11] For a detailed catalog of the history of this project and its disastrous consequences, see Isabel Macdonald's "10 Years Ago, We Pledged to Help Haiti Rebuild. Then What Happened?".

Indeed, the US government deployed all their resources after the earthquake to make sure that Haitians did not attempt to reach the United States. The US coastguard, which received $50 million for its role in "earthquake response," spent a sizable amount of that money patrolling the shores of Haiti to prevent such attempts, while the Department of Defense flew cargo planes broadcasting the following announcement in Creole: "If you think you will reach the U.S. and all the doors will be wide open to you, that's not at all the case. They will intercept you right on the water and send you back home where you came from" (Macdonald). This small piece of post-earthquake imperial activity demonstrates, quite effectively, how borders work to enable the movement of capital and the confinement of labor in particular ways. Much more could be said about the massive environmental costs of projects similar to the Caracol Industrial Plant—the amount of water used to manufacture garments, the release of toxic chemicals, rampant aquatic pollution, and so on, but needless to say, any "development" that takes place has little to do with actually improving the quality of the lives of the Haitian people and much more to do with enriching US corporations and client states such as South Korea. Many of the Haitians who left the country at this point ended up in Chile, as it offered itself as a haven for migrants. However, this openness soured over the last several years, especially after billionaire Sebastián Piñera was reelected as President in 2018. Driven by increasing exploitation, racial discrimination, and a hardening line on immigration, thousands of Haitians arrived at the US–Mexico border hoping for refuge from a new American administration, who they thought would be more welcoming than the previous one. Most of them were then deported to Haiti, a country they had not seen in ten years. At every level, over the last decade, a Haitian's path toward security and mere survival has been jeopardized by the vagaries of border rule.

There are two points worth reiterating here. One is that neoliberal development politics and border rule are inexorably linked. The second point is that border rule is a necessary component of a global system that relies on racially differentiated forms of exploitation set in place by colonial and neocolonial structures and reproduced by neoliberal economic formulas. Thus, the development paradigm does not just reinforce the imperial control of labor and resources; it also draws from and reproduces preexisting colonial racial structures that enable and require the division of a population into governable sections. When these populations resist, as when President Aristide suggested in 2004 that France and the United

3 THEORIZING BORDERS IN THE SHADOW OF IMPERIAL VIOLENCE   79

States pay back their debt to Haiti, they are immediately "disciplined." Shortly after seeking reparations, Aristide was overthrown in a right-wing coup. Once again, Haiti was designated by Western powers as a failed state, ungovernable and incapable of responsible self-rule.[12] Military involvement, structured aid, and other forms of intervention, then, become ways to bring order from disorder.

As we see in the case of Haiti, preexisting colonial structures, put in place and maintained via massive indebtedness or a series of military occupations prepared the ground for its continuing exploitation. Thus, it is important to understand that border politics, whether in Haiti or in almost any nation of the Global South, are not confined to policies about territorial borders; rather, much as I argued in the previous chapter, border rule should be understood as a mode of domination, as a set of social relations that produces and enables exploitation, drawing from and reinforcing a hierarchy of racialized difference. Moreover, this hierarchy of difference is reproduced in wealthy metropolitan centers as well; they, too, as we know, are bordered and policed in particular ways, and not unlike other sites of control, border rules are about access to resources, the control of wealth, the regulation of labor, all accomplished through racially differentiated modes of control. Of course, border rule is not just limited to the West's domination over the Global South or in its domestic policies but operate between countries in the Global South as well; for instance, in the Indian subcontinent, between, say, India and Nepal; in the Middle East, between Saudi Arabia and Yemen; and in the Asia-Pacific, between Singapore and Indonesia. In each of these cases, neoliberal arrangements determine policies that impact labor migration, business investment, and environmental degradation. Here, too, racial politics, a legacy of the colonial era, play a role in determining how power, wealth, and the exploitation of labor are delineated across national and territorial lines.[13]

These regional examples problematize the common assumption about racial differentiation, contesting the notion that these hierarchies only exist between the imperial North and the Global South, suggesting, instead, the notion of global raciality. So, for instance, Chilean hostility to Haitian migrants or an Indian mill owner's treatment of Nepali workers

---

[12] Please see Peter Hallward's *Damming the Flood: Haiti, Aristide, and the Politics of Containment.*

[13] For a specific iteration of this kind of border rule, see for further details: Philippe Revelli's "Singapore, Malaysia and Indonesia: A Triangle of Growth or a Triangle of Inequality?".

reflect the racial policies inherited by postcolonial regimes, along with a global mode of devaluation of particular populations. This hierarchy, reproduced through a migrant's national identity and origin, produce modes of raciality that must be acknowledged. In a recent collection, *Global Raciality*, the editors conclude: "Raciality is produced not in isolation but rather in connection with other contextual relations of power, such as colonialism and empire, capitalism, gender, sexuality, class, caste, queerphobia, religion, indigeneity, ageism, and disability" (9). While this conclusion supports my claim that raciality should not be viewed in isolation, I would argue that it is also necessary to contextualize these intersections. As Kevin Floyd and the other editors of a new collection, *Totality Inside Out: Rethinking Crisis and Conflict Under Capitalism* remind us, "the specific form of totality that capitalism organizes, as Susan Ferguson has argued, cannot be arrived at by simply assembling additive lists of oppressions or by reducing the material specificity of these oppressions to underlying class relations" (2). Instead, the editors call for a "deeper engagement with the categories of capitalist political economy and the determinants of capitalist crisis … to scrutinize how oppressions are not only interlinked through but historically altered by their imbrication within capitalist structures" (3). I would concur that this particular attention to "capitalist structures" is a much-needed corrective to an acknowledgment of the more generalized abstraction of "contextual relations of power."[14]

And this corrective is certainly not a new one. This is an appropriate moment to remember W.E.B. Du Bois's words about the color line at the dawn on the twentieth century. As is well known, Du Bois had announced in *The Souls of Black Folks* (1903) that "[t]he problem of the twentieth century is the problem of the color-line." What is less known is how he amends this statement 50 years later for the anniversary edition of the book, alluding to what he "then [in 1903] did not know or did not realize." One was the influence of Freud and the other was "the tremendous impact on the modern world of Karl Marx" (43). Having made this qualification, he reflects on his famous statement, commenting:

---

[14] Satnam Virdee's gloss on Stuart Hall's conception of race and articulation is useful here as well: "treating a social formation as a complex structured totality of parts, each with a degree of relative autonomy from the other yet linked to form a contradictory unity. We can then empirically distinguish the multiple determinants of racism at different levels and plot the connections between the different parts of the social formation" (Virdee).

3 THEORIZING BORDERS IN THE SHADOW OF IMPERIAL VIOLENCE   81

I still think today as yesterday that the color line is a great problem of this century. But today I see more clearly than yesterday that back of the problem of race and color, lies a greater problem which both obscures and implements it: and that is the fact that so many civilized persons are willing to live in comfort even if the price of this is poverty, ignorance, and disease of the majority of their fellowmen; that to maintain this privilege men have waged war until today war tends to become universal and continuous, and the excuse for this war continues largely to be color and race. (43)

In this formulation, Du Bois doesn't just catalog the various relations of power that produce the color line, but also stresses how that line is inextricably connected to the acquisition of wealth and the immiseration of others.[15] One way "men have waged war," to continue, as Marx put it in *The German Ideology*, the "present state of things" is to ensure the consolidation of borders and the division of the world into the owners of wealth and those who create that wealth.

This interrelationship is truly a global one and must be seen as such. So, not only does global raciality play out in different contexts, but there are also ways in which these ideologies circulate and get reproduced in the global space. As I have indicated, domestic racial politics are mirrored in imperial racial politics, and the way populations are designated as disposable are often linked to their dispossession of their land and resources. In other words, imperialists and settler colonialists take their ideologies with them when they travel. It is worth citing an example here to illustrate both this point and the long historical continuity of global raciality. It is likely, for instance, that very few Americans know that more Filipinos were killed in the conquest of their island by the United States (1899–1903) than died in the entire American Civil War. Estimated figures of the loss of Filipino lives are 775,000 (Immerwahr 103). By contrast, the US military lost a little over 4000 men, three quarters to disease (Immerwahr 103). This was also the war in which waterboarding as a form of torture was

---

[15] In chap. 20 *of Capital, Volume 1*, Marx describes the process that would later be termed immiseration: "[W]ithin the capitalist system ... all means for the development of production transform themselves into means of domination over the producers; they mutilate the labourer into a fragment of a [human], degrade [the worker] to the level of an appendage of a machine ... they transform life-time into working-time, and drag [the worker's whole household] beneath the wheels of the Juggernaut of capital. But all methods for the production of surplus-value are at the same time methods of accumulation .... Accumulation of wealth at one pole is, therefore, at the same time accumulation of misery ... at the opposite pole, *i.e.,* on the side of the class that produces its own product in the form of capital" (799).

82   K. CHOWDHURY

used for the first time by a Major Edwin Glenn. Not surprisingly, the chief destroyer in this war was a General Jacob Smith, who had honed his murderous skills during the massacre at Wounded Knee. Upon arriving in the Philippines, Smith announced his intentions: "'I want no prisoners,' Smith allegedly told his subordinate. 'I wish you to kill and burn, the more you kill and burn the better you will please me.' All rice was to be seized, Smith insisted, and any male over the age of ten who did not turn himself over to the U.S. government should be killed. 'The interior of Samar [where resistance was particularly strong],' he ordered, 'must be made into a howling wilderness'" (Immerwahr 100). When his actions were investigated in 1902, he was not tried for war crimes or wanton murders, but because of "conduct to the prejudice of good order and military discipline" (qtd. in Immerwahr 101). The punishment imposed by President Roosevelt was to demand Smith's retirement from the Army. Today, General Smith is buried in the National Cemetery at Arlington. The fact that this "war" and the multiple atrocities committed during it have been erased from history textbooks is not surprising. Nor is it surprising that the white supremacist and imperial settler logic of the "Indian wars" continued to be practiced in Philippines, Cuba, or Puerto Rico, or indeed, in the more recent past, in Vietnam and into the present occupations of Afghanistan and Iraq. In short, the twenty-first-century atrocities at Abu Ghraib, Guantanamo, and Fallujah should have surprised no one. Current expressions of global raciality are inextricably tied to imperial practices of the past, and, as I have suggested, reify border rules, strengthening or reforming them, as the situation warrants.

Having interrogated the paradigm of development that informs current border practices by emphasizing the imperial lineage of border ideology and practice, manifested most tellingly in its extractive and racial forms, let us now navigate the many theoretical road maps that have been drawn up by a range of scholars as they chart the space of the border.

BORDER CRITIQUES: SCAPES, EDGES, AND OTHER NEGOTIATIONS

Perhaps an appropriate place to begin this discussion is by examining an influential piece by Étienne Balibar, "What is a Border?" published in 1995. Writing shortly after the Schengen agreement came into force in 1995, Balibar offers three prominent ways to consider the function of borders. First, he points out that borders are overdetermined, "in that sense, sanctioned, reduplicated and relativized by other geopolitical divisions. This feature is by no means incidental or contingent; it is intrinsic. Without the *world-configuring* function they perform, there would be no borders—or no lasting borders" (79). Departing from the banality of "there were always borders" claim, such a position clarifies the imperial/ capitalist function of borders as a distinctive one, going as far back as the Iberian control of the Americas and Portuguese forays into Africa and Asia. Second, he emphasizes the "*polysemic nature* of borders. In practical terms, this simply refers to the fact that they do not have the same meaning for everyone" (81). Needless to say, borders work "actively to *differentiate* between individuals in terms of social class" (81–82). This function, of course, leads to possible contradictions, as I pointed out in the previous chapter, where the powers that be must cater to the interests of a transnational class even while maintaining the popular legitimacy of the nation state through nationalist strivings and dramatic performative gestures. Finally, Balibar points to the "*heterogeneity* and ubiquity of borders or, in other words, the fact that the tendency of borders, political, cultural, and socioeconomic, to *coincide*—something which was more or less well achieved by nation-states, or, rather, by some of them—is tending today to fall apart." "The result of this," he points out, "is that *some borders are no longer situated at the borders at all*" (84). Certainly, the last point is proving to be increasingly the case, as imperial centers attempt to prevent migrants from arriving at their shores by extending their security apparatus further and further away from the immediate site of the border. Likewise, as the reach of capitalist financialization moves to all corners of the planet, so-called regulatory apparatuses work both to contain and to enable movement of capital, irrespective of the limits of territorial boundaries.

Reflecting on the Balibarian claim that "borders are everywhere," a collective of scholars in a piece "Interventions on rethinking 'the border' in border studies" attempts to concretize what that statement might actually mean. According to one of these scholars, Anssi Paasi, Balibar's statement can be elaborated on in two ways: one, "borders are rooted in historically contingent practices and discourses that are related to national ideologies and identities. These can be labeled as discursive/emotional landscapes of social power that often draw on various forms of nationalism. The site of the border is therefore not only the borderland but also the complex nation-building process and nationalist practices that can have material manifestations" (63). In this sense, borders are wide ranging and exist

84   K. CHOWDHURY

everywhere. Meanwhile, since 9/11, "technical landscapes of control and surveillance, monitored by increasingly technical devices and biometrics ... associated with border control to prevent terrorism or illegal immigration are not located solely in border areas but may indeed exist 'everywhere'" (63). Both practices work to strengthen state power.

Louise Amoore offers us a way to resist such state-based dominations: "To intervene in the writing of the contemporary border, then, is to speak back to the automated decision, the algorithmic rules and the risk-based judgment, to reinstate its irreducible difficulty, and to write the associations and relations of border lives differently" (63). Some ways in which borders can be seen as not merely enforcing and reaffirming dominant modes of control but also as avenues for reinventing a liberatory space are described in the following strategies suggested by Chris Rumford. One, "People can construct the scale of the border for themselves; as a 'local' phenomenon, a nation-state 'edge', or as a transnational staging post: the border can be reconfigured as a portal." Two, "Citizens, entrepreneurs, and NGOs are active in constructing, shifting, or even erasing borders." Finally, "Borderwork can also be associated with a range of claims-making activity, not only claims to national belonging or citizenship, but also demands for transnational mobility, assertions of human rights, and demonstrations of political actorhood, all of which can comprise acts of citizenship" (67–68). While all these possibilities grant a certain amount of agency to the citizen actors at the borderlands, these actions, in somewhat contradictory fashion, end up legitimizing these borders since all the "activity" is in relation to the affirmation of borders and states rather than a negation of their role in determining peoples' lives. Also, needless to say, affirming the role of "entrepreneurs, and NGOs" in helping to "erase" borders is surely a fanciful gesture? Many of these actors rely precisely on borders to fulfill and promote their interests.[16]

One such example where agency is being exercised, although without any discernable difference in actual power equations can be seen in the Edem Adotey's analysis "An imaginary line? Decolonisation, bordering and borderscapes on the Ghana–Togo border." In this article, Edem Adotey describes the multiple ways in which the border is performed at

---

[16] For a thoughtful recounting of the role of NGOs in furthering the interests of global capitalism, see Stephanie McMillan and Vincent Kelley's "*The Useful Altruists: How NGOs Serve Capitalism and Imperialism* and the more recent "Role of NGOs in Promoting Neo-Colonialism" by Syed Ehtisham.

the Ghana-Togo border. In this case, it is not just the state who makes the border what it is. The Ewe people of this region who have historically moved across these international borders created by the colonial powers also contribute to the making and unmaking of the border through their performances that include rituals based in community and commercial ties. As Adotey puts it,

> Bordering and borderscapes for the border inhabitants are fluid and contextual. In certain cases the precolonial border is evoked, while in others the postcolonial is also evoked. In the performance of these borders, the performers take on various identities—family, community, ethnic and national. Which is privileged depends on the motivations, which may be economic, political or social. While in certain cases family or ethnic identities may be privileged over national identities, in other contexts national identities may matter more. The audience is also important, as it also affects how the bordering is carried out. (1080)

While Adotey illustrates the ways in which the border is made and unmade, highlighting, specifically, the Ewe peoples' ability to perform the border through their own agency, their actions do not change the fact that Ghana has staggering levels of inequality, especially between the rural and urban populations, and that more than 50 percent of the Togolese people live below the poverty mark. Moreover, given Ghana's relatively higher position on the global gross domestic product list of nations in comparison to Togo ($65.6 billion versus $5.4 billion), a "status," which has all kinds of implications in its standing within global financial markets, there is little doubt that despite the ingenuity of border dwellers, there is unlikely to be any actual fluidity in the borders between the two countries.[17] Both states will continue to enforce border rules to protect their own interests, as well as the financial interests of the global market.

Indeed, even as scholars such as Adotey celebrate the ways in which borders are made and unmade by those who live in its interstices, and others point to its fluid characteristics, it is necessary to foreground the real material work done by borders. Too often, critics stop at the theoretical threshold of fluidity as a point of liberatory opposition to dominant border rules. Christopher Sohn, for instance, in "Navigating borders' multiplicity: the critical potential of assemblage," points out a few problems

---

[17] For a range of economic and other points of comparison between the two nations, please see the Georank page "Ghana vs Togo: Economic Indicators Comparison."

with Balibar's all encompassing "borders are everywhere" position, electing, instead, to use the framework of the assemblage to understand the "ontological multidimensionality" and the "fluid and manifold nature" of the border" (184). "The assemblage perspective," according to Sohn, suggests that the identity of a border is not of an essential nature but must be framed in relative and provisional terms" (187). There is undoubted merit to this argument, but it also disavows the real, material consequence of borders and their punitive role in regulating the movement of peoples from low-income zones on the planet to high-income ones. In short, there are always imperial networks that determine how "fluid" or "relative" a border scape can be. Also, even if the forces of deterritorialization can unsettle an assemblage, as we have seen with the arrival of the refugees in Europe in 2014–2015, these assemblages very quickly reterritorialize themselves. The growing militarization of borders across the world is a testament to this reality. In fact, one could argue that the fluidity of border rules enables states to solidify power as they continue to reinvent their own surveillance and carceral apparatus. Consider, for instance, Italy's introduction of a "blocked ports" policy in 2018–2019, when the government prevented sea vessels from disembarking migrants who had been rescued at sea. Many such occurrences of negation and reinvention allow little creative latitude for improvising social actors who may benefit from any apparent fluidity of the borderline.

Notions of fluidity and the "assemblage perspective" can also be seen in another popular mode of border analysis: the critical framework of the borderscape.[18] Elena dell'Agnese and Anne-Laure Amilhat Szary identify three versions of the borderscape as used by critics: the first is inspired by performance artist, Guillermo Gómez-Peña. In this iteration, a "borderscape is an area, shaped and reshaped by transnational flows, that goes beyond the modernist idea of clear-cut national territories" (6); the second, developed by Arjan Harbers, an urban planner, is described by dell'Agnese and Szary as an approach that "focuses on the role of the nation-state in shaping and reshaping the area surrounding the boundary" (6). More specifically, "the borderscape is the material output of the difference in sovereignty marked by the international boundary" (6); finally, Gabi Dolff-Bonekämper and Marieke Kuipers's notion of the borderscape emphasizes "the role of boundaries in transforming the territorial

---

[18] For a comprehensive introduction to this subject, see *Borderscapes: Hidden Geographies and Politics at Territory's Edge*, edited by Prem Kumar Rajaram and Carl Grundy-Warr.

configuration of adjacent lands … [or a] 'borderland', that is to say a portion of land surface influenced by the presence of an international boundary" (6).

Just as the ideas regarding the border as a site of fluid meanings or as an assemblage bring with them the notion of "openness," so, too, does the borderscape convey a sense of motion and changeability. Dina Krichker in "Making Sense of Borderscapes: Space, Imagination, and Experience" points to the limitations of this openness. Even as she describes a "'borderscape', as a fluid, mobile, open zone of differentiated encounters—a border zone without borders," she also acknowledges the "'irresistible vagueness' of the concept" (1225). Nonetheless, she believes that "[t]he idea of the borderscape allows us to extend our vision of border performance away from the border, and to grasp bordering exclusion dynamics in their continuity" (1229). In a particularly relevant insight for my study of cultural texts, she cites Art, as an example, for having "a capacity to reproduce the dynamics of bordering, distancing or challenging the separation dynamics in different spaces, constituting a unique cultural spatiality and temporality" (1228). Certainly, as my analysis of murals in Chap. 6 will attempt to demonstrate, art has the potential to challenge the "separation dynamics in different spaces" (1228).

In an effort to ground the concept of borderscapes to something more concrete, Krichker looks to Henri Lefebvre for his theoretical understanding of the production of space. As he said famously in his groundbreaking text, "Social relations, which are concrete abstractions, have no real existence save in and through space. *Their underpinning is spatial*" (404). Lefebvre, of course, sees the production of space, especially abstract space as that produced by capital for the organization of abstract labor and exchange; it is "the space of the bourgeoisie and of capitalism" (49, 57), a "space of calculation and quantification" (49). In this formulation, it is appropriate to extend Lefebvre's reading by seeing the border as instituted by the nation state for the management of "abstract labor, money, commodities and capital" (348). This space of domination and abstraction contrasts with the lived spaces of everyday life. For Lefebvre, only class struggle will destroy these dominant spaces. Krichker, eschewing the language of class struggle, speaks of the "interaction between space, imagination and experience in the process of borderscapes production" (1238). Based on her field research in Melilla, she argues "that imagination and experience both produce and are produced by space, and have the capacity to infuse space with the 'borderscaping' conditions" (1238). Her attention to the migrants and residents of Melilla offer us the "space of 'subjects' rather than of calculations" (362). However, despite this Lefebvrian framework, Krichker can only claim that "[i]n order for a borderscape to be constituted, it needs to be experienced and/or imagined as such" (1238). While granting precedence to social relations, Krichker does not emphasize the role of capitalist economic arrangements in producing spaces nor does she inquire into the ways in which relations of productions determine how people "experience" these borderscapes.

Krichker's call to bring a greater methodological and theoretical clarity to the concept of the borderscape is echoed by David Newman in "Borders and Bordering: Towards an Interdisciplinary Dialogue." Newman, in a similar vein, attempts to apply the actual fluidity of borders to the study of borders themselves. He urges border scholars not to accede to disciplinary compartmentalization in their studies of the border; limiting our studies to certain methodologies or forms of analysis, according to Newman, is in tension with the ways in which borders work. A more fluid approach to border studies will capture their elasticity and their multiple impacts on how individuals navigate their lives. An attention to both the territorial and the non-territorial reach of borders, for instance, is necessary to draw out the complexities of this construct. Ultimately, though, according to Newman, analysis should not just replicate the status quo. He urges border scholars "to acquire, and actively promote, an understanding of the processes through which all types of borders can be opened even further and how they can be crossed with greater ease. It is by no means a given and it requires a mutual willingness to cross the disciplinary divide and to learn each other's border language, if we are to move beyond the common, but not necessarily shared, discourse interaction space which has been created during the past decade by border scholars" (183). Newman's call for an interdisciplinary approach is apposite, particularly given the multiple ways in which borders impinge upon the political, cultural, economic, and psychic lives across the globe, but the actuality of colonial/material relations are flattened by an approach that lacks any specificity. Opening "all types of borders" is a process that will take concerted, collective action, one that will not just be about how borders "can be crossed with greater ease," but instead, how they can be abolished.

One of the reasons to be skeptical about a focus on easing border crossings, as I have argued, is because they do not necessarily undermine the authority of the state, a structure that relies on historically embedded forms of access and exclusion. Dimitris Papadopoulos is one such critic who draws our attention to the many historical layers that underwrite any discussion of contemporary borders. Refusing to refer to the arrival of migrants in Greece after the Syrian war as an ahistoricized "crisis," he points to the multiple ways in which Greeks themselves have been refugees in the same spaces that are now designated as sites of crisis. "Fluidity," for Papadopoulos, does not necessarily point to a liberatory future or an access to reinvention for migrants. Reflecting on different border episodes in Greece's history and drawing from analyses of the "border as technique and process" and the "concept of borders as both rooted and rhizomatic," Papadopoulos uses the term "bordering" to "emphasize boundaries both as anchored divisions and as ever-active instruments of propagating fragmentation and internalizing differentiating relations" (135–136). Papadopoulos accurately captures the simultaneity of border work. On the one hand, borders are the material manifestation of state rigidity and authority; all too often, a mere transgression of this fixed line can end in detention or death. Yet, on the other hand, borders work most effectively for the state when they are fluid, literally moving across space and time to enact regulation and control, allowing for maximum flexibility. The external and the internal work done by the border are always interrelated. At the same time, however, Papadopoulos is willing to concede that this flexibility also allows for transborder resistance and alliances whose goal is to undermine the state's ability to dictate, surveil, and control.

In general, most of these critics agree that borders are not confined to rigid dividing lines that operate in mechanical ways. Scholars in border studies recognize this fluidity, and as we have seen, writers such as Rumford, Rohn, or Adotey argue that border dwellers resist the hegemonic reach of the border to constitute varying relationships with border spaces, even if, as I argue, these relationships cannot bypass the dominance of the state or the reach of capital. The nature of these relationships is acknowledged in particular modes of analysis, such as the structuration method, which, Emmanuel Brunet-Jailly describes thus: "Bounded territories and borderlands are the outcome of the continual interactions and intersections between the actions of people (agency) within the constraints and limits placed by contextual and structural factors (structure)" (3). This method does not prioritize the universal or the specific nor the structure or the agent, paying equal attention to both. Borders, in short, are part of this dialectic between those who must live with its implications and laws and thus constantly have to remake them. Consequently, the border itself continuously shifts meaning and assigns value to these subjects when necessary. Md Azmeary Ferdoush, similarly, uses the notion of structuration to position the border as the edge of the state structure. He defines "edge" as a place in which different ideas of space, territoriality, sovereignty, citizenship, and identity are formulated, practiced, and negotiated" (184).

In a similar vein, Luca Tateo and Giuseppina Marsico, in their piece, "Signs as Borders, and Borders as Signs" emphasize the site of the border as a point of negotiation and argue that borders function as signs through which humans act out and perform interpsychic relations and regulate their own conduct and the conduct of others. Borders, according to Tateo and Marsico, operate in microscopic ways, such as a child learning about safe and unsafe zones, and in more dominant ways in creating identity markers once a border is recognized as such. Some of these behaviors become internalized and function as a system of self-regulation. What becomes evident in their description is that the border is a sign that operates in both the intrapersonal and the interpersonal psychic domain. As Tateo and Marsico put it,

> Different meanings and values are produced as the border creates an asymmetry between what is inside and what is outside. A border acquires its meaning from goals: a line may become a border depending on people's purposes, actions, and intentions. Borders do not exist as fixed in time; they emerge, unfold, develop, and disappear in time .... It is a place of both tension and pacification, of meeting and potential clash, of discrimination and desire, of violence and dialogue. It marks and puts into relationship what is possible to know, to say, or to do with what is unknow-able, unspeakable, or unworkable. (722)

Even while emphasizing the inevitable contingencies and uncertainties that characterize the border space, Tateo and Marsico are too apt to see an almost natural rhythm to the border. It ebbs and flows, it provides opportunities and ruptures, it harbors dreams and desire. There appears to be little emphasis on the forces of history, capital, or colonialism in this web of bordered life.

Brunet-Jailly, Ferdoush, and Tateo and Marsico correctly emphasize the many ways in which the border is a site of negotiation, and in granting agency to border dwellers and border crossers, they acknowledge the myriad possibilities that are available both to undermine and to unsettle the hegemony of the state. However, even while accepting the fact that ordinary people who must navigate the border on a regular basis, perform the border every day, and thus play a role in making and unmaking the border at multiple levels, it is necessary to point out that the state, too, has a unique and powerful role in enacting and ritualizing its performance of the border and that these negotiations at the "edges" are never on equal terms. The recent militarization of borders across the world, the building of walls and fences, and deportation of those who seek refuge, are just some of the ways in which violent border practices by the state have accelerated in the last several years. Likewise, even though Adetayo and Ferdoush are correct in implying that notions of citizenship or sovereignty are being reinvented at the "edges" of the state, we cannot assume the stability of such categories, which, in the end, are constantly being reshaped to fulfill the benefits of the state. Moreover, not only are the stability of categories, such as citizenship and sovereignty elusive, but relying on these categories as markers for negotiation indirectly legitimize the state, granting it the authority to validate claims or rights according to the terms that have put in place by the state itself.

Nancy Wonders alludes to this centrality of state performance in her essay, "Global Flows, Semi-permeable Borders and New Channels of Inequality": "Although states attempt to choreograph national borders, often in response to global pressures, these state policies have little meaning until they are 'performed' by state agents [and] by border crossers. Border agents and state bureaucrats play a critical role in determining where, how, and on whose body a border will be performed" (66). Such performances, as I point out in Chap. 2, not only happen at the border line, but as Wonders specifies, the "where" of the borderline has become increasingly wide ranging and expansive in both its juridical and its military reach. ICE agents in the United States, for instance, appear to have free ranging jurisdiction to conduct raids whenever and wherever they please.[19] Ferdoush's attention to "Borders, borderworks, and bordering practices ... as the outcome of a complex interaction between the state, state actors, border-landers, citizens, non-citizens, and multiple other factors both internal and external to the state" is a necessary reminder of the process of making and performing a border, yet these processes must always be seen through the lens of political economy and the mutations and contradictions that accompany the life of this process. In other words,

---

[19] For a recent example, see Caitlin Dickerson's "'Flood the Streets': ICE Targets Sanctuary Cities with Increased Surveillance" in the *New York Times*.

I am in sympathy with Ferdoush and other critics who remind us that the border is not a place of closure, where meaning is not just finalized through state dictates. Indeed, in my analysis of border texts, I will demonstrate how artists and activists, alike, resist border rules and the border as a place of closure; however, I will also point to the ways in which these acts of resistance and refusal must always be seen in the context of border abolition.

As a cautionary note, I will briefly comment on how such qualifications are necessary even in a disciplinary category such as critical border studies. In their introduction, "Critical Border Studies: Broadening and Deepening the 'Lines in the Sand' Agenda," Noel Parker and Nick Vaughan-Williams describe Critical Border Studies as advocating for "two twinned moves: a shift from the *concept of the border* to the *notion of bordering practice*; and the adoption of the lens of *performance* through which bordering practices are produced and reproduced" (729). Focusing on practice "emphasises attention to 'the everyday'—the processes through which controls over mobility are attempted and enacted—and the effects of those controls in people's lives and in social relations more widely" (729). Similarly, "Reconceptualising borders as a set of performances injects movement, dynamism, and fluidity into the study of what are otherwise often taken to be static entities" (729). Both moves clearly attempt to depart from the idea that the border is a "line in the sand," an immovable static place, attached to the notion of territoriality, the only relevant point where subjects can come into being as participants in the rituals of the border as a bounded space. While the "task of developing new border imaginaries, theories, and methodologies," is to be lauded, as is the call for the border to "become a field of action on the part of non-state actors—notably, the ordinary citizens who dismantled the Wall or have been involved in numerous less vaunted episodes before and since" (733), it is important to keep center front the need to consistently question the fiction of the nation state, which often is manifested in the state's performative modes, as well as capital's requirement to keep fluid border practices in place.

An illustration of why this move is necessary can be seen in the concrete situation of the US–Mexico border and the multiple ways in which this border functions through maintaining a certain degree of fluidity and fixity at the same time. So, undoubtedly, many of the critics are correct in suggesting that borders often work in contrasting ways, and that they are sites of negotiation, but these practices, as I have argued, primarily suit the interests of the power elites. Fluidity and statis are generally interrelated

3 THEORIZING BORDERS IN THE SHADOW OF IMPERIAL VIOLENCE 93

and interdependent upon each other. Take, for example, the passing of North American Free Trade Agreement (NAFTA) in January 1994. As soon as this celebratory borderless North American world was put into motion, the physical borders of the United States were tightened against the movement of people from the South to the North. This was no coincidence. These same power elites who designed the treaty knew full well that the provisions of NAFTA would have a devastating impact on Mexican farmers and those involved in most forms of agricultural work. The erosion of subsidies for Mexican farmers, the continuation of subsidies for US farmers, and the flooding of Mexican markets with American corn could only lead to one end. As the saying in Mexico goes, "Sin maiz, no hay pais" (without corn, there is no country). Farmers were forced to migrate to cities where there was very little hope for long-term survival. Those who would inevitably seek economic survival through the journey north would then have to be held back at all costs. This is when a *large-scale* militarization of the border began.[20] It was also during this period that the Antiterrorism and Effective Death Penalty Act and the Illegal Immigration Reform and Immigrant Responsibility Act were passed in 1996. Both these acts saw a massive increase in deportation, arrests, and incarceration.[21] These contrasts, thus, are not accidental. The so-called opening of

[20] Of course, the militarization of the US/Mexico border did not just begin in the 1990s. For a comprehensive account of this history, see Greg Grandin's *The End of the Myth: From the Frontier to the Border Wall in the Mind of America* and his earlier piece, "The Militarization of the Southern Border Is a Long-Standing American Tradition."

[21] Tanya Maria Golash-Bozai in *Deported: Immigrant Policing, Disposable Labor and Global Capitalism* points out that "[d]eportees are, in some ways, the ultimate example of surplus labor. Whereas the United States will eventually free most prisoners, it banishes deportees, typically for life. This keeps them from competing for scarce jobs or diminishing public aid" (253). In their home countries, they fulfill different purposes, from serving as "convenient scapegoats for rising crime" or "as ideal laborers for transnational call centers, an outgrowth of global capitalism" (219). Golash-Bozai also points out the racialized nature of deportations, which are a significant contributing factor to the larger inequities of global apartheid: "Mass deportation helps to maintain [the] system of global apartheid by removing mostly nonwhite people from the United States—a land of plenty—to much poorer nations where most people are not white. Global apartheid is part of the larger system of global capitalism. The role of the United States in the maintenance of global apartheid is a continuation of its highly racialized history of immigration policy (261). The bare numbers that characterize mass deportations are startling in their racial singularity. Golash-Bozai informs us that 'today 97 percent of all deportees are sent to Latin America and the Caribbean" in a process that "primarily affects nonwhite people; is carried out without due process; and separates millions of children from their parents" (264).

borders, whether it is the United States or Europe, usually results in borders tightening as well. It is no coincidence, likewise, that Fortress Europe arrived with the implementation of Schengen in March 1995—roughly the same time as the implementation of NAFTA. As always, flexibility for some, fixity for others.

An attention to such material realities informs possible criticisms of the methodologies of critical border studies. Some of these criticisms also implore us to shift our glance from the center to the periphery. In a spirited analysis of the limitations of critical border studies, "Inverting the Telescope on Borders that Matter: Conversations in Café Europa," Dorte Andersen, Oliver Thomas Kramsch, and Marie Sandberg describe that project as questioning the conventional studies of borders, decentering these studies as being an "anchorage in the apparatus of the state, as a merely epiphenomenal expression of state territoriality and sovereignty" (459). In this iteration, then, according to Andersen et al. critical border studies scholars make the following claims: "borders are 'manifold and in a constant state of becoming'; they are defined by 'bordering practices' rather than as stable, objective 'things,' the former clearly visible in practices of 'the everyday'; and they are captured most vividly through acts of 'performance' in and by which bordering practices are produced and reproduced" (Andersen et al. 459–60). Andersen et al., however, find these scholars' analyses, though "supposedly mov[ing] beyond the violent and exclusionary cartographical imaginaries of the nation-state line … serves nevertheless to reinscribe that line, including its disciplinary effects" (460). "Borders here," they argue "are indeed ceaselessly practiced and performed, but violence, domination (and, ultimately, death) somehow fails to enter the imaginative repertoire of Europe's most reflexively critical border scholarship" (460). They charge these scholars with an attempt to court the "neutrality of a la carte perspectivalism (i.e., one that places the border scholar in a God's eye position to objectively canvas myriad border perspectives, standing above the political fray while casually erasing the problem of political exclusion and violence from her stories)" (461). Instead, Andersen et al.

> argue for the need to fashion a robust normative lens capable of locating our research in the multiplicity of interconnected tensions between large-scale dynamics of capitalist globalization, widespread cultural transformation and macro-shifts in European territorial governance, on the one hand, and particular expressions of bordering in precisely those places where bordering

3 THEORIZING BORDERS IN THE SHADOW OF IMPERIAL VIOLENCE   95

truly matters, at the interface of localized practices and globalizing designs. (461–62)

An attention to the totality of capitalist globalization at the "interface of localized practices" is a salutary step in view of the more flattened and neutralized categories employed by many critical border theorists, as is an attempt to decenter Europe.

In fact, Andersen et al. reach back to Benedict Anderson's metaphor of an "inverted telescope" to oppose critical border studies scholars. This approach, they argue, "displaces and de-centers the reality of European bordering processes as a matter determined exclusively from the designs of an internally driven, territorially homogeneous European governmental norm," instead "opening analysis of bordering practices to a multiplicity of encounters whose localized effects cannot be easily re-domesticated into any determinate European fold (462). Ultimately, Andersen and his colleagues "attempt to develop critical comparativist accounts of borders able to relate disparately located bordering processes as co-constitutive elements of wider material and symbolic circuits of exchange, transmission, and exploitation (462). This, in turn, allows them to engage in "an affective and worldly solidarity with those for whom the violence of bordering has real, material consequences" (462). Proposing a "real-and-imagined space" called Café Europa, where this is possible requires "a change of vision, an inversion of the telescope by which we normally apprehend borders and bordering processes as derivative appendages of state territorial power" (462–63).

Of course, merely turning the telescope can just reassert the binary, so it is important that "the process of self-othering invoked by the inverted telescope, while perhaps dizzying and disorienting, can nevertheless be re-signified not as a constitutive lack or a renewed power move but as a fruitfully ambiguous vantage point, a space of ontological up-rooting and tension: the essence of Café Europa" (464). Turning the telescope also enables an envisioning of "multiple discursive–material assemblages enabling migratory processes rather than, as is often done in migration studies, focusing on choice-making individuals (472). In the end, it is in this "collaborative, politicized and ontologically-grounded writing praxis ... that multiple border realities can be both perceived and enacted" (473). This, they claim, can be done "by training attention on localized bordering practices that contest naturalization and re-appropriation within the logics of global, European, and state-centered geopolitical designs

(473). Andersen et al.'s attention to the "spectral presence of a European imperial past" and to the "mechanisms of labor migration flows across time and space" appropriately places the materiality of border spaces and border experiences center front. Moreover, the metaphor of the inverted telescope forces us to rethink the space that is called Europe.

While I applaud the decentering of Europe, glancing aslant at it from its peripheral spaces and delinking it from its privileged perch, I am less convinced by the writers' investment in what they call the "ontological politics of bordering" (473). An attention to a situated, localized politics is necessary, but it must be attached to a larger collective struggle against the border rituals that trap people in exploitative situations. What Kevin Floyd calls "totally thinking" is a necessary antidote to a fixation on localized ontologies. Here is Floyd's definition of this critical stance, which counters the more abstract totality of "global, European and state-centered geopolitical designs" (Andersen et al. 473): "The Marxian critique of capital ... endeavors to comprehend what this ontological and epistemological atomization makes it impossible to apprehend: capital as the systemic global source of this enforced social dispersal" (6). It is this form of "totality thinking" that informs my study of border practices and rituals, and I will conclude this critical review by focusing briefly on the work on three theorists, who foreground the material politics of borders, paying special attention to the role of capital and its exploitation and regulation of labor through the mechanics of exclusion and inclusion.[22] These writers also identify and name the colonial structures and hierarchies of racial difference used to construct narratives of nation, place, and identity. These narratives, they contend, further the mythology of whiteness, which, in turn, augments and runs parallel to the needs of capital.

BORDERS: A MATERIALIST CRITIQUE

The most powerful voice in this trio is Harsha Walia, a Canadian author and activist, who published *Undoing Border Imperialism* in 2013. Walia's new book, *Border and Rule: Global Migration, Capitalism, and the Rise of Racist Nationalism* (2021) reiterates the point she had made in her previous work, *Undoing Border Imperialism*: "Borders are an ordering regime,

---

[22] Gracie Mae Bradley and Luke de Noronha's *Against Borders: The Case for Abolition* (2022) was published as I was completing my final revisions. I look forward to engaging with their ideas in the future.

both assembling and assembled through racial-capitalist accumulation and colonial relations" (2). Like most other border theorists, she does not view borders as "fixed or static lines." Rather, "they are productive regimes concurrently generated by and producing social relations of dominance" (6). Walia's analysis is framed by an understanding of the totality of capital accumulation. For this reason, she does not view migration as a self-generated "crisis" in the mode of Betts and Collier. Instead, for Walia, "contemporary migration is *itself* a mode of global governance, capital accumulation, and gendered racial class formation" (6). In this reading, migrants and refugees are not the objects of humanitarian aid for the West, but "a constitutive outside to bordering regimes whose journeys are largely an accounting of debts, reparations, and redistribution long due" (15).

Walia focuses on four border governance strategies that "solidify racism": "exclusion, territorial diffusion, commodified inclusion, and discursive control" (78). The first operates by containing and expelling, using "walls, detention centers, and deportations. Governance through exclusion works to fortify territorial control, solidify racialized nationalist identity, and criminalize migrants and refugees as 'undesirables' and 'trespassers'" (79). Walia connects this border governance to the broader issues of "wealth hoarding, deindustrialization and outsourcing, the dismantling of public services," and many other forms of neoliberal segregation (83). Neoliberal dictates, according to Walia, make it necessary for border scholars to connect the dots between, say, illegality and criminality. Who is excluded and for what reasons generate discussions of the border within the totality of capital relations. The second form of governance, territorial diffusion, similarly, makes connections between "disciplinary practices *within* the state, as well as imperial outsourcing beyond the state's borders" (84). In short, the border can exist anywhere, and its impact continues far from the "magical line" of the border (84). One way in which these punitive measures operate describes the third form of governance: having at hand an available pool of labor with "deliberately deflated labor power to guarantee capital accumulation" (85). This form of commodified inclusion ensures that even if the "workers are declared illegal, the surplus value they create is never deemed illegal" (85). It is no surprise, then, that deportations of workers increase if there is ever a threat of unionization. Finally, "discursive governance" ensures that terms such as "migrant crisis" and "refugee crisis," and myriad ways of designating who is worthy of protection and refuge, based on Eurocentric and anti—Communist ideologies, allow the state to codify and regulate the terms for granting asylum and for creating a "slew of legally distinct categories and a hierarchy of rights in order to manage, divide, and control people on the move" (87). Walia's precise attention not only to the dynamics of capital accumulation, but also to a global totality that must be put center front if any theory of the border must be constructed is an admirable reminder that the border remains an essential piece of the global exploitative chain that reproduces hierarchies of difference and enables the generation and shifting of resources and people that are essential to the efficient production and circulation of capital.

Also published in 2021, Justin Akers Chacón, a professor of US History and Chicano Studies at San Diego City College, in *The Border Crossed Us: The Case for Opening the US-Mexico Border*, underwrites his analysis of the US–Mexico border buoyed by many of the same theoretical foundations. In the neoliberal mode of accumulation, Chacón argues, "state action has been taken to internationalize capitalist mobility, force open once-protected national markets, and to otherwise eradicate the vestiges of previous revolutionary advances, social reforms, and policy structures that embodied the accumulated gains of past episodes of class struggles" (6). Much of the accumulated wealth in the last three decades of US-led capitalist globalization has come through the exploitation of migrants, "through everything from ownership of the largest productive firms that use migrant labor to selling weapons or prison beds to the state or charging migrants exorbitant prices for sending remittances" (13). Border enforcement makes this extraction possible and furthermore ensures the international division of labor which enables differential modes of exploitation and disposal of surplus labor. As Chacón puts it, through the "subdivision of production across borders, capital can intensify the rate of exploitation of all segments by lowering the wage threshold to the lowest possible denominator. This is made possible by reinforcing national boundaries [which then] ... ideologically divide the workers along national lines by making them compete with each other for jobs" (137).[23] Perhaps

---

[23] Of course, the history of this attempt to divide workers is as old as the history of industrial capitalism in the United States. For an excellent documentary of this history, see Scott Noble's *Plutocracy: Political Repression in U.S.A.*

the most startling rates of exploitation are visible in the field of electronics and technology.[24]

Of course, this division also operates *within* the nation state. Chacón reminds us that "[m]ost farmworkers are born outside of the United States, primarily in Mexico but also in Central America and the Caribbean. Over half of the workforce is undocumented, although many have lived and worked in the US for over a decade .... The exploitation of a highly skilled, undocumented workforce is the cornerstone of accumulation for this industry and increasingly in others" (167).[25] As Walia also notes, this exploitative pattern has ensured that the state brutally represses any labor activity; indeed, "at the core of the migra-state," Chacón argues, "is labor repression.[26] It is precisely designed to repress that labor power among immigrant workers" (231). Underlining the connection between workers' rights and movements to abolish border regimes, Chacón believes that "it will likely take the reemergence of a militant workers' movement to open the borders, which is a precondition to rebuilding a labor movement within and across boundaries" (231–32). The fight to "abolish the migrant repressive apparatus and, by necessity, the system of capitalism as a whole ... will also require a convergence and reintegration of socialist politics as a guiding framework of the class struggle, rooted in internationalism and a concrete vision for building working-class unity within and across borders" (235). Throughout his analysis of the specific contexts of the US–Mexico border, Chacón persistently identifies the border as a problem rooted in the organization of the world to maximize profits for the few. To this end, the planet's most vulnerable are at the receiving end of repressive border politics. As I asserted in Chap. 1, populations are kept in place, moved, or disposed of according to the needs of capital. Meanwhile,

---

[24] For a staggering example of this rate of exploitation, see a piece from *The Tricontinental* entitled "The Rate of Exploitation: The Case of the iPhone."

[25] As the recent pandemic has further emphasized, immigrant workers are employed in some of most precarious forms of employment. Not only does the nature of their work expose them to the greatest risks, but they also have the fewest social security nets to assist them if they are to get sick or lose their employment. For an example, see Michael Sainato's "'A Lot of Abuse for Little Pay': How US Farming Profits from Exploitation and Brutality."

[26] Michael Dear points out that because so many "migrants held in detention centers often work in kitchens and laundry rooms, for which they usually get paid one dollar per day," the "federal government—which prohibits hiring undocumented workers—[is] the largest single employer of unemployed migrants in the country" (166). This, too, is the central contradiction of the migra-state, but entirely in keeping with the analysis suggested in Chap. 2 regarding the role of disposable labor.

finance capital rains down ruination through debt, extraction, and speculation. Any attempt at cross border solidarity is undermined by concerted and collaborative attempts by states to destroy such movements. However, these repressive actions also suggest that the state understands that acts of transborder solidarity are one of the most effective ways to organize against the rapacity of global capitalism. Chacón reminds us that they remain a potent way in which an unbordered future can be imagined.

Finally, political geographer at the University of Hawaii, Reece Jones, in *Violent Borders: Refugees and the Right to Move* (2016) **looks at various border zones—the European Union, US–Mexico, the West Bank, Australia-Pacific, India-Bangladesh, Bangladesh-Myanmar—to emphasize that borders produce violence. As he puts it, "drawing a border is an inherently violent act that relies on the threat of force to support a territorial claim" (9).** Jones identifies five types of violence produced by the border. The first three are the ones we are most familiar with: "overt violence," "the use of force or power—threatened or actual—that increases the chances of injury, death, or deprivation," and forms of violence that impinge upon peoples' rights to land and resources (9). The remaining two means of violence are largely ignored by the Western media and policy makers but have devastating consequences for those affected by it. Although not viewed through a directly Marxist lens as practiced by Walia and Chacón, Jones does point to the structural violence "that deprives the poor of access to wealth and opportunities through the enclosure of resources and the bordering of states" (9). This structural violence is also related to the fifth category of violence: the damage done to the environment not only through the technologies of surveillance, such as walls and fences, but also by creating "separate jurisdictions that allow the ideology of resource extraction to become pervasive by preventing uniform environmental regulations" (9).

Throughout, Jones reminds us about the materiality of walls and borders, a materiality that is translated into economic and human terms. So, for example, "walls are built on borders where there is a sharp wealth gap across them. In 2012, the gross domestic product per capita of countries building walls was more than $14,000 while on the other side it was $2,900" (203). Not only does this lay bare some real divides, but raises the question whether borders are designed to separate nations or whether they are at the core a class project. Another material reality that Jones points to is the reality of thousands who die trying to traverse these borders. According to Jones, "more than 40,000 people died attempting to cross a border from 2006 to 2015." In 2016, "there were more than 8,000 deaths" (208). Since 2014, there have been almost 23,000 migrants who have lost their lives just in the Mediterranean crossings (Missing Migrants Project). It is worth noting that these large numbers of deaths are a result of Western countries deliberately directing migrants to more dangerous routes, whether they be to the central Mediterranean or regions of the Arizona desert. These policies are an instantiation of the fact that borders, although constituting an existing line of separation, can be repurposed to spell the difference between life and death.

Jones's attention to the inherent violence produced by borders, especially in terms of describing the politics of wealth and power that determine how this violence is inflicted on the most vulnerable is a salient point in any discussion of border practices, but unlike Walia and Chacón, the power of his analysis is somewhat limited by his attention to the concrete impact of the "magical line." Much of the violence, one could argue, happens through the social relation that is not confined to the actual space of the border or to the violence that occurs in that space. So, for instance, the question of who labors in the most exploitative jobs, who has access to health care, or whose family is harassed by ICE is connected to the much wider structural violence of global capitalism, and this gap in Jones's analysis may also explain why Jones does not emphasize the ways in which race and gender play a significant role in producing particular forms of differential violence. Finally, Jones puts too much faith in the free movement of labor as a solution for many of the ills of the current crisis. Exploitation will not cease because migration becomes easier. As I argued in Chap. 1, the dynamics of wealth accumulation can accommodate and even desire a certain amount of movement on the part of the global workforce. True liberation for workers must include the abolition of borders.

However, for Jones, a more humanitarian, open borders policy seems to be the immediate goal. In a recent, edited collection, *Open Borders: In Defense of Free Movement* (2019), Jones confirms that his aim in the book is to "denaturalize movement restrictions at borders by questioning their necessity and demonstrating how they damage people and the environment (3). He argues "that there is not a moral, legal, philosophical, or economic case for limiting the movement of human beings at borders" (3). The book, he tells us "brings together theorists for open borders with activists working to make safe passage a reality on the ground to put forward a clear, concise, and convincing case for a world without movement restrictions at borders (4–5). Ultimately, then, the collection, even though containing essays by activists who want to abolish borders, primarily advocate for "making the positive case for the benefits of free movement for countries on both ends of the exchange." The argument of the book, according to Jones, "is very simple: movement is a fundamental human right, and the right to move freely should be protected at the global level (13). This is where I depart from Jones's position, which is primarily a reformist one, advocating for more humanitarian border policies. Such an end, leaving in place the structural formations of the nation state and its fundamental quest to enable the accumulation of wealth isn't a productive goal for the present moment.

WORKS CITED

Adotey, Edem. "An Imaginary Line? Decolonisation, Bordering and Borderscapes on the Ghana-Togo Border." *Third World Quarterly,* vol. 42, no. 5, 2021, pp. 1069–1086.

Alexis, Yveline. *Haiti Fights Back: The Life and Legacy of Charlemagne Péralte.* Rutgers University Press, 2021.

Andersen, Dorte, et al. "Inverting the Telescope on Borders that Matter: Conversations in Café Europa." *Journal of Contemporary European Studies,* vol. 23, no. 4, 2015, pp. 459–476.

Bacchetta, Paola, et al. *Global Raciality: Empire, PostColoniality, DeColoniality.* Routledge, 2018.

Balibar, Étienne. "What is a Border?" *Politics and the Other Scene.* Verso, 2002, pp. 75–86.

Basit, Abdul. "Why Did the Afghan Army Disintegrate so Quickly?" *Al Jazeera,* 17 Aug. 2021, https://www.aljazeera.com/opinions/2021/8/17/why-did-the-afghan-army-disintegrate-so-quickly.

Betts, Alexander, and Paul Collier. *Refuge: Rethinking Refugee Policy in a Changing World.* Oxford University Press, 2017.

Bradley, Gracie Mae, and Luke de Noronha. *Against Borders: The Case for Abolition.* Verso, 2022.

Brunet-Jailly, Emmanuel. "Special Section: Borders, Borderlands and Theory: An Introduction." *Geopolitics,* vol. 16, no. 1, 2011 pp. 1–6.

Carayannis, Tatiana and Louisa Lombard, editors. *Making Sense of the Central African Republic.* Zed Books, 2015.

Chacón, Justin Akers. *The Border Crossed Us: The Case for Opening the US-Mexico Border.* Haymarket Books, 2021.

Dalleo, Raphael. *American Imperialism's Undead: The Occupation of Haiti and the Rise of Caribbean Anticolonialism,* University of Virginia Press, 2016.

3 THEORIZING BORDERS IN THE SHADOW OF IMPERIAL VIOLENCE   103

Dear, Michael. *Why Walls Won't Work: Repairing the US-Mexico Divide.* Oxford University Press, 2013.

Dell'Agnese, Elena, and Anne-Laure Amilhat Szary. "From Border Landscapes to Border Aesthetics." *Geopolitics,* vol. 20, no. 1, 2015, pp. 4–13.

Dickerson, Caitlin, et al. "'Flood the Streets': ICE Targets Sanctuary Cities with Increased Surveillance." *New York Times,* 5 Mar. 2020, https://www.nytimes.com/2020/03/05/us/ICE-BORTAC-sanctuary-cities.html.

Downes, Alexander B. *Catastrophic Success: Why Foreign-Imposed Regime Change Goes Wrong.* Cornell University Press, 2021.

Du Bois, W. E. B. "Preface to the Jubilee Edition of *The Souls of Black Folk* (1953)." *Monthly Review: An Independent Socialist Magazine,* vol. 55, no. 6, 2003, pp. 41–43.

Edmond, Charlotte. "84 Percent of Refugees Live in Developing Countries." *World Economic Forum,* 20 June 2017, https://www.weforum.org/agenda/2017/06/eighty-four-percent-of-refugees-live-in-developing-countries/.

Ehtisham, Syed. "Role of NGOs in Promoting Neo-Colonialism." *Counter Currents,* 16 Feb. 2021, https://countercurrents.org/2021/02/role-of-ngos-in-promoting-neo-colonialism/.

Ferdoush, Md Azmeary. "Seeing Borders Through the Lens of Structuration: A Theoretical Framework." *Geopolitics,* vol. 23, no. 1, 2018, pp. 180–200.

Floyd, Kevin, et al., editors. *Totality Inside Out: Rethinking Crisis and Conflict Under Capitalism.* Fordham University Press, 2022.

Forgie, Keir. "US Imperialism and Disaster Capitalism in Haiti." *Good Intentions: Norms and Practices of Imperial Humanism,* edited by Maximilian C. Forte. Alert Press, 2014, pp. 57–75.

Gani, Aisha. "An Afghan Refugee Commuted Hours for His Uber Job. Then He Was Shot in His Car." *The Guardian,* 31 Dec. 2021, https://www.theguardian.com/technology/2021/dec/31/an-afghan-refugee-commuted-hours-for-his-uber-job-then-he-was-shot-in-his-car.

"Ghana vs Togo: Economic Indicators Comparison." *Georank,* https://georank.org/economy/ghana/togo.

Gibbons-Neff, Thomas, et al. "The Afghan Military was Built Over Twenty Years. How Did it Collapse So Quickly?" *New York Times,* 13 Aug. 2021, https://www.nytimes.com/2021/08/13/world/asia/afghanistan-rapid-military-collapse.html.

Golash-Bozai, Tanya Maria. *Deported: Immigrant Policing, Disposable Labor and Global Capitalism.* New York University Press, 2015.

Grandin, Greg. *The End of the Myth: From the Frontier to the Border Wall in the Mind of America.* Metropolitan, 2020.

———. "The Militarization of the Southern Border is a Long-Standing American Tradition." *The Nation,* 14 Jan. 2019, https://www.thenation.com/article/archive/the-militarization-of-the-southern-border-is-a-long-standing-american-tradition/.

Hallward, Peter. *Damming the Flood: Haiti, Aristide, and the Politics of Containment*. Verso, 2008.

Immerwahr, Daniel. *How to Hide an Empire: A History of the Greater United States*. Farrar, Straus and Giroux, 2019.

Johnson, Corey, et al. "Interventions on Rethinking 'the Border' in Border Studies." *Political Geography*, vol. 30, no. 2, 2011, pp. 61–69.

Jones, Reece, editor. *Open Borders: In Defense of Free Movement*. University of Georgia Press, 2019.

———. *Violent Borders: Refugees and the Right to Move*. Verso, 2016.

Krichker, Dina. "Making Sense of Borderscapes: Space, Imagination and Experience." *Geopolitics*, vol. 26, no. 4, 2021, pp. 1224–1242.

Lefebvre, Henri. *The Production of Space*. Translated by Donald Nicholson-Smith, Wiley-Blackwell, 1992.

Macdonald, Isabel. "10 Years Ago, We Pledged to Help Haiti Rebuild. Then What Happened?" *In These Times*, 12 Jan. 2020, https://inthesetimes.com/features/haiti_earthquake_recovery_us_aid:anniversay_military_waste.html.

Marx, Karl. *The German Ideology*. Marxists.org, https://www.marxists.org/archive/marx/works/1845/german-ideology/.

Marx, Karl. *Grundrisse*. Translated by Martin Nicolaus. 1857-58. Random House, 1973.

Marx, Karl. *Capital: A Critique of Political Economy, Vol. 1*. 1867. Translated by Ben Fowkes, Penguin, 1983.

McMillan, Stephanie, and Vincent Kelley. "The Useful Altruists: How NGOs Serve Capitalism and Imperialism." *Counterpunch*, 20 Oct. 2015, https://www.counterpunch.org/2015/10/20/the-useful-altruists-how-ngos-serve-capitalism-and-imperialism/.

Merriam-Webster. "Honeypot." *Merriam-Webster*, https://www.merriamwebster.com/dictionary/honeypot.

Missing Migrants Project. "Migration Within the Mediterranean." *Missing Migrants*, https://missingmigrants.iom.int/region/mediterranean.

Newman, David. "Borders and Bordering: Towards an Interdisciplinary Dialogue." *European Journal of Social Theory*, vol. 9, no. 2, 2006, pp. 171–186.

Papadopoulos, Dimitris C. "Boundary Work: Invisible Walls and Rebordering at the Margins of Europe." *Walling In and Walling Out: Why Are We Building New Barriers to Divide Us?*, edited by Laura McAtackney and Randall H. McGuire. University of New Mexico Press, 2020, pp. 131–154.

Parker, Noel, and Nick Vaughan-Williams. "Critical Border Studies: Broadening and Deepening the 'Lines in the Sand' Agenda." *Geopolitics*, vol. 17, no. 4, 2012, pp. 727–733.

Plutocracy: Political Repression in the U.S.A. Directed by Scott Noble. Metanoia Films, 2015.

Prashad, Vijay. *Washington Bullets: A History of the CIA, Coups, and Assassinations.* Monthly Review Press, 2020.

Rajaram, Prem Kumar, and Carl Grundy-Warr, editors. *Borderscapes: Hidden Geographies and Politics at Territory's Edge.* University of Minnesota Press, 2008.

Renda, Mary A. *Taking Haiti: Military Occupation and the Culture of U.S. Imperialism, 1915–1940.* University of North Carolina Press, 2001.

Revelli, Philippe. "Singapore, Malaysia and Indonesia: A Triangle of Growth or a Triangle of Inequality?" *Equal Times,* 4 Oct. 2016, https://www.equaltimes.org/singapore-malaysia-and-indonesia-a?lang=en#.Ykn8-ejMJdh.

Robinson, Nathan. "McKinsey and Company is an Elitist Cult. Why is Buttigieg Defending it?" *In These Times,* 31 July 2019, https://inthesetimes.com/article/pete-buttigieg-mckinsey-consulting-firm-2020-election-elitism.

Roniger, Luis, et al., editors. *Exile, Diaspora, and Return: Changing Cultural Landscapes in Argentina, Chile, Paraguay, and Uruguay.* Oxford University Press, 2017.

Saif, Salem. "When Consultants Reign." *Jacobin,* 9 May 2016, https://www.jacobinmag.com/2016/05/saudi-arabia-aramco-salman-mckinsey-privatization.

Sainato, Michael. "'A Lot of Abuse for Little Pay': How US Farming Profits from Exploitation and Brutality." *The Guardian,* 25 Dec. 2021, https://www.theguardian.com/us-news/2021/dec/25/us-farms-made-200m-human-smuggling-labor-trafficking-operation.

Schake, Kori. "Why the Afghan Army Folded." *The Atlantic,* 17 Aug. 2021, https://www.theatlantic.com/ideas/archive/2021/08/us-afghanistan-taliban-training/619774/.

Schmitt, Eric. "Military Can't Find ISIS Safe House That Prompted Kabul Drone Strike." *New York Times,* 8 Nov. 2021, https://www.nytimes.com/2021/11/08/us/politics/isis-military.html.

Sohn, Christopher. "Navigating Borders' Multiplicity: The Critical Potential of Assemblage." *Area,* vol. 48, no. 2, 2016, pp. 183–189.

"Somali Population." *Minnesota Compass,* https://www.mncompass.org/topics/demographics/cultural-communities/somali.

Tateo, Luca, and Giuseppina Marsico. "Signs as Borders and Borders as Signs." *Theory & Psychology,* vol. 31, no. 5, 2021, pp. 708–728.

"The Rate of Exploitation: The Case of the iPhone." *The Tricontinental,* 22 Sept. 2019, https://thetricontinental.org/the-rate-of-exploitation-the-case-of-the-iphone/.

Virdee, Satnam. "The Longue Durée of Racialized Capitalism: A Response to Charlie Post." *Identities: Global Studies in Culture and Power,* 23 June 2021, https://www.identitiesjournal.com/blog-collection/the-longue-duree-of-racialized-capitalism-a-response-to-charlie-post.

Walia, Harsha. *Border and Rule: Global Migration, Capitalism, and the Rise of Racist Nationalism.* Haymarket Books, 2021.

———. *Undoing Border Imperialism*. AK Press, 2013.

Wonders, Nancy. "Global Flows: Semi-permeable Borders and New Channels of Inequality: Border Crossers and Border Performativity." *Borders, Mobility and Technologies of Control*, edited by Sharon Pickering and Leanne Weber, Springer, 2006, pp. 63–86.

Wu, Lawrence, and Michelle Lanz. "How the CIA Overthrew Iran's Democracy in 4 Days." *NPR*, 7 Feb. 2019, https://www.npr.org/2019/01/31/690363402/how-the-cia-overthrew-irans-democracy-in-four-days.

CHAPTER 4

Narrating the Border: Fluidity, Gender, and Resistance in Rabih Alemmedine's *The Wrong End of the Telescope* and Yuri Herrera's *Signs Preceding the End of the World*

[O]ne of the basic human rights possessed by those who pick up the tab for the progress of civilization is the right to be remembered. Theodor Adorno

My skepticism toward Reece Jones's position emerges from many of the claims I have made in the first three chapters, principal among which was to establish the multiple ways in which the social relations engendered by the border enable and are enabled by the work of capital accumulation. As we have seen, this work is accomplished by the implementation of actual economic rules, state practices, and the forces of capital. These rules not only comprise actual policies and forms of governance but also operate in less overt ways through the production and circulation of dominant representations of bordered subjects. However, characterizing these rules as "less overt" does not imply that they are any less effective in creating the conditions for expropriation, exploitation, and expulsion. In this chapter, I will turn to a discussion of the multiple ways in which the border is being represented and narrated in the popular imagination and focus on the ways in which these representations and, in effect, border rules themselves are being challenged by oppositional artists and activists.

Oppositional activism to border rules is forged through street protests, union work in sweatshops, solidarity programs in community centers, and the tireless strivings of multiple (im)migrant and refugee advocacy organizations. These oppositional politics are also disseminated broadly through

© The Author(s), under exclusive license to Springer Nature Switzerland AG 2023
K. Chowdhury, *Border Rules*, Politics of Citizenship and Migration, https://doi.org/10.1007/978-3-031-26216-6_4

107

cultural works, whether they be novels, songs, murals, or films. If the dominant logic of the border is to be overturned, these representations will play a role not merely in destroying borders that have been made to appear natural and ordered but also help us imagine what that borderless future may look like. Moreover, the global reach of many of these cultural forms and their impact on countless communities often make them more effective means of generating transnational discussions about a bordered world and alternatives to that world. Certainly, a music video or a photograph posted on social media, even if arriving via the compromised circuits of global capital, is seen by millions in comparison to a United Nations document on migrants' rights that is only ever circulated in the corridors of power.

As I have indicated in the first chapter, any discussion about borders must necessarily be a discussion about the millions who are most affected by the violence they produce. According to the United Nations Refugee Agency, by the end of 2021, there were 89.3 million displaced people in the world. One way of comprehending such a number is that if this group constituted a country's population, it would match that of Germany (19th on the list of most populous nations).[1] It is also true that this number is a conservative estimate, so the actual figures point to a far more devastating reality. However, the so-called refugee crisis is not just about numbers. It is also about the hard evidence that the systems that sustain populations in the Global South have been eroded over the last 30 years through war, brutal economic tariffs and barriers, structural debt paid out to global banks and institutions, the impact of climate change on food security, and a wholesale capitulation of the local elite to the needs of global capital in return for their own personal enrichment. Whether they be mechanisms devoted to the availability of health care, employment, education, safety, and food security, and protection from environmental ruination, these programs have ceased to exist. Under these conditions, the distinctions often made in the West between economic migrants and "legitimate" asylum seekers is a purely artificial one. Indeed, there is little doubt that this

---

[1] See "Refugee Statistics" from the United Nations High Commissioner for Refugees (UNHCR).

4 NARRATING THE BORDER: FLUIDITY, GENDER, AND RESISTANCE... 109

distinction is made to elide the rapacity of a global system that makes it necessary for a person to leave their place of habitation merely to survive.[2]

Likewise, the omnipresent designation for the present situation—the refugee crisis—is only thus characterized since it is viewed through a Western lens. The presence of brown and black bodies at the borders of predominantly white nations constitutes a crisis when seen from the latter's perspective.[3] For the migrant, the crisis is quite different. The real crisis for them is the systematic destruction that has been carried on by banks, armies, and institutions of power. By pinpointing the crisis precipitated by these institutions as one that is a result of a finite conflict, the powers that be can claim that once the overt unrest has become less severe, those seeking refuge can "return" to their original homes. This is increasingly the case with Syrian refugees in Europe, for instance, or the Rohingya, who are being forced by the Bangladeshi government to return to Myanmar.[4]

More recently, in October 2021, only a couple of months after the Taliban regained power in Afghanistan, six European countries "wrote to the European Commission claiming that halting returns 'sends the wrong signal and is likely to motivate even more Afghan citizens to leave their home for the EU.'"[5] This instance is a particularly egregious one since there is usually a rationale that is used to characterize so-called normal conditions, and in the case of a Taliban-ruled Afghanistan, such a rationale can hardly be said to exist. In the case of Iraq, for instance, the judgment

---

[2] For an assessment of the impact of neoliberal policies in Iraq, post-occupation, see "Iraq's Security 2003–2019: Death and Neoliberal Destruction Par Excellence." The authors of this piece point out: "When Saddam Hussein's regime was defeated and replaced by the Coalition Provisional Authority (CPA), headed by Paul Bremer, a series of extensive neoliberal measures were quickly introduced in its first month without any waiting period, from privatisation of 200 Iraqi state-owned companies to reducing corporate tax from 45 percent to 15 percent, and from allowing foreign firms to retain 100 percent of their Iraqi assets to a complete restructuring the Iraqi banking system."

[3] For a thought-provoking account of the ways in which "crisis" narratives function, see Janet Roitman's *Anti-Crisis*. In her view, invoking crisis narratives allows certain forms of action to be prioritized while others can be forestalled. See, also, Serena Parekh's *No Refuge: Ethics and the Global Refugee Crisis*.

[4] See the recent report (September 7, 2021) by Amnesty International: "Syria: Former refugees tortured, raped, disappeared after returning home."

[5] In 2021, Greece, Denmark, Belgium, Austria, Germany, and the Netherlands argued for the continued deportation of Afghan refugees. For more information on this situation, see *Euronews* article "Six EU countries want to keep forced return of Afghans despite Taliban offensive."

that a country has returned to "normal" is based on the impoverished idea that all that is necessary for renewal and safety is for some version of liberal democracy to be imposed, represented by a leader selected by the West, backed with ideas about development and free trade—ideas and policies that led to many of the problems in the first place—to be put in place. These so-called initiatives, as we know, were tried in Afghanistan and Iraq, and both countries, during these processes of rebuilding, still accounted for a huge majority of the global displaced population.

Contexts and Labels

Consequently, as I attempt to analyze cultural texts over the next few chapters, it is necessary to pause and reflect on the problems that confront us as we use terms that bring with them a whole set of assertions, presumptions, and elisions that enable acts of border violence. What becomes apparent in any discussion about migrants is that they are a constructed category, so it becomes even more important to reassess and contest the labels that are used widely to categorize and describe populations. These labels, as we will see, do the work of repressing the economic and political conditions that create these categories in the first place. It is equally crucial, however, that we do not fetishize the "refugee" population as an abstract, disembodied category of the excluded. As I asserted in Chap. 2, millions have been dispossessed and expelled, but they do not exist outside the parameters of exploitation. To isolate refugees into a category of workers outside of capital or outside of the realm of the employed plays into the hands of capital, which wants this division. Let us remember that as a surplus population, they are vitally connected to the ways in which the work of labor exploitation continues.

It is, likewise, a mistake to see refugees primarily as a hyperracialized group, one that is made up of the racial outcasts of the Global South. Of course, this cautionary statement comes with its own qualification. There is undoubtedly a consistent refusal to acknowledge migration as a process that brings with it assertions about white supremacy and colonialism within debates about migration both in the United States and in Europe.[6] However, it is equally true that migrant "authenticity" is overdetermined in the western media through their representation as dehistoricized racialized bodies. This representational gesture, I suggest, has the following effects. One, it confines the migrants' plight to one calling for a moral or affective response. This response can range from pity over their abject status to fear roused by the very fact of their difference. The victim and the economic competitor/potential criminal binary obviates any need to find a solution for the displacement of people based on a structural analysis of actually existing conditions. Two, by representing migrants as an undifferentiated mass from the Global South, there is little attempt to map the links between the specific contexts of postcolonial abjection and continuing colonial domination. Viewing an undifferentiated mass of people from sub-Saharan Africa aboard a boat on the Mediterranean, there is little reason to ask why one of the wealthiest countries in the world (in terms of resources), the Democratic Republic of the Congo, has seen the displacement of over five million people in 2017–2019. This elision of colonial history leads me to my third point. Racialization is also key in deferring the text of exploitation—race explains why certain regions of the world are "chaotic," disorganized, and mired in poverty, since such "inadequacies" can be easily accommodated to the logic of white supremacy. Thus, for instance, "economic" migrants are not considered "legitimate" refugees since economic mismanagement and corruption are the hallmarks of racially subordinate groups. Placing them within this racial strongbox obscures any analysis of these migrants as historically produced subjects.

[6] De Genova describes these entanglements in *The Borders of Europe*: "the borders of Europe are simultaneously entangled with a global (postcolonial) politics of race that redraws the proverbial color line and refortifies European-ness as a racial formation of whiteness, and a comparably global (neoliberal) politics of transnational labor mobility and capitalist labor subordination that produces such spatialized (and racialized) differences, above all, to capitalize upon them" (21).
In another essay, "The 'migrant crisis' as racial crisis: Do *Black Lives Matter* in Europe?" Nicholas De Genova reminds us in the European context that "[d]espite the persistence of racial denial and the widespread refusal to frankly confront questions of 'race' across Europe, the current constellation of 'crises' presents precisely what can only be adequately comprehended as an unresolved *racial crisis* that derives fundamentally from the postcolonial condition of 'Europe' as a whole, and therefore commands heightened scrutiny and rigorous investigation of the material and practical as well as discursive and symbolic productions of the co-constituted figures of "Europe" and "crisis" in light of racial formations theory" (1765).

Consequently, even as racialized structures are clearly a determining factor in any analysis of the movement of people from the South to the North, one must undertake a more complex methodological task of positioning refugees within a world historical framework. Certainly, there are historical and economic factors that unite refugees from South Asia, the Middle East, Sub-Saharan Africa, or Central America. Their role within a global economy that has shifted the point of production to the Global South, where it has acquired super-exploitative form, has destabilized their lives through regimes of debt and exploitation. In addition, structural adjustment policies, which have led to massive cuts in education and health care, and direct acts of war and violence have created conditions that have forced millions to flee their homelands. Moreover, many of the migrants hail from regions that are not just marked by the recent impact of imperial policies but have suffered the yoke of neo/colonialism for many decades. Despite their differences, then, these factors unite the refugee from El Salvador, Nigeria, and Afghanistan. The fact of their racialization is not without significance, undoubtedly, since the politics of migration are inseparable from the way "race" becomes a dominant factor in dehumanizing and erasing a vast number of people; however, as I have suggested, to limit our analysis in this fashion would be a serious error.

Nonetheless, taking such matters into account makes it evident that analyzing cultural narratives that focus on the lives of migrants is not merely about navigating and evaluating aesthetic categories. Instead, our analysis must always highlight the political and economic contexts within which these representations take place. A good place to begin is to delineate what it might mean to use the terms refugee and migrant. In the essay "What's in a name?" Tazreena Sajjad points to the different ways in which the state, NGOs, and the media represent the experiences of those who are forced to leave their original homes. Whether these individuals are accorded the title of migrant or refugee, for instance, has an enormous bearing on the possibilities of their settlement in a host country. Labeling a person a "migrant,", Sajjad argues, "speaks to an association of 'choice' and confers the idea of opportunistic decision-making that generates little sympathy when considering questions of the rights and dignity of the individual in question. It also strikes at the very heart of the politics of belonging" (46). Likewise, labeling a person an (im)migrant has implications about that person's rights to citizenship. This is not to imply that a "refugee," will not, similarly, face doubts about their right to belong; however, as Sajjad points out, a "refugee" does lay a "claim on a state for action and exposes the complexity of values and judgements involved in, essentially, a subjective categorisation. There is now extensive scholarship that clearly establishes that the label 'refugee' is highly changeable, dependent on context and inextricably linked to ideas of citizenship, the state, and understandings of the 'self' and the 'other' in any given period of time" (46).

Sajjad contends that all labels, including those that directly condemn the person seeking refuge, by terming them "illegals" or "fraudulent" or "bogus" asylum seekers have direct consequences, "given that such labels carry heavy normative weight and generate a climate where verbal, physical and institutional violence become commonplace *and* legitimized" (47). The multiplication of categories, Sajjad demonstrates, has not led to an improvement in governments' response. Quite the contrary, in fact. It has, instead, "reinforced the power of the state to create systems of hierarchy, making hyper-visible those who have transgressed a range of boundaries, and violated the natural order of the state–citizen relationship (56). Labeling is thus an essential regulatory function of border politics, one that determines categories of belonging and non-belonging, a process, which, in the imperial centers is always embedded in constructions of racial difference. "What becomes evident," Sajjad points out, "is that the increasing preoccupation with borders emphasises a revisionist interpretation of history that is monolithic and dismissive of the historical connections between European and non-European people" (52), confirming what Dominic Thomas, for instance, establishes in his essay on "Fortress Europe." As he puts it, "Contemporary debates and policy initiatives pertaining to ethnic minorities, immigrants, race relations and 'European' identity are inextricably connected to a much longer European colonial history" (455).

In their essay "Refugees, migrants, neither, both: categorical fetishism and the politics of bounding in Europe's 'migration crisis,'" Heaven Crawley and Dimitris Skleparis, similarly, warn us against a reliance on already existing analytical categories. These categories, they argue, that are used to make political decisions about granting asylum and other migration related matters in the midst of "Europe's 'migration crisis' are not simply inadequate tools for capturing the complex drivers of migration across the Mediterranean but also serve to perpetuate and reinforce a simplistic dichotomy which is used to distinguish, divide and discriminate between those on the move" (49). Equally troubling for those of us who write on these matters is the fact that "[t]aking the dominant categories as the basis of our analytical approach can limit our understanding of migration and make us potentially complicit in a political process which has, over recent years, stigmatised, vilified and undermined the rights of refugees and migrants in Europe" (50). In short, our analyses of the existing situation concerning migrants is always already compromised by the categories that we have accepted as normative starting points. Indeed, as in the previous sentence, using the word "migrant" establishes certain assumptions about the people in question. Instead, the authors caution, "we should be challenging where the boundaries between categories are placed and the differential value—and rights—assigned to those who are situated accordingly" (60). Perhaps it is not realistic to completely abandon categories, but, according to Crawley and Skleparis, we need "to explicitly engage with the politics of bounding, that is to say, the process by which categories are constructed, the purpose that they serve and their consequences" (60). Such scholarly engagements, of course, should not be limited to the pages of academic journals, but ought to find their way into popular discourse, enlarging and amending the way categories circulate in the non-academic sphere.

Over the last ten years, narratives about refugees and borders have proliferated, and, as a result, categories, such as migrants, have met with various forms of critical interrogation. Perhaps the most rigorous and fruitful efforts to combat the popular representation of refugees and borders and contest and amend labels and categories have been in the realm of cultural production. Artists' attempts to represent the lives of the refugees have found expression in almost every cultural arena: films, paintings, sculpture, music, and literary texts depicting the movement of people across borders have been produced in several languages all over the world, often securing prizes and attention at the global level.[7]

Part of my argument in this book is that the hegemony of border rules must be contested in multiple way. Artists, many of whom make little secret of their political convictions about contesting border rules, provide us with the language and utopian imaginings of a borderless future. The process of refusal and attempts at transformation will not occur in a void, and these imaginings will inform our progress toward abolition. I am not

---

[7] See, for instance, the sculpture "Angels Unaware" unveiled in the Vatican in 2019; the 2021 Danish film *Flee*, which received three Academy Award nominations for Best Animated Feature, Best Documentary Feature, and Best International Feature; and Banksy's 2019 installation "Child in Venice."

suggesting a causal trajectory here, where the impetus for change emerges from the forceful interventions of artists; clearly, the artists themselves are constantly grappling with the present moment and their art is evolving in unpredictable ways at a world historical moment, a characteristic of which is the unparalleled displacement of people. However, in the spirit of Raymond Williams's words, art and literature can represent the structure of feeling of a historical moment. As he put it in his *Preface to Film*: "The structure of feeling ... lies deeply embedded in our lives; it cannot be merely extracted or summarized; it is perhaps only in art ... that it can be realized, and communicated, as a whole of experience" (40). In a sense, then, artists' rendition of an emergent social experience communicated in some of these works may allow for a wider political engagement involving potentiality and change.

The two literary texts I have selected to analyze in this chapter offer the readers border landscapes that are mottled with contradictions. Characters in both novels traverse spaces that are marked by violence, and the traces of exploitation, despoilation, and dispossession are everywhere. Yet, these landscapes also offer hope for unlikely solidarities; despite the surface differences between characters who hail from varied geographic and cultural landscapes, the potential for alliances across boundaries is ever present. There are no palliatives here, however, for a bordered world. The violence and inevitable loss that have been created by war and the ravages of global capitalism cannot be transcended or hidden from but must be confronted. Both writers force the reader to extend some of the questions that I have already raised in the first three chapters of this book. How might these novels help us think about the political economy of the border, and the ways in which race and gender play a pivotal role in shaping the politics of displacement? I consider whether the authors' presentation of these bordered worlds contest the positions of some of the critical voices, who were reviewed in the previous chapter. For instance, how would the description of a borderscape as a "fluid, mobile, open zone of differentiated encounters" help us comprehend the landscapes described in both novels (Krichker 1225)? What are the aesthetic and political limitations that must be confronted in an attempt to represent those whose lives have been destroyed by the rapacious inroads of capital and state oppression? Can those on different sides of the global power divides navigate a bordered world in ways that do not reproduce systems of domination? What does it mean to assist or be in alliance with those who are most affected by the violence engendered by borders? Are liberatory and potentially revolutionary alliances possible at these intersections?

Decentering the Gaze: Rabih Alameddine's *The Wrong End of the Telescope*

I begin addressing these questions with an analysis of *The Wrong End of the Telescope* (2021), Lebanese American writer Rabih Alameddine's sixth novel. Although the novel focuses on the refugees arriving on the Greek island of Lesbos, a place where Alameddine had volunteered during the time when many thousands of refugees were arriving there, he had already encountered many refugees before that point, listening to accounts of their lives and journeys, while in Lebanon, a country which hosts over 1.5 million refugees, which is almost a third of its population.[8] By his own account, Alameddine found it almost impossible to write about the lives of displaced people until he "discovered" his protagonist, Mina Simpson. While there is an "author" figure in the novel, who similarly confronts his own doubts and misgivings about telling the stories of the refugees, it is Mina, a volunteer doctor who provides the reader a path into the narrative. *The Wrong End of the Telescope* (*WET*) is, for many reasons, an ideal text for navigating political and ethical questions around the border. Without offering any pat solutions about how outsiders and Westerners might intervene in ethical ways to mitigate the tremendous hardships experienced by those seeking refuge, Alameddine makes it clear that inaction is not the answer. He shares his disquiet about those who volunteer, but he does not pretend to have any moral clarity about the "right" way to address the monstrous scale of injustice that confront the migrants.

The novel begins with the arrival of Lebanese American surgeon, Mina Simpson, as a volunteer, on the island of Lesbos hoping to alleviate the conditions confronting the many desperate migrants who have arrived after dangerous and deadly journeys across the waters separating Turkey from Greece. Thus, right from the first page, the spotlight shines directly on the outsider, the one who enters and departs at their own leisure. Alameddine's text maintains this stance throughout the text and is unfailingly critical of aid workers, charitable organizations, and NGOs, in terms of their self-centered approach to the arrival of refugees on their shores. Set in Skala Sikamineas, a fishing village in Lesbos, Greece, Alameddine does not flinch as he depicts the "help" offered by groups and individuals for

---

[8] For more information on the refugee situation in Lebanon, see the UNHCR's Lebanon Fact Sheet and UNHCR article by Leo Dobbs, "The number of Syrian refugees in Lebanon passes the 1 million mark."

4 NARRATING THE BORDER: FLUIDITY, GENDER, AND RESISTANCE... 117

the refugees arriving in Lesbos. One of the residents, Nikolas, describes the volunteers, "be they European or American," as behaving "exactly like the German tourists who arrived every summer full of imperious airs and left with shellacked skin and complaints about the chaos that was the island (37). Indeed, one can understand Nikolas's attitude; after all, Greece "was in "the worst recession in recent memory, no thanks to the Germans, yet villagers opened their homes, shared their meals, donated their clothes" (38). Then the "NGOs and volunteers came. They thought they were doing God's work and they expected the villagers to serve them" (38).[9]

This strange world of volunteering is seen through the eyes of Mina, a surgeon, who grew up in the neighborhood of Ain el-Mraisseh in Beirut (36). Mina arrives in January of 2016, missing her 30th anniversary with her partner, Francine, who is in Chicago. This was at a moment when tens of thousands of refugees were attempting to reach Lesbos.[10] She has come to the island in answer to a call sent out by her friend, Emma, who is working for an NGO on the island. Even though the protagonist is a volunteer, Alameddine wants us to consider both the benefits and the limitations of transnational alliances, ranging from the work of Doctors Without Borders to Spanish lifeguards and the Seventh Day Adventists. Emma, who herself works for a Swedish NGO, has perhaps the harshest denouncement of the young people who volunteer during their vacations, taking selfies with the

[9] While Alameddine comments on the volunteers in his novel, Omar El Akkad's *What Strange Paradise*, published the same year, takes to task the actual tourists on such Greek islands, who continue with their rituals as the lives of thousands crumble around them. In a particularly effective passage, El Akkad describes the tourists and their vacuous daily rituals at a hotel aptly named Xenios. El Akkad does not spare us the irony here. Zeus Xenios is the protector of strangers, and the word xenia encompasses an ancient Greek concept of hospitality: "The tourists sit under beach umbrellas, picking at their food and nursing elaborate tropical drinks. Vänna overhears little snippets of conversation about the wreck on the beach; the incident has ruined the tourists' day, confining them to the grounds of their hotel. She hears a middle-aged couple argue about whether to demand a refund" (76). In the final section of the book, El Akkad captures the contrast between the desperation of those dying at sea and those who "come here for what is tranquil, what is undisturbed .... They come to see time autopsied, to marvel from the safety of the present from the endlessly dying past" (234). Most of all, though, they come for the sea. For them, the surf is "harmless," and it "makes them children again, returns them to a time when the world was an unbounded thing, made only to be immersed in, made only for joy" (234-35). Not since Jamaica Kincaid's *A Small Place* has a novel captured so aptly the different worlds inhabited by the rich and the poor, between those who have been cast adrift and those who enjoy the "safety of the present," between those who are the engines and those who are the fuel.

[10] According to *al Jazeera*, refugees in Lesbos's largest refugee camp, known as Moria, have long been subject to extreme heat and cold, police violence, and unhygienic conditions.

arriving boats: "That's all they really want. The perfect photo for Facebook or Instagram or whatever's the latest stupid thing. Look at me. I am not useless. I'm a humanitarian. Aren't I wonderful?" (48). The unnamed author in the novel, as described by the narrator, is even more damning in phrasing his condemnation: "You loathed their selfies, their self-flattery, their patronizing righteousness, their callous self-regard, everything … you resented much about them. You felt they had all the wrong reasons to come to the island. They wanted to help in order to feel better about themselves" (331).

However, the volunteers are not without their moments of awareness. Along with this realization comes the need—sometimes—to redefine one's purpose. An American recalls his years of volunteering in Malawi. The "longer he stayed," however, "the more he realized that something about what he was doing in Africa was dishonest …. He began to understand that he was using the pain of others to alleviate his own … he could no longer live with the fact that he was using the suffering of poor villagers to satisfy his sentimental needs. He needed them to suffer … in order to feel needed, in order to reinforce his privilege" (271). The subjective shifts inspired by these border crossings constitute a significant feature of the novel, and indeed, Alameddine depicts borders at every level. Not only is Lesbos literally a border land between the East and West, inhabited by the "sons and daughters of refugees themselves, arriving on the island after the Greco-Turkish War in 1922"; it also lays bare the superficiality of such geographical and cultural markers. Moreover, borders, as we have seen, are not just territorial lines to be crossed, but ways of maintaining certain power relations. Those who travel the edges of these bordered spaces are often the ones who must contend most vigorously with the irrationalities and cruelties of border rules.

The protagonist, Mina, for instance, has to occupy different gender identities and roles in her life. At age 11, as Mina moved into adolescence, she was given a lesson in the world of maps and borders and the boundaries that should not be transgressed: "My father, in a kind yet unequivocal tone, proceeded to trace the borders I was not to cross. In private, when I got older, I could do what I wanted, but discreetly, he said. In private, eat according to your taste, but in public, behave according to the public's …. Boys like me needed guidance to grow into men like him—guidance and direction and a clear map" (355). In this instance, we have a melding of gender and national boundaries and the public and the private. Is it too much of a leap to conclude that Alameddine sees a continuity between the cartographies of gender oppression and those that create a world of refugees and disposable human beings? Can a world that adheres to the rigidity of political borders ever accommodate other forms of border crossings? As I attempted to demonstrate in Chap. 2, the boundaries of the capitalist world system are buoyed by and dependent on a patriarchy and the maintenance of a system of racial difference that sustain and reproduce a social form that enables particular modes of accumulation, one that enforces an international division of labor and the production and maintenance of sexual and racial hierarchies.

Meanwhile, the island troubles the borders between the outsider and the insider, between those who are mere visitors, those who are en route, and those who live there. As a novel that tries to tell the stories of refugees, it is also very conscious of the representational problematic, that is, the divide between the one whose tale is to be told and the one who gets to tell the tale. In the novel, this is not just a problematic embedded in the complexities of translation, but one rooted in the experience of different realities. Mina, a transnational, privileged citizen, stretches across class and national divides to befriend Sammy and Sumaiya and their three children, who are "from a village outside of Hussainiyah, north of Deir ez-Zor [in Syria]" (54–55). Although Mina's relationship with Sumaiya, who is in the final stages of liver cancer, may be characterized as one between a doctor and patient, it is much more than that. As one of the central relationships presented in the novel, their pact, one based on mutual trust and respect, demonstrates what is possible if "feeling better about oneself" is not the motivation for an act of solidarity.

What inhibits such interactions, Alameddine suggests, are the predetermined structures of representation—labels and categories play a significant role in buoying up these structures—that influence how we "see" the other. The border separating the Western journalists and volunteers from the refugees is probably one of the hardest ones to cross. The former arrives with particular ways of seeing set in place, well and ready to position the refugees within social and political categories. One of the best examples of this is the chapter, appropriately titled "Who Is Us and Who is Them?" when Sammy is being interviewed by a group of journalists, who ask him "Are you an Islamist?" (178). Studiously ignoring his wife, assuming she has nothing to recount, they insist that Sammy is a "hero" for saving his family. When Mazen, Mina's brother, says "most of the people in this camp are here because they wanted to save their families. They're all heroes," the journalist replies, "Not all. This man wanted to

120   K. CHOWDHURY

save his daughter. He endured much hardship because he loves his daughter." "What father doesn't?" says Mazen. She responds: "Well, they don't really love their daughters. Not all of them" (192). This assumption about "them" comes from an embedded knowledge system that has been formed based on a particular understanding of "Middle Eastern" men, one that then places "them" in a container that is built on unbending notions concerning gender, family relations, religion, region, and race.

These predetermined beliefs regarding modes of being also force upon others the need to perform an identity in order to conform to these expectations. Seeking asylum based on persecution for one's sexual orientation, for instance, isn't enough to receive consideration. One must "prove" one's sexual identity. As one of the volunteers, Rasheed, tells a gay Iraqi man: "don't just point to your ring to indicate that you are married to your partner. Point to the ring in a certain way." Rasheed plays a Beyoncé video, "Single Ladies (Put a Ring on It)," for the couple and explains that he must "memorize how she moved her hands. I told them if they could Beyoncé, everyone would know they're gay. Smile nervously and Beyoncé" (233). These performative gestures hold true for establishing religious identity as well. A Lebanese priest assists Syrian Christian refugees to settle in Europe and Australia. The latter country "had refused to accept any Syrian refugees who were not Christian" (286). The priest had encouraged a Syrian Muslim couple to convert to Christianity because "most countries in the West would move their application in front of the line if they were Christian. Unlike Australia, most European countries were discreet about their discrimination" (286). For migrants, then, crossing borders is never simply a journey across physical territories but one that entails movement across territories of belonging, mapped by a declaration of specific allegiances and loyalties. These declarations, of course, must be performed through recognizable—as determined by those who grant asylum—rituals of identity.

Opposing such prescribed categories, Alameddine makes it abundantly clear that he cannot write a "refugee" novel. In fact, he does not even claim to know what that might be. "Keys are not found in literature," as his writer persona puts it (348). He is even more pessimistic about the audience for such a book:

> Did you believe that if you wrote about Syrian refugees the world would look at them differently? Did you hope that readers would empathize? Inhabit a refugee's skin for a few hours? As if that were some kind of panacea. You still hoped even though it had never happened. At best, you would

4 NARRATING THE BORDER: FLUIDITY, GENDER, AND RESISTANCE... 121

have written a novel that was an emotional palliative for some couple in suburbia. For a few moments, they'd think how terrible it was for the refugees. They'd get outraged on social media for ten minutes. But then they'd pour another glass of chardonnay. Empathy is overrated. (348–49)

What, then, may looking through the wrong end of a telescope accomplish? Consider the Greek etymology of the word, telescope: Tele = far, and skopein = to see. One task that this way of seeing may perform, such as the one advocated by those in Café Europa (see Chap. 2) is to decenter the gaze of the West, frozen on telegenic moments and images of life vests and boats. Decentering the gaze leads to two, intertwined realities. One is to recognize the subject as a human being, whose ontological existence is not always already marked or fixed by others, and the second is the understanding that this human being exists within a chain that it is part of a greater global totality. Thus, at one point, for instance, the unnamed author reveals a list that he had "copied by hand off Wikipedia, a list of wheel-well stowaway deaths," a list of "only those who fell from the skies." When Mina asks why he keeps such a list, he replies, "someone has to, don't you think" (150–151). Similarly, most of us have seen the photograph of Aylan (Alan) Kurdi lying face down on the sand. But there are thousands whose deaths haven't been marked. The author memorializes another unknown migrant, one whose name isn't easily recognizable, such as Baris Yagzi, age 22, who drowned on April 23, 2017, off the coast of Turkey. All he wanted was to be a musician: "Baris washed up on the Turkish shore clutching his violin case, his fingers squeezing the life out of what gave him life" (311).[11]

Alameddine then supplements these moments of intimacy, of a recognition that each human being on these deadly journeys have their own stories, with an effort to locate the migrants' stories in the context of wider imperial relations. Mazen puts it thus: "I loathe these Westerners who have fucked us over and over for years and then sit back and wonder aloud why we can't be reasonable and behave like they do with their noses up in the air as they're smelling shit. I hate their adulation of their own imaginary virtues" (204). Much of the book also reflects on the immigrant experience, one hardened by the xenophobia of the post-9/11 years and the "global war on terror." Mina reflects on Bush's speech on September

---

[11] For more information on the death of Baris Yagzi, see "The story of the Kurdish musician who drowned clutching his violin after trying to reach Europe" in *The Independent*.

122   K. CHOWDHURY

20, 2001, to the Joint Session of the Congress, where he announces: "This is civilization's fight. This is the fight of all who believe in progress and pluralism, tolerance and freedom" ("Address to a Joint Session"). On that day, Mina knew what the new war would look like:

> Hell, every immigrant knew. Our country was redefining the enemy and it was us. But first let's bomb them over there. Shock and awe, baby. Let all of us who *believe in progress and pluralism, tolerance and freedom* blindly destroy their countries, shatter their political systems, economies, infrastructures, and create millions of refugees for generations to come. Bush called that civilization's fight.[12] (229)

Fifteen years later, as the refugees from "that civilization's fight" flee their homes, they arrive at the gates of Europe, where they find crowded camps and NGOs "handing out large gift boxes with dried cereal and Barbie Dolls" (111).[13] Very soon after the initial moment of humanity, "Europe all but closed the borders."[14] As Mina puts it, "Lesbos was a somewhat

---

[12] As part of "civilization's fight," the Council on Foreign Relations states: "According to the U.S. Air Force, during the initial 76 days of bombing, some 6500 strike sorties were flown, with 17,500 munitions dropped on over 520 targets."

[13] Civilization's fight included the dropping of food "bombs," along with real bombs when bombing commenced in Afghanistan in October 2001. The Pentagon admitted that it was possible for the Afghans to mix up one with the other. The cluster bombs and the Humanitarian Daily Rations (HDR) were both colored blue and similarly sized.

[14] "Closing" borders and forcibly "returning" asylum seekers also violate the basic principle of refugee law, non-refoulement, which refers to the obligation of states not to refoule, or return, a refugee to "the frontiers of territories where his life or freedom would be threatened on account of his race, religion, nationality, membership of a particular social group or political opinion." (1951 Convention relating to the Status of Refugees, Article 33.1). The French "refoulement" means turning back. Refouler is to "push back," from (re) again and (fouler) to trample.

Non-refoulement is universally acknowledged as a human right. It is expressly stated in human rights treaties such as Article 22(8) of the American Convention on Human Rights (1969): "In no case may an alien be deported or returned to a country, regardless of whether or not it is his country of origin, if in that country his right to life or personal freedom is in danger of being violated because of his race, nationality, religion, social status, or political opinions. Finally, Article 3 of the OHCHR Convention against Torture declares: "No State Party shall expel, return ('"refouler"') or extradite a person to another State where there are substantial grounds for believing that he would be in danger of being subjected to torture."

humane mess when we were there. Shortly thereafter it became an inhumane one" (161). [15]

Mina and those who have departed for the West are caught in these intertwined realities, where the intimacy of the personal encounter exists in the shadow of imperial relations. On the one hand, they see past the fetishistic representations of those with whom they share the familiarities of home and language, but on the other hand, Sumaiya and the others who flee their homelands are also worlds removed from them. Consequently, even if Mina sees the volunteering world in all its inadequacies and recognizes the effects of imperial violence, she is aware that her structural position creates psychic borders, ones that reflect the material realities of the characters' worlds. When Mina tries to help a woman, for instance, who shows no detectable medical problems and is experiencing no pain, the woman explains: "Ever since we left home ... I haven't been able to speak." Even though she is speaking, it is "not the right way. My words seem heavy and slow, much too slow." She claims that she doesn't "sound normal ... Not like before. My tongue has expanded. It's quite swollen, much too big for my mouth" (235). The best Mina can do is recommend a dentist. All Mina can say to herself is: "I wished to say kind words to her, anything. My words were too heavy" (236). The heaviness of words, words that are never enough to convey the scale of the disaster confront the writer at every turn, and this failure is compounded by a realization that these words will be consumed in the way that many cultural commodities are—as another form of bourgeois leisure: "You tried to find a way to write about refugees and break the wall between reader and subject. You said you wanted people not to dismiss the suffering, not to read about the loss and sorrow, feel bad for a minute or two, and then

---

[15] See the Aegean Boat Report for an account of illegal deportations by Greek authorities: "It's time for European politicians to take off their blindfolds, it's time to see that what is going on the borders of Europe is a crime against humanity, to say 'we didn't know' is no longer an option. We must stop pretending that this doesn't concern us, that's it's 'their' rights that are being violated, not ours .... It is an attack on us all: when a government strips a Somali teen, a Syrian child, an Iraqi man, an Afghan woman of their human rights, you have to know that they are reserving the right to do the same to you, to your son, daughter, brother, sister, parents, grandfather and grandmother. Those rights belong to us all: once they are taken from one of us, they can be taken from us all. It must stop. We cannot simply turn a blind eye to this—the disgrace of Europe. Instead, we must stand, together, and demand better: from our governments, from the EU, from the international community."

124 K. CHOWDHURY

go back to their glass of overly sweet chardonnay. But you failed, of course" (293).

Later, speaking of his experiences conversing with refugees in Lebanon, in comparison to his time in Lesbos, the author confides, "There was a barricade between the person I was talking to and me. I could hear the stories, and no matter how sickening they were, I felt protected. I was able to listen dispassionately, impersonally. They were stories, after all, simply stories. I deal with stories all the time" (327). This was possible, he surmises, because there was a "handler from the UNHCR" with him and thus "there was a barricade between the person I was talking to and me." In Lesbos, it was different: "Metaphor seems useless now, storytelling impotent" (327). In June of 2021, Alammedine had shared his thoughts on his encounter with refugees in Lebanon, based on the stories refugees had recounted to him: "This is when I realized, again, that the service that I was providing was just as an ear …. There is absolutely not one thing I can do, but not doing something is a crime" (Khatib "Refugees are Suffering"). In a more recent interview with the *New York Times*, Alameddine summed up the conflicts of telling these stories: On the one hand, his "outsider perspective helps him find the 'Goldilocks distance' from his subjects," but with "*Telescope*, he set out to write a novel that encompassed his own experiences and the stories of the refugees he met, but, unable to extricate himself enough, he developed the character of Mina, someone whose life differed from his own" (Khatib). The novel ends with the writer passing on the burden to Mina, both of them knowing full well that she, too, would have to confront failure: "Maybe I could understand what happened, you said. I could unravel the mystery and find the key. Maybe I could come to terms with my past and heal my wounds. Ever delusional you" (350).

It may be appropriate to pause here and reflect on the artistic and political dilemma presented at the conclusion of this novel, since, I believe, a consideration of these dilemmas is also at the heart of our encounter with the other oppositional texts that I will be analyzing throughout this book. In a sense, the writer's pessimism about the potential impact of his work points to a fundamental contradiction about producing politically committed art in a world where it becomes a commodity from its moment of conception to its future life in controlled forms of circulation. Its movement and distribution are tightly structured by commercial imperatives, and although Alameddine does not stress this commercial aspect of "failure" in writing about refugees, he does point to the middle-class milieu in

4 NARRATING THE BORDER: FLUIDITY, GENDER, AND RESISTANCE... 125

which art, especially the novel form is consumed. What, indeed, can be achieved by an art form which offers "an emotional palliative for some couple in suburbia" (349).

But, one wonders, if this a problem that is particular to the art form chosen by its creator? Are other cultural texts being consumed in the same manner or does the method of production, circulation, and distribution determine whether that work has the potential to transform the boundaries of one's imagination and to awaken the desire for political change? Later in this book, I will examine different art forms, suggesting that the mode of cultural production does play an important role in how that art form comes to life and acquires political significance. Moreover, Alameddine is also indicating that the unnamed writer may be producing art for all the wrong reasons. In an amazing riposte to the frustrated writer, the narrator lists some of these short sighted reasons: for "absolution"; "to help you understand what happened"; "that'll you'll be able to figure things out"; that writing would "force coherence into a discordant narrative"; "for dreams of respite"; to "heal your pain"; that "you'd come across a clue that would unravel the puzzle, the one key that would unlock your mystery"; that the "world would look at" Syrian refugees differently; that "readers would empathize? Inhabit a refugee's skin for a few hours?" (348). Not surprisingly, all these reasons have little to do with the refugees themselves, but more to do with putting the artist center stage, where *he* can willfully and objectively craft a reaction to the refugees' predicament through his control of words and language.

Alameddine's skepticism about the transformative role of art at the ending of the novel may suggest an impasse, indicating that neither can the world of borders be transcended nor can the lives of those who face its ravages ever be accurately represented. However, the world of the novel does offer us the potential space for solidarity between those with differing national or class origins, even as it lays bare the realities of what must be confronted if borders are going to be contested and abolished. Acts of solidarity are made even more difficult by the multiple levels of entrapment that envelope the lives of refugees, particularly as so many millions are placed in limbo in makeshift camps, in-between places, where the strictures of official time and space confine them to a formless existence. Both the temporal and spatial shackles of these borderscapes are captured by Dina Krichker in her article "Making Sense of Borderscapes": "These are the sites where border infrastructure constitutes social exclusion through institutional borders and camps within the transit spaces. The bureaucratic mechanisms of asylum applications' processing take indefinite time and generate peculiar temporality of uncertainty and stress within Melilla and Lesvos. Here borderscape appears as a place in between, neither inside, nor outside" (1230). Of course, the in-between space can also be a space of resistance; there have been countless acts of resistance in many of these camps, but as I argued in Chap. 2, the immediacy of state violence and the threat of deportation limit these scapes as possible sites of liberation.[16] Umut Ozkaleli, however, in her conversations with four Syrian women in "2016 in Gaziantep, Turkey, a border city to Aleppo, Syria," offers us some hope:

> If a social structure keeps people detached, discriminated against and excluded, their selves experience displacement. Similarly, the circumstances and access that one finds in a host community may shape individual's agency in a way that the person re-invents the self. Displacement may become a transforming experience of personal revolution, liberation or strength for envisioning and aspiring a future for the self in the host community, or envisioning a future in the home country. Such an approach encourages a reflective analysis where refugees are active and empowered people with unique subjectivities and agency. (23)

Unlike the labels and categories that are often used to negate or deemphasize the agency of refugees and their potential for resistance, Ozkakeli demonstrates in her conversations with these women that they are active agents who, if provided the right circumstances and the support of an alliance of transnational actors, may be able to overturn the insidious power of borders to entrap many thousands behind barbed wires. *WET*, with its description of the conditions on Lesvos, presents us with the monumental challenges that confront those who undertake this task. However, even if the scale of that overcoming may seem daunting, the presence of a protagonist, Mina, who had been instructed to stay within the confines of socially constructed borders early in her childhood and whose life has since

---

[16] In September 2020, a fire devastated Moria, leaving many refugees unhoused and without food, water, and hygiene in the midst of the COVID-19 pandemic. For more information on this disaster, see NPR's "Fires Gut Europe's Largest Migrant Camp on the Greek Island of Lesbos." After the fire, refugees in the camp began a protest over the death of an Afghan woman. A Doctors Without Borders officer is quoted in the *Guardian* attributing the death to "a brutal policy that is trapping 13,000 people in a camp meant for 3000." In Pakistan, homeless Afghan asylum seekers fleeing the Taliban protested their living conditions by wearing shirts urging the Pakistani government to "kill [them] or rescue [them]."

4 NARRATING THE BORDER: FLUIDITY, GENDER, AND RESISTANCE... 127

highlighted the meaninglessness of those borders suggests a path toward abolition.

"MORBID PHENOMENA" IN THE BORDERLANDS: YURI HERRERA'S *SIGNS PRECEDING THE END OF THE WORLD*

Yuri Herrera's *Señales que precederán al fin del mundo* (2009) was translated by Lisa Dillman into English under the title *Signs Preceding the End of the World* (2015). It received the "Best Translated Book Award" in 2016.[17] Herrera's second novel offers us a protagonist, Makina, who takes a trip across what is ostensibly the Mexican-US border, and her journey highlights not only the material act of crossing over and the violence that accompanies this crossing but also the surreal elements of existing in a time and space made more hallucinatory because of the crossing over experience. After all, as we have seen in *WET*, and as so many migrants have suggested in their experience of border landscapes, there is a fantastical element in border politics as seen from the perspectives of migrants. International law gives them the right to seek asylum, to cross over, but the state criminalizes them as soon as they leave their place of abode. In other words, what does the world of real policies matter when those laws and proclamations hold little value to those in power? Border crossing, then, is experienced both as an affirmation of the irrationality and cruelty of border rules and as a negation of the self, a point made quite early during Makina's preparations to leave.[18]

During the course of her journey, Makina passes through lines that indicate different sides, but, as "one of the rules Makina abided by," she is also the portal herself: "You are the door; not the one who walks through it" (18). Those who make the crossing and stay away too long also encounter a form of objective negation, as experienced by a friend of Makina's: "when he came back it turned out that everything was still the same, but somehow all different, or everything was similar but not the same" (20).

---

[17] The Best Translated Book Award is conferred by Three Percent, the online newsletter for the University of Rochester's translation press, Open Letter Books.

[18] For a considered understanding of the border literature genre, see Christina L. Sisk's "How to Cross the Border: Instructions for a Fronterizo and for a Migrant." Sisk argues that migration is not simply a US–Mexico border issue. Because there are so many different groups from the country and from across the world attempting to cross, "Mexican migration must be considered a transnational issue, not just one of the U.S.–Mexico border, of the originating states, or of the United States" (87).

This lack of fixity, of any kind of certainty is also the case when one measures the material promises of crossing. A young man who returns with a cellphone for his mother is unable to get a connection as he hands the phone over to his mother and attempts to call her. "Maybe you should have bought a few cell towers, too?" says Makina to the hapless young man. Consoling him, she offers a wry comment: "Don't worry, kid, they will get here one day" (45–46). Labor, resources, and profits flow North, but their exchange value, or, in this case, even their use value, does not return to the point of origin. Makina knows the twisted contours of these stories since she is the only phone operator in town: "She ran the switchboard with the only phone for miles and miles around. It rang, she answered" (18). She was also familiar with the "native tongue or latin tongue." Those "who'd often already forgotten the local lingo," she "responded to them in their own new tongue" (18–19).

This combination of the material and the surreal, of real history and its spectral presence becomes established in the very first pages of the novel. The novel begins with Makina's first thought: "I'm dead" (11). This is because the earth opens up in front of her, swallowing a "man, and with him a car and a dog, all the oxygen around and even the screams of passers-by" (11). The sudden appearance of this sinkhole is not just a whimsical happenstance, an idiosyncrasy of the Gods, who must remind ordinary beings of their tenuous grip on mortality, their brief sojourn on this earth. The sinkhole, in fact, is a direct reminder of 500 years of colonial violence. This "Little Town was riddled with bullet holes and tunnels bored by five centuries of voracious silver lust, and from time to time some poor soul accidentally discovered just what a half-assed job they'd done of covering them over" (11–12). The ground beneath one's feet recedes and disappears because the violence of the past is ingrained in the very terrain.

Of course, as we see later, the violence is not confined to the past nor is it located within specific borders. Makina must cross over to the other side to find her brother, who has returned to locate and lay claim to their family's land, a reminder of what was lost when the border lines were drawn, dispossessing millions of people of their birthright. The historical trajectory of violence and dispossession does not end here. On the other side, the land that belonged to Makina's family has become a new place of extraction. What confronts Makina, instead of her birthright, "when she arrived and saw what she'd come to find it was sheer emptiness" (69). Here were "excavators obstinately scratching the soil as if they needed urgently to empty the earth; but the breadth of that abyss and the clean cut of its walls didn't correspond to the modest exertion of the machines. Whatever once was there had been pulled out of its roots, expelled from this world; it no longer existed" (70). In this scene, Herrera conveys with irresistible force the ceaseless rapacity of capital, tearing up the earth in its inexorable centuries-long search for resources. This site is not just evidence of a despoliation of the land, but a void, "sheer emptiness," a space of negation.

On the other side, she also sees a different form of negation, captured in "signs prohibiting things." These signs "thronged the streets, leading citizens to see themselves as ever protected, safe, friendly, innocent, proud, and intermittently bewildered, blithe, and buoyant; salt of the only earth worth knowing" (56). Yet, she also notices how "miserable" the "anglogaggle at the self-checkouts … looked in front of those little digital screens, and the way they nearly-nearly jumped every time the machine went bleep! at each item" (56–57). Far more disturbing, however, is the other presence, "scattered about like bolts fallen from a window: on street corners, on scaffolding, on sidewalks; fleeting looks of recognition quickly concealed and then evasive. These were her compatriots, her homegrown, armed with work; builders, florists, loaders, drivers; playing it sly so as not to let on to any shared objective, and instead just, just, just: just there to take orders" (57). What Makina sees is a landscape of alienation, of labor exploitation, of being "armed with work," of just-survival, and even though the anglogaggle are separated from their fellow workers who are "just there to take orders," both groups are in thrall to the forces who remain invisible.

Yet, there is also joy in this landscape of loss and rupture. When Makina comes across a marriage ceremony of gay couples, she finds that there is "rejoicing galore" (81). But, even here, the shadow of social norms casts a pall. She wonders why, even though she had "witnessed other ways to love," everyone was "acting just the same … imitating people who've always despised them" (82). As a border crosser, she then concludes, "perhaps they just want the papers … any kind of papers, even if it's only to fit in; maybe being different gets old after a while" (82). Significantly, though, by encountering another marginalized communities' attempts to secure legitimacy, Herrera forces us to question the world of social relations set up by the border regime itself. The reader is left to wonder whether we can only access forms of joy or fulfillment within the limits set by the state. Is our potential for happiness always to be held hostage based on our access to the right papers? Is our agency to be always determined by the demands made by the state? In other words, does our access to state-approved forms of rights, be they in the guise of citizenship, marriage, or property ownership, constitute our only guarantee of personhood? It is no surprise, then, that in this chapter, "The Place Where the Flags Wave," the only flags that are in evidence are the multicolored flags at the wedding ceremony and "another array of flags" that she sees shortly afterward, "equally pretty but all lined up and all the same size. This was where the soldiers were" (82).

In a world governed by borders rules, then, there are those who will never have the proper documents or access to rights or resources. These are the people who are subject to vicious abuse and threatened by vigilantes and those who enforce the law of the border. At one point, Makina is forced to join a group of men who are on their knees, interrogated by a "patriot" cop who tells them, "Fall in and ask permission. Civilized, that's the way we do things around here! We don't jump fences and we don't dig tunnels" (97). When the cop attempts to get one of the men to write "why you think you're up the creek, why you think your ass is in the hands of this patriotic officer," Makina grabs the paper and pencil and writes a rejoinder that leaves the cop dumbfounded? Encapsulating and parroting the paranoiac fears of the nativist, she writes, "We who came to take your jobs …. We who fill your shiny clean streets with the smell of food …. We, the dark, the short, the greasy, the shifty, the fat, the anemic. We the barbarians" (100). She speaks here for the wretched of the earth. This is not the borderscape of possibility—it is, more accurately, a space marked by violence, where one is subject to the random brutality of patriots. Yet, it is also a space where Makina claims solidarity with "her compatriots, her homegrown." Perhaps this possibility for resistance is the reason for them "playing it sly so as not to let on to any shared objective" (57).

Makina's rejoinder to the cop offers this hope for resistance but the others "looked at one another, half-glad, half mistrustful, then looked at Makina but couldn't say anything to her because she'd started walking again and all they could make out was her silhouette against the sun" (100). This moment is reminiscent of a crisis Gramsci spoke of—"*il nuovo non può nascere*" (the new that cannot be born), where "*i fenomeni morbosi più svariati*" (the most varied morbid phenomena) reigns (*Quaderni del Carcere*, vol. 1, § 311–312, *Prison Notebooks* 276).[19] Thus, in this interregnum, it is not unusual to find those that are in between political action and political quiescence, in between the coordinates of settled time and space. Yet, all is not lost in the interregnum. Herrera shows us that the borderlands create worlds that are inhabited by those who are both neither/nor and either/or. There are, for instance, the in-between people, who

> are homegrown and they are also anglo and both things with rabid intensity .... Their gestures and tastes reveal both ancient memory and the wonderment of a new people .... They speak an intermediary tongue that Makina instantly warms to because it is like her: malleable, erasable, permeable; a hinge pivoting between two like but distant souls, and then two more, and then two more, never exactly the same ones; something that serves as a link. (65)

The border here is not some clear "midpoint between homegrown and anglo." Rather, in Gramscian language, "their tongue is a nebulous territory between what is dying out and what is not yet born" (65). Those who live in the borderlands express in their language "nostalgia for the land they left or never knew." Their way of saying things is "not another way of saying things; these are new things. The world is happening anew, Makina realizes; promising other things, signifying other things, producing different objects" (66). Even if the "new" does not promise abolition, the presence of those who "say new things" signifies the failure of the border regime to implement a stark duality between here and there, a line of difference that is clearly distinguishable, a point of no return. Thus, we may have people navigating worlds that are forever indeterminate or envisioning futures that are forever deferred, but their accession to newness marks a refusal to subscribe to the tyranny of a singular belonging.

---

[19] Gilbert Achcar makes the point that these lines are often misinterpreted: "Thus, rather than referring to the surge in far-right barbarism in the context of the capitalist crisis and the gap between its depth and the weakness of the working-class forces that could replace capitalism with socialism it is quite likely that "morbid symptoms" was actually referring to the ultraleft symptoms that emerged against this backdrop." Achcar clarifies, however, that in the present moment, the "weakness and fragility of the forces of progressive change have meant that the accelerating crisis of global capitalism's socioeconomic and political conditions has until now mostly benefitted the rise of the Far Right around the globe. It is hence on the far right of the political spectrum that we are witnessing at present the most spectacular "morbid symptoms" produced by the degeneration of capitalist politics" ("Morbid Symptoms").

Despite enacting a certain kind of refusal, however, what becomes abundantly clear during Makina's journey is that the border enables an endless exploitation of brown bodies. Not only are these bodies used as laboring units of value, but they are also ultimately disposable, sacrificed on the altar of the nation so that white bodies may survive. Makina's brother's story illustrates this reality. On the Anglo side of the border, Makina's brother has taken the place of a young man who, "without consulting his family [had] decided to do something to prove his worth as a man and had joined the army, and in a few days they were going to send him to the other side of the world to fight against who knew what people that had who knew what horrific ways of killing" (88). According to the terms drawn up by the boy's family, "Makina's brother would pass himself off as the other." On his return, "the family would pay him a sum of money." Of course, they do not expect him to return, so when he does, they "stared at him with eyes like saucers, astonished to see him there, alive and decorated: alive" (90–91). And "Since they'd assumed he wasn't coming back, they didn't have the money they'd promised." Instead, they give him their son's identity. "[We] will go someplace else," says the mother. "We'll change our name, reinvent ourselves" (91). So, now Makina's brother is left behind with "no clue what to do, where to go, what the path of the person with that name should be." When his sister asks him why he does not leave, he says, "Not now. Too late. I already fought for these people. There must be something they fight so hard for. So I'm staying in the army while I figure out what it is" (93). He is another lost soul, lost not just as a physical sacrifice for an imperial war fought on distant shores, but lost also because he sees no purpose in a return and little to gain in the warmth of a mother's or a sister's embrace.

Unlike her brother, Makina does not wish to remain on the other side. Everywhere Makina turns, she is confronted by physical barriers, by vigilantes or emissaries of the state. In her search for her brother, Makina encounters "barricades that held people back for the benefit of cars" (69). She is also shot by a police officer (50). While traveling north in the quest for their lost land, she encounters "disdain" and "suspicious looks" (69). She is called "scum," by a "huge red headed anglo who stank of tobacco .... Makina knew the bastard was just itching to kick her or fuck her" (73), and when she leaves the barracks, having bid goodbye to her brother, she is ordered by a cop to get in line with "half a dozen men staring at the ground" (97). Fortunately, these acts of outright hostility are countered by a similar cast of outsiders, those who recognize her as a kindred spirit of the borderlands: Chucho, who helps her cross over and saves her from a vigilante; an old man who takes her to the place where she has to deliver a package she is carrying; her traveling companion who introduces her to Doña, an innkeeper, who in turn tells her where to find her brother.

Cordelia E. Barrera, using an Anzaldúan reading of the text, argues: "As a border dweller, Makina exists in a liminal, borderlands space that Anzaldúa describes as a 'vague and undetermined place created by the emotional residue of an unnatural boundary' in a constant state of transition" (479). Certainly, this is evident from the very beginning of the text, where we see Makina navigating crossings and real spatial barriers such as a river, mountain passes, and the gates behind which the gangster overlords lurk, whose blessings she must gain in order to make the journey to the Big Chilango. In addition, she is also adrift in a world that is cut through with disquiet, unrest, and violence. The violence that confronts her during the crossing over is very real and the evidence of the losses on that journey is apparent from the moment she crosses over. Soon after she crosses, for instance, she sees what she thinks is a pregnant woman resting under a tree. Instead, it turns out to be "some poor wretch swollen with putrefaction, his eyes and tongue pecked out by buzzards" (44). Alongside this very urgent evidence of the real, however, is a dream world, a world where instability and undecidability rule. Barrera reaches back to Anzaldúa to further elucidate on her drawing on the ideal of "Nepantla, a Nahautl word meaning tierra entre medio, or the 'space between worlds'" (479). For Anzaldúa, Neplanta "signifies unstable, transitional landscapes lacking clear boundaries. Border dwellers, queers, women of color, and those defined as Other in established patriarchal societies dwell in these unstable spaces of dis-placement" (479). However, this is not a space of ennui or atrophy—quite the opposite, in fact—and this is quite evident when we witness Makina's navigation of this *tierra entre medio*. Barrera specifies: "The middle, or nepantla, state is a terrain of potential change that signifies 'temporal, spatial, psychic and/or intellectual points of crisis' and is situated within a spatial dynamics of social ordering and liminality that is unsettling" (479).

Arguably, Makina ends her journey at this point of crisis and her final words, her words to herself, as she is handed a file with "another name, another birthplace. Her photo, new photo, new numbers, new trade, new home,"—"I'm ready"—can only be taken to mark a particular moment rather than a reconciliation with the world of borders (106–107). We must remember her "readiness" is clouded with ambiguity. Recall the moment, as she prepares for departure to the other side, when she steps from Mr. Q.'s office to the mirrored hall: "She looked into the mirrors: in front of her was her back: she looked behind but found only the never-ending front, curving forward, as if inviting her to step through its thresholds. If she crossed them all, eventually, after many bends, she'd reach the right place; but it was a place she didn't trust" (22). It's worth remembering Mr. Q's words as Makina had prepared for departure: "you'll get desperate, of course, but you'll see wonders and in the end you'll find your brother, and even if you're sad, you'll wind up where you need to be. Once you arrive, there will be people to take care of everything you require" (21). Yet, her final descent is categorically different from the lines she crosses during the rest of her journey. Her movement into a different world is not dictated only by the linear topography of political borders. We are, moreover, not to be beguiled into believing Makina's troubles are over because she no longer feels "the weight of uncertainty and guilt" (107). Is a reconciliation with the violence of the bordered world available only at a heavy cost, where one has "been skinned," and has "another name, another birthplace" (106)? Does the "newness" allow for a certain kind of liberation or is the loss of the memories of a "lovely landscape" a recognition of what must "fade away" for something new to be born? Is this the only "ending" that the bordered world offers us?

Makina's final descent raises the question: What might we make of the mythological elements in the book? How do the tropes of the journey, the crossing over, and the final descent illuminate the lives of border dwellers? Elizabeth Fielder argues: "Mythological realism fits as a genre for migration literature since antiquated texts—such as the Greek and Latin epics, the Bible and medieval quests—place refugeeism, exile and being lost in new lands at the centre of human experience" (333). She places Herrera's text within the framework of what she calls a "*stowaway aesthetic*, to describe both a method of storytelling (to *stow away* mythological references within the text) and an aesthetic in contemporary fiction about migration that draws attention to what is hidden or unsaid in narrative about refugees (333). Fielder draws on Herrera himself for this framework; he alludes to the mythology employed in his work in the following terms: "This is the thing with this mythology: Its meaning and its depth and its force is like a stowaway. It's not supposed to be the main thing in the story." Using this perspective, it is possible "to embrace the unknowns and to replace the desire to seek out answers with the sustenance from tales and mythologies. Feats of escape have an air of mystery and magic

4 NARRATING THE BORDER: FLUIDITY, GENDER, AND RESISTANCE... 135

out of necessity, and these stories call on us to recognize and respect what we cannot know" (343). Consider Makina's impressions as she considers the distinctive language of the borderlands: "Using in one tongue the word for a thing in the other makes the attributes of both resound …. It's not another way of saying things; these are new things. The world happening anew, Makina realises: promising other things, signifying other things, producing different objects" (66). Makina's final descent into newness offers possibilities, but one wonders about the many others, including her brother, who, though far from the actual border, is forced to live in its shadows and endure an endless search and experience an endless longing, all while surviving on the state's ability and desire to fight wars.

In an interview with Aaron Bady, Herrera adds a few more insights on some of the mythological elements in the book. He explains that for the Mexica, "the place where most people went after they died, was called "Mictlán." Alluding to the nine chapters in the book, he mentions: "In order to get there, you would have to go through nine underworlds. In each one of these underworlds, you would have to face a challenge. Nobody knows the exact meanings of these challenges, because this is a world that disappeared, that was destroyed by the Spaniards." Makina confronts these challenges and in the last chapter, she is placed at "The Obsidian Place With No Windows or Holes For the Smoke" (101). Herrera elucidates that "when you get to the last underworld, there is only silence; no others and no sounds and no life. The first Spanish priests identified that point as hell, even though there was no such thing as "hell" among the Mexicas. That place is the place of re-creation. In this world, you didn't die and disappear, and you weren't reincarnated: You came to this place of silence to somehow be part of a re-creation." What Herrera attempts to do in this book, in his own words, is to "take this narrative as a found object and place it in a different context to see how it would work. I thought of it as similar to something my father liked to do: go to an outdoor market, buy things, and put them to some other use in the house. This is something like that, it's a narrative that is mythological in its meaning, but I hope I somehow reactivated its utility" ("Literature")

Perhaps one of the most notable ways in which Herrera captures the ambiguities present at the border is with his use of a particular word, "Jarchar." "*Jarchar* is a word," he explains that defines a part of a poem in the Middle Ages, in what is now Spain, in poems that were written in Arabic characters, but when they sounded like what would later be called the Spanish language …. I would use it very loosely, as a synonym for going out, going between one place and another …. It is not simply going through a door or exiting; it's what this process is doing to you" (Bady). Lisa Dillman, the translator, uses the verb, "to verse" to signify what Herrera is attempting in the novel. She elaborates: "Used in context it is easily understood, and has the added benefits of also being a noun-turned-verb, a term clearly referring to poetry, and part of several verbs involving motion and communication (traverse, reverse, converse) as well as the 'end' of the universe. Makina, the protagonist, is the character who most often 'verses,' as well as the woman who serves as a bridge between cultures, languages and worlds" (113). Makina's exit or "versing" at the end of the novel emphasizes for Herrera "that this kind of moving from one place to the other is not just a displacement but is a whole transformation, just like what happens to the characters in the book" (Kim). Rather than offering us any pat solutions about borders or advocating for their removal, Herrera wants us to consider how lines force us to confront the new. As he puts it, "what I can say is that for many people the crossing of a border and the starting of a new life after crossing it implies facing challenges that were inconceivable before" (Kim).

Signs is a book in which the countries the "United States," and "Mexico," or the word, "border" are never mentioned. In an interview, Herrera explains that "I make a lot of lists before I prepare a book: lists of stories, lists of words I like, lists of words that I won't use. That last one might be the most important list, and that has to do with the need to avoid clichés, to not repeat certain predigested concepts in place of problems or emotions that are much more complex than those concepts" ("Literature as a Political Responsibility"). It is not a paradox, then, that a book that never mentions a border offers us both a flash of recognition and a moment of defamiliarization when we consider that well known line of division. As we accompany Makina on her journey, we immediately understand the material forms of violence engendered by the border, even as those same borders appear fantastical and grotesque. Like Alameddine, Herrera does not suggest a path forward; instead, in a vein similar to Alemeddine, he makes visible the violence engendered by lines that reinforce power and enable exploitation. Perhaps Makina's attraction for the in between people, those whose "gestures and tastes reveal both ancient memory and the wonderment of a new people" and who speak "an intermediary tongue" hints at a liberatory border subject—one who is like Makina: "malleable, erasable, permeable; a hinge pivoting between like but distant souls, and then two more, and then two more, never exactly the same ones; something that serves as a link" (65). At the moment of transition, all remains possible.

Yet, Herrera, just as we see at the conclusion of *WET*, is steadfast in his refusal to offer a clearly drawn road map that one can follow for accomplishing a world free of borders. By presenting us with characters who both confront and challenge the dominant social relations that have been put in place by borders, they show us the possibility of an alternative set of relations that can exist outside the parameters determined by race, capital, gender, and religion. Without pretending to affirm that acts of human kindness and the ability of people from different backgrounds to work together are enough to transform our contemporary realities, they do demonstrate the possibility that alliances, acts of solidarity and myriad forms of resistance can be necessary guides for the way forward. One of the ways in which they accomplish this is by troubling the labels and "lists of words" that place a vast range of people in simplified categories that obviate such solidarities. Moreover, by laying bare the multiple ways in which border rules are enforced, whether it is through the war-making capacity of imperial nations or through a chain of exploitative practices, we see that abolishing borders, as will become evident throughout this study, cannot be accomplished in a magical moment of change. Rather, it will constitute a political process that will involve a large-scale transformation of the present set of relations. Alameddine and Herrera help us imagine what the emergent moments of this process may look like.

Works Cited

Achcar, Gilbert. "Morbid Symptoms: What did Gramsci mean and how does it apply to our time?" *International Socialist Review,* vol. 108.

Adorno, Theodor. *Aesthetic Theory* (1970). Translated by C. Lenhardt, Routledge, London, 1984, p. 72.

Alameddine, Rabih. Interview by Kara Walker. *Bomb Magazine,* 17 Sept. 2021. https://bombmagazine.org/articles/rabih-alameddine/.

Alameddine, Rabih. *The Wrong End of the Telescope.* Grove Press, 2021.

Armstrong, Mark. "Six EU countries want to keep forced return of Afghans despite Taliban offensive." *Euronews,* 10 Aug. 2021, www.euronews. com/2021/08/10/six-eu-countries-want-to-keep-forced-return-of-afghans-despite-taliban-offensive.

Bady, Aaron. "Border Characters." *The Nation,* 2 Dec. 2015, https://www.the-nation.com/article/archive/border-characters/.

Barrera, Cordelia E. "Utopic Dreaming on the Borderlands: An Anzalduan Reading of Yuri Herrera's *Signs Preceding the End of the World.*" *Utopian Studies*, vol. 31, no. 3, 2020, pp. 475–493.

Bush, George W. "Address to a Joint Session of Congress and the American People." *White House Archives*, https://georgewbush-whitehouse.archives.gov/news/releases/2001/09/20010920-8.html.

Crawley, Heaven, and Dimitris Skleparis. "Refugees, migrants, neither, both: categorical fetishism and the politics of bounding in Europe's 'migration crisis.'" *Journal of Ethnic and Migration Studies*, vol. 44, no. 1, 2018, pp. 48–64.

Dearden, Lizzie. "The story of the Kurdish musician who drowned clutching his violin after trying to reach Europe." *The Independent*, 4 May 2017. https://www.independent.co.uk/news/world/europe/refugee-boat-sinking-turkey-aegean-baris-yazgi-kurdish-violinist-belgium-musician-story-family-disaster-turkey-a7718551.html.

De Genova, Nicholas. "The Borders of 'Europe' and the European Question." *The Borders of "Europe": Autonomy of Migration, Tactics of Bordering*, edited by Nicholas De Genova. Duke University Press, 2017.

———. "The 'migrant crisis' as racial crisis: do *Black Lives Matter* in Europe?" *Ethnic and Racial Studies*, vol. 41, no. 10, 2018, pp. 1765–1782, https://doi.org/10.1080/01419870.2017.1361543.

Dobbs, Leo. "The Number of Syrian Refugees in Lebanon Passes the 1 Million Mark." *UNHCR*, 3 Apr. 2014, https://www.unhcr.org/en-us/news/latest/2014/4/533c1d5b9/number-syrian-refugees-lebanon-passes-1-million-mark.html.

El Akkad, Omar. *What Strange Paradise*. McClelland and Stewart, 2021.

Fallon, Katy, et al. "How my dream of freedom died in Greece's 'holding pens.'" *The Guardian*, 5 Apr. 2020, https://www.theguardian.com/world/2020/apr/05/how-my-dream-of-freedom-died-on-the-road-to-greeces-gulag.

Fielder, Elizabeth Rodriguez. "Stowaway stories and mythological realism in Yuri Herrera's *Signs Preceding the End of the World* and Mohsin Hamid's *Exit West.*" *Crossings: Journal of Migration & Culture*, vol. 12, no. 1, 2021, pp. 331–346, https://doi.org/10.1386/cjmc_00035_1.

Gramsci, Antonio, *Quaderni del Carcere*, vol. 1, Quaderni 1–5, Q 3, § 34, 311–312; *Selections from the Prison Notebooks*, 275–276.

Gonzáles-Ramírez, Andrea. "This is What Life is Like for Refugee Mothers Living in Greece." *Refinery29*, 26 Jan. 2017, https://www.refinery29.com/en-us/2017/01/138017/syrian-refugee-mothers-pregnant-greece-camps.

Hamourtziadou, Lily, and Bülent Gökay. "Iraq's Security 2003–2019: death and neoliberal destruction par excellence." *Open Democracy*, 7 Jan. 2020, https://www.opendemocracy.net/en/north-africa-west-asia/iraqs-security-2003-2019-death-and-neoliberal-destruction-par-excellence/

Herrera, Yuri. *Trabajos del reino (2004)*, translated by Lisa Dillman as *Kingdom Cons.* And Other Stories, 2017.

———. "A Word with Yuri Herrera." *New Internationalist*, 1 Nov. 2017. https://newint.org/columns/finally/2017/11/01/yuri-herrera.

Herrera, Yuri, et al. "Literature as a Political Responsibility: An Interview with Yuri Herrera." *Latin American Literature Today*, https://latinamericanlit-eraturetoday.org/2017/04/literature-political-responsibility-interview-yuri-herrera-radmila-stefkova-and-rodrigo/.

Herrera, Yuri. *Señales Que Precederán al Fin del Mundo*, translated by Lisa Dillman as *Signs Preceding the End of the World*. And Other Stories, 2015.

"Hiding a humanitarian crisis on Greece's Lesbos." *Al Jazeera*, 12 Oct. 2015, https://www.aljazeera.com/features/2015/10/12/hiding-a-humanitarian-crisis-on-greeces-lesbos.

Kakissis, Joanna. "Fires Gut Europe's Largest Migrant Camp on the Greek Island of Lesbos." *NPR*, 9 Sept. 2020, https://www.npr.org/2020/09/09/911201270/fires-gut-europes-largest-migrant-camp-on-the-greek-island-of-lesbos.

Khatib, Joumana. "Refugees Are Suffering. This Novelist Won't Look Away." *New York Times*, 1 Sept. 2021, https://www.nytimes.com/2021/09/01/books/rabih-alameddine-wrong-end-telescope.html.

Kim, Elizabeth Sulis. "Yuri Herrera: Interview." *New Orleans Review*, n.d., https://www.neworleansreview.org/yuri-herrera/.

Krichker, Dina. "Making Sense of Borderscapes: Space, Imagination and Experience." *Geopolitics*, vol. 26, no. 4, 2021, pp. 1224–1242.

"Lebanon." *UNHCR*, Jan. 2023, https://reporting.unhcr.org/document/4449.

Office of the High Commission for Human Rights (OHCHR), *Convention against Torture and Other Cruel, Inhuman or Degrading Treatment or Punishment*, Article 3, 10 Dec. 1984, United Nations, https://www.ohchr.org/en/instrumentsmechanisms/instruments/convention-against-torture-and-other-cruel-inhuman-or-degrading, accessed on 26 Mar. 2023.

Olsen, Tommy. "It's Time for European Politicians to Take Off Their Blindfolds." *Aegean Boat Report*, 11 Sept. 2021. https://aegeanboatreport.com/2021/09/11/its-time-for-european-politicians-to-take-off-their-blindfolds/.

Organization of American States (OAS), American Convention on Human Rights, "Pact of San Jose", Article 22.8, Costa Rica, 22 November 1969, https://treaties.un.org/doc/publication/unts/volume%201144/volume-1144-i-17955-english.pdf, accessed on 26 Mar. 2023.

Ozkaleli, Umut. "Displaced selves, dislocated emotions and transforming identities: Syrian refugee women reinventing selves." *Women's Studies International Forum*, vol. 70, 2018, pp. 17–23.

Parekh, Serena. *No Refuge: Ethics and the Global Refugee Crisis.* Oxford University Press, 2020.

"Rabih Alameddine: *The Wrong End of the Telescope.*" *Between the Covers, TinHouse,* https://tinhouse.com/podcast/rabih-alameddine-the-wrong-end-of-the-telescope/.

Ramalho Da Silva, Beatriz and Corrine Redfern. "Fruit pickers lured to Portugal by the dream of a 'raspberry passport,'" *The Guardian,* 30 Jan. 2022, https://www.theguardian.com/global-development/2022/jan/30/fruit-pickers-lured-to-portugal-by-the-dream-of-a-raspberry-passport.

"Refugee Statistics." *UNHCR,* https://www.unrefugees.org/refugee-facts/statistics/.

Roitman, Janet. *Anti-Crisis.* Duke University Press, 2013.

Sajjad, Tazreena. "What's in a Name? 'Refugees', 'migrants' and the Politics of Labelling." *Race and Class,* vol. 60, no. 2, 2018, pp. 40–62.

Sisk, Christina. *Mexico, Nation in Transit: Contemporary Representations of Mexican Migration to the United States.* University of Arizona Press, 2011.

Smith, Helena. "Riots at Greek refugee camp on Lesbos after fatal fire." *The Guardian,* 30 Sept. 2019, https://www.theguardian.com/world/2019/sep/30/riots-at-greek-refugee-camp-on-lesbos-after-fatal-fire.

Sullivan, Eileen and Mariam Jordan, "Illegal Border Crossings, Driven by Pandemic and Natural Disasters, Soar to Record High." *New York Times,* 21 Oct. 2021, https://www.nytimes.com/2021/10/22/us/politics/border-crossings-immigration-record-high.html.

"Syria: Former Refugees Tortured, Raped, Disappeared after Returning Home." *Amnesty International,* 7 Sept. 2021, https://www.amnesty.org/en/latest/news/2021/09/syria-former-refugees-tortured-raped-disappeared-after-returning-home/.

Thomas, Dominic. "Fortress Europe: Identity, Race and Surveillance." *International Journal of Francophone Studies,* vol. 17, no. 3, 2014, pp. 445–468.

UN General Assembly, Convention Relating to the Status of Refugees, Article 33.1, 28 July 1951, United Nations, https://www.unhcr.org/en-us/3b66c2aa10, accessed on 26 Mar. 2023.

"U.S. changes color of food aid." *CNN,* 1 Nov. 2001, https://edition.cnn.com/2001/US/11/01/ret.afghan.fooddrops/.

Williams, Raymond, and Michael Orrom. *Preface to Film.* Film Drama, 1954.

Wood, Tony. "In-Betweenness." *London Review of Books,* vol. 38, no. 29, 2016.

Yousafzai, Sami. "'Rescue us,' beg Afghan refugee families as they protest their 'slum life' in a Pakistani park." *CBS News,* 21 June 2022, https://www.cbsnews.com/news/afghan-refugees-pakistan-islamabad-slum-life-protests/.

Zenko, Micah, and Amelia M. Wolf. "Tracking Eight Years of Airstrikes in Afghanistan." *Council on Foreign Relations,* 8 Jan. 2015, https://www.cfr.org/blog/tracking-eight-years-airstrikes-afghanistan.

CHAPTER 5

Documenting the Migrant Journey in Ai Weiwei's *Human Flow* and Diego Quemada-Díez's *La Jaula de Oro*

If Alammedine and Herrera help us imagine—through the literary landscapes that they craft—what the emergent moments of a borderless future may look like, the two films I examine in this chapter offer a somewhat forbidding roadmap to that future. Both filmmakers are aware of the catastrophic consequences of border rules, but they do not attempt to propose pathways that will guide us toward border abolition. They do, however, interrupt and interrogate the normalization of border rules and the attendant narratives that support them, forcing viewers to question their logic. Of course, as artists whose works are embedded in global commodity circuits, their own positions within these circuits must also be considered. Moreover, since films have a far wider reach than literary texts, I will explore the role of films within the larger—often problematic—economic contexts of their production and circulation. I will also reflect on the possibilities and limitations of the cinematic form to represent the many forms of bordered violence, as well to produce a visual reimagining of border spaces as potential sites for liberation.

HUMAN FLOW AND POETIC PROTEST

Ai Weiwei, the Chinese artist, became a refugee in 2015, when he left China after several years of conflict with the government over his criticism of official policies. In 2011, he had been detained for "economic crimes"

© The Author(s), under exclusive license to Springer Nature Switzerland AG 2023
K. Chowdhury, *Border Rules*, Politics of Citizenship and Migration, https://doi.org/10.1007/978-3-031-26216-6_5

141

and imprisoned for 81 days. His passport was seized, and he was unable to travel during this period.[1] Over the last ten years, he has become a well-known global figure, particularly in the West, where he is held up as the model dissident artist, opposed to the arbitrary actions of Chinese authoritarian rule. Other than his many pieces of installment art and exhibitions across the world, produced in the last 20 years, Ai has also made a series of documentaries, including *A Beautiful Life* (2009), *So Sorry* (2011), *Stay Home* (2013), and *Fukushima Art Project* (2015).[2]

The documentary *Human Flow* (2017) made with Andy Cohen focuses primarily on the massive humanitarian crisis on the shores of Europe in 2015–2016, but also includes vignettes of people on the move or stuck in limbo in refugee camps in Africa, Asia, and North America. The film is a tour de force, both from a technical point of view—it was shot with the help of iPhones, drones, and conventional cameras—and in terms of sheer scale. Not only does it cover borders and refugee camps across three continents, including places such as Gaza, which functions as an open-air prison, cut off from the rest of the world, but the production of the film also involved over 200 crew members who crisscrossed the globe capturing a range of images. In concrete terms, Ai "visited more than 40 refugee camps in 23 countries" in order to make this film (Rosler). His film combines stark moments of real footage, such as a tear gas attack by Greek police at a refugee camp and the destruction of the Calais "Jungle" by the French authorities, along with poetic set pieces, such as horses being bathed in the sea in Gaza.

Human Flow, at one level, is a showpiece for its creator, Ai Weiwei to engage at a personal level with the people and places who constitute the current landscape of migration. The film also serves as a platform for Ai to comment on the failure of Western states to provide a humanitarian response for the many who are seeking refuge. Clearly, as a refugee

---

[1] For more information on Ai's arrest and detainment, see the BBC article "Chinese artist Ai Weiwei held for 'economic crimes.'" See also Ai's installation, "S.A.C.R.E.D.," in which he portrays the circumstances of his detainment via six dioramas.

[2] Ai is recognized for serving as artistic consultant for the National Stadium in Beijing, also known as the Bird's Nest, which has been used for both the 2008 Summer Olympics and Paralympics and the 2022 Winter Olympics and Paralympics. Other notable works include *Sunflower Seeds* (2010), an installation consisting of "millions of individually handcrafted porcelain sunflower seeds," and *Hansel and Gretel* (2017), in partnership with Jacques Herzog and Pierre de Meuron, which explored the idea of public surveillance with drones watching and recreating visitors' every moves.

himself, even if one with a rare set of privileges, Ai is well aware of the vicissitudes of exile and displacement. He is also an appropriate person to question the West's commitment to human rights since he is held up as an example of their celebration of an individual's right to freedom of expression and for their promotion of democratic and humanitarian values. As a poster child, then, of Western liberalism and its opposition to Chinese totalitarianism, Ai's riposte to the West in *Human Flow* is apposite. By laying bare Western governments' utter failures to offer refuge to those escaping war and by highlighting their moral culpability and silence in the face of human suffering, and indeed their unwillingness to live up to the principles of international law, Ai succeeds in debunking the West's self-congratulatory narrative of itself as a defender of human rights.

One way in which Ai attempts to personalize what can otherwise become a series of images constituting faces, places, scenes of loss, and moments of sadness is by inserting himself into the narrative. He does this in various ways, frequently demonstrating compassion for the refugees he interacts with, injecting humor into his exchanges with individuals, showing himself using his iPhone to record images in camps or of boats arriving on the shore, and by his own actual movement through borders and barriers. Not surprisingly, such insertions result in a set of contradictory effects. On the one hand, we are conscious of the fact that we are not watching news footage or a documentary presenting information in a dispassionate, apparently neutral tone. The director, through his interactions with the refugees, makes it clear that the individuals in the film are not just part of an undifferentiated group of "refugees" to be pitied and looked at. There is, after all, a long tradition in documentary film where "the use of 'objective' or 'neutral' conventions (such as long takes, wide-angle shots, and explanatory third-person commentary) to represent non-Western and indigenous cultures nonetheless marked them as authentic, timeless, and untouched by civilization—that is, as other" (Rangan 5). The personalization effect also highlights the contradictory ways in which film can both humanize and produce a subject.

On the other hand, putting aside what may or may not be the director's intentions about this mode of filmmaking, Ai's insertion in the documentary is certainly one of the most troubling elements of his approach to telling the individual's story. Let us examine a few examples of this technique from the film: in one scene, subjects stand, without uttering any words, in front of a white background; in other scenes, subjects speak directly into the camera about their harrowing journeys; on frequent occasions, Ai directly interacts with the migrants, often with what appears to be contrived set pieces, such as one where he exchanges his Chinese passport with a migrant's Syrian passport or one where he accompanies a young man, who has just come ashore, and acquires for him a hot cup of tea; in one affecting scene, he finds a piano and has it brought to a camp so that a young woman can play a few notes of Beethoven. It is possible to view these moments as examples of the director centering those whose stories make up the fabric of this film.[3] Yet, it is difficult not to get the impression that these moments are also about the director performing his role as the compassionate observer/participant. Quite often, he is filmed directly full face while his subject's face is removed from the camera. In one scene, for instance, he comforts a woman who is recounting her story. Her back is turned to the camera (to preserve her anonymity), and when she begins to cry, overwhelmed by sorrow, Ai crosses over from behind the camera, sits next to her, hands her tissues and comforts her. Clearly, breaking through the wall that separates the subject from the director/observer can be seen in a positive light as that filmmaker's objectivity is seen to be a transparent, constructed one. Yet, in the remainder of the scene, once the woman is unable to speak, Ai, effectively, becomes the subject of the scene.[4]

The critic Eszter Zimanyi has a more sympathetic reading of Ai's interventions in the film. She argues that "[b]y maintaining this self-reflexivity, Ai provides audiences with an opportunity to discuss how all political and social identity categories are constructed, performed and policed, and indicts not only viewers but also himself (a high-profile artist who benefits from continuous media exposure) as complicit in maintaining unequal

---

[3] The scene where he accompanies the young man is a selfie video, thus enhancing the centrality of the director in this scene.

[4] Ai, of course, has become the subject of his own creation at other moments. In an earlier piece of performance art, soon after the famous photograph of Aylan Kurdi had circulated the globe, Ai had invited a photographer, Rohit Chawla, from the Indian magazine *India Today* to take a photograph of him lying on a beach in Lesvos in the same position as the young child. Responding to a backlash over his actions, Ai declared that the world had more interests in his actions than in paying attention to the atrocities that led to the death of Kurdi. His defenders, moreover, point out that his actions are not divorced from his "performances." He had closed an exhibition in Denmark a week before this photograph appeared because the government had announced a plan to confiscate the possessions of refugees to pay for their upkeep.

hierarchies that have significant and ongoing material consequences (378). Such a reading opens up the liberatory and oppositional possibilities of Ai's interventions into the narrative, but the overall effect of his interventions, I would argue, is not of unsettling hierarchies but of reestablishing them.

There is undoubtedly a point to be made that Ai's forays into scenes allow for a defamiliarization effect that bolsters some of the larger political points he attempts to establish. Ai, like the unnamed narrator in *The Wrong End of the Telescope*, is concerned that a humanitarian crisis of this scale may be impossible for his audience to comprehend fully or that scenes documenting this crisis will appear too similar to the many images circulating worldwide of people fleeing their homelands. Niels Pagh Andersen, the film's Danish editor, comments that he instructed his fellow editors to make their selections from the hundreds of hours of film based on the following criterion: "If you see an image that could be in a normal television program, don't use it. Or if it's so powerful you think you must use it, give it double the length you normally would. We read an image on the surface in two to five seconds, but if it's a very strong image, then there are layers in it that encourage a new interpretation when it remains on the screen longer than we expect." Thus, a face remains on camera for several seconds, often accompanied by complete silence. Sometimes we know them by name; other times, nameless individuals gaze back at the camera. Ai's intrusion, then, can be seen not just as a way to mark a "break," a "rupture," unsettling the typical television narrative, but it can also serve as a contrast to the shots that do remain on the "screen longer than we expect."

Another striking defamiliarizing technique employed by Ai is the juxtaposition of images, foregrounding both the absurdities of the current situation and the world's criminal response to them. He interviews a group of young women in Gaza who comment on their prison-like existence. Many of them evince an interest in seeing the world—they speak with enthusiasm about their hopes for traveling and then returning to their homes. The next sequence focuses on the solitary tiger in the Gaza Zoo, Laziz, confined in a small cage. We then see the tiger being shipped out to Johannesburg so that it can be freed from its confines, a journey that is made possible by the cooperation of a number of nation states and

146   K. CHOWDHURY

organizations.[5] Is this a comment on the humanity of a world that sees a violation in the predicament of a caged tiger and is willing to do all it can do to improve its condition, but then can remain silent in the face of the everyday brutalities that the residents of Gaza have to endure?[6] Are we supposed to cheer for what is possible if nations come together or be appalled that an animal merits this much attention in the face of human suffering? Clearly, it is not an either/or question, but juxtaposing the scenes in this manner has the effect of unsettling the viewer.

Perhaps the most compelling use of defamiliarization is Ai's use of cinematic form, whether it is shot composition, use of music, or length of a shot. These techniques, arguably, disallow the viewer from experiencing the familiar comfort of a settled narrative form. Thus, as I have already mentioned, Ai uses motion within and between frames in combination with long takes of landscapes or faces. These patterns are most distinctive when the viewer is subject to the disorienting handheld iPhone camera footage taken by Ai, including extended shots of destroyed houses, graves of those who have died at sea, and tents rustling in the wind. Ai also uses overhead long shots in juxtaposition with intense close-ups of faces. The sounds of the wind and the waves break into moments marked by the dulcet chords of a violin or a cello. These combinations have the desired effect of encouraging contemplation even as it jars the viewer out of that contemplation. In a sense, what we are seeing on the screen is the

---

[5] Consider the language used to describe the tiger's captivity by a representative of the organization Four Paws: "I believe it's not nice for a tiger to hear [...] the bombs around them. They don't understand this. To keep the animal here during any war or any conflict, for 15 days not being able to come here to feed the animal... I believe that's not nice for the animal. To keep an animal in a place like this where it never touches the grass, I don't believe this is the correct place for an animal. A wonderful creature like this deserves to be freed from these conditions" (*Human Flow*). See also the Four Paws article detailing the rescue of Laziz from Khan Younis Zoo in which the conditions are described as "desolate," with animals "starving and lacking fresh water" for years.

[6] In a 2022 United Nations report on the "increase in the levels of mental disorders amongst the population of the Gaza Strip, especially among children" the authors mention that "[m]ore than 65 percent of the population of Gaza live below the poverty line, and more than 60 percent are unemployed." As for help for those who need to be treated for the psychological traumas they experience as a result of the Occupation: for the "more than two million people [who] live in the Gaza Strip: there is only one mental health hospital" ("One Third of Gaza Strip").

5 DOCUMENTING THE MIGRANT JOURNEY IN AI WEIWEI'S... 147

desperate urgency of those who have lost their homes, side by side with the torpor of global inaction as millions of people wait endlessly for refuge.[7]

A final technique that interrogates the ways we see is through Ai use of drone shots. In Chap. 2, I used the image of Branson's space flight as an embodiment of global capital's attempt to break through the restrictive borders of space and time. The obscene importance granted to Branson's "ascent" into space as I pointed out, on a day that the bodies of several migrants were found in the Arizona desert, acquires greater significance since this achievement is celebrated even as the names and faces of those who lost their lives in the desert are obscured for us. One of Ai's cinematic techniques accomplish quite the opposite effect: employing drone shots, his point of view begins in the skies, so to speak, focusing on wide panoramic view of camps, vast bodies of water, and moving vehicles. As the camera moves in, zooming in on the actual elements that compose the image, we see the specificity of migrants on a boat or of hundreds of tents in a desert landscape or of children playing. In a sense, this opposite movement—from space to earth—unlike Branson's journey, forces us to reckon with what we would rather consign to the realm of the fantastical. Indeed, in Branson's account, capital erases its devastations on earth even as it reaches for an imaginary new life in the clouds. Taking this metaphor a step further: if ascending to space signifies an erasure of borders, descending to earth makes real those borders and their effects.

In one spectacular shot, for instance, at the exact midpoint in the film (1:07:30), we look down from a vast distance over what appears to be an unidentifiable row of rectangles. In the middle of the frame are tiny, indistinguishable dots. As the shot zooms in closer to the image, we realize that we are looking at a row of tents and that the small, unrecognizable shapes

---

[7] Attempting to determine the average length of time that refugees and asylum seekers spend in camps proves difficult. A commonly cited statistic states that refugees spend, on average, 17 years in camps, but Benjamin Thomas White disputes this claim on the BBC podcast *More or Less*. White tracks the mysterious statistic to a 2006 UNHCR publication, but he notes that the statistic does not, in fact, refer to refugees living in camps but rather to individuals in all refugee situations. With this figure incorrectly attributed and over a decade out of date, the initial question of average amount of time spent in refugee camps is unclear. The interviewer on *More or Less* sums up the problem of determining such a figure, stating that "Dr. White argues that there's no point in even trying to measure the average length of time in a refugee camp. It doesn't help refugees, and it doesn't help humanitarian agencies plan their response to crises. In fact, it might even deter governments from taking in refugees if they think they'll be encamped for 17 years."

are children gathered together. As the camera approaches the ground, the children move aside, providing a place for it to land. What the director accomplishes in this shot is not just an aesthetic tour de force that leads the viewer from disorientation and distance to familiarity and proximity. More significantly, I believe, Ai manages to take an abstraction—the sheer enormity of the numbers that comprise the movement and displacement of people—and reconstitute it as a concrete reality that makes up the lives of the millions impacted by the catastrophic conditions. For the rest of the world, and certainly for the West, these lives and their dwellings are the stuff of fiction and sensationalized media coverage.

Just as in this example, a significant element of current coverage of the movement of people has been the employment of drone shots. They are now commonplace in documentaries. As one of the film's cinematographers comments, "dealing with a massive scale, drones have a superior ability to capture scale in a very short time. We all know how [documentarians] generally approach filming in poorly structured camps. It's nothing new. You've seen one, you've seen them all. Drones change the point of view, show the camp in relation to the landscape (Silberg). It is true that the use of drone shots in this film appears to have a specific purpose—one connected to relationality. But what exactly does an awareness of this relation accomplish? Does it aim to align the vastness of the landscape with the absence of compassion, of humanity? Does it make the refugees' expulsion from the world appear in even more stark terms? Can a drone shot highlight the relation between appearance and essence? Consider the final shot of the film, which consists of a drone shot that moves back into space, unlike the shot of the refugee camp that becomes familiar as we descend from space. In this instance, we begin with a recognizable object: a discarded life vest; as the camera ascends, we see thousands of these life vests. The sheer numbers are staggering. Gradually, we can no longer recognize what we see. In both these examples, Ai conveys the totality of the refugee crisis through the centripetal and centrifugal movement of the camera, guiding our relationship to the image so that we misrecognize the familiar. A bordered world is visible in all its material effects; yet this world also remains firmly in the realm of the abstract since nature offers no signals for the points at which borders appear and disappear. In this way, technique is vital to the politics of the film.

What, then, more specifically, are the politics of the film? Without gesturing to a simple assessment based on an existing set of criteria, I want to offer a close reading of the first ten minutes of the film, suggesting that certain aesthetic and political choices are put in the place early in the film and these help us determine the overall effectiveness of the film as a piece of oppositional art.

The film begins with an overhead shot of a vast body of water. We then notice a tiny speck; it is a white bird flying from the top of the screen toward the bottom right of the screen. We follow the bird as it exits the frame at the bottom of the screen. The same image of a wide blue sea is now disrupted by a boat full of people that appears from the right of the screen. As the boat moves across the water, we cut to a still shot of what appears to be sunrise on the shores of an unnamed place. The words of the Turkish communist poet Nâzım Hikmet appear on the screen: "I want the right of life / of the leopard at the spring / of the seed splitting open— / I want the right of the first man." Gradually, the camera pans to the left where we see the blinking lights of a lighthouse. The stillness is interrupted by small signs of activity: what appears to be a small coastguard boat glides across the water; a helicopter flies by overhead; a man in a bodysuit in the water gestures, and then we see a dinghy approaching the shore. Other volunteers appear, offering a rope to one of the men on the dinghy. As the boat moors, volunteers help young children and the elderly from the boat. We then see Ai Weiwei lying by the side of the road, camera in hand photographing the arrivals.

Suddenly the tempo shifts, and our perspective is guided by a handheld phone that captures the urgency of the moment as people help each other off the boat. We then follow Ai as he films himself accompanying a young man to find him a "hot cup of tea." The man looks into the camera, smoking a cigarette as he answers Ai's questions: "your name?" "from where?" The young man responds: "My name is Muhammed Hassan from Iraq, Salah ad-Din." The director then asks him if he is from the camp there, but Hassan doesn't catch what he is asking.[8]

---

[8] Salah al-Din is in an area just north of Baghdad. In a report by the European Agency for Asylum, last updated in 2021, summarizing the dire security situation there and the lack of infrastructure and viable living conditions, the drafters conclude: "Looking at the indicators, it can be concluded that indiscriminate violence is taking place in the governorate of Salah al-Din, however not at a high level and, accordingly, a higher level of individual elements is required in order to show substantial grounds for believing that a civilian, returned to the territory, would face a real risk of serious harm within the meaning of Article 15." For further information on Article 15, see https://eur-lex.europa.eu/legal-content/EN/TXT/?uri=celex%3A32011L0095. These are, then, the unrealistic standards that must be met in order to receive asylum.

150 K. CHOWDHURY

We then glimpse another dinghy moving across the open water, and the title "*Human Flow*: A Film by Ai Weiwei" appears on the screen. After pausing for a few moments on this image, we are presented with a drone shot of what appears to be a series of tents on a desert landscape. The word Iraq appears on the screen, followed by these statistics: "Iraq hosts 277,000 refugees, most of whom are fleeing Syria." As the camera descends, we see countless number of tents, shots of children playing, and then a shot of a young girl, taken from the back of a tent, showing her in silhouette, standing at the entrance of tent. On the screen appears the statement: "Following the US-led invasion, 268,000 people have been killed in violent conflicts in Iraq. More than four million Iraqis have been displaced from their homes." We then observe a group of women making bread, followed by a scene showing an army official handing out identity cards to a group of assembled men. The official has an exchange with one of the men, but we are not told what the discussion is about. The scene then shifts to two women who relate their stories: the younger woman tells us that "we left four years ago because the situation was so horrible." The other woman joins in and adds "because every place was being hit by missiles coming from Jobar ... yes, missiles were coming from Jobar without warning ... missiles from Jobar falling like rain."[9] The camera lingers on her face for a few seconds and then we see drone footage of a town entirely destroyed by bombs. We are not given the identity of the town, suggesting that this is not an uncommon sight for those fleeing Syria.

The tempo shifts once again and we see a single figure, a young woman, standing in front of a white background. The camera stays with her for a few seconds. This image is then followed by five other individuals (one of a mother and her child) standing in a similar position, staring directly into the camera. As the last image disappears, we hear the sound of water with the following statement from the UN Refugee Convention (1951) on the screen: a refugee is a person with a "well-founded fear of being persecuted for reasons of race, religion, nationality, membership of a particular social group, or political opinion." As the screen darkens into nighttime, we see the flash of the lighthouse lights once again. We glimpse people gathered

---

[9] According to research by the United Nations Satellite Centre (UNOSAT), in 2018, 93 percent of buildings in Jobar have been severely damaged due to fighting between the Syrian Army and several different rebel groups. For more information and relevant UNOSAT maps, see the BBC article, "Syria War: UN Security Council truce vote delayed."

on the shore by a fire, and then we hear voices and shouts, and it is apparent that another dinghy has just reached the beach.

I have given a fair amount of attention to these first ten minutes since I believe that this section of the film offers us both a cogent articulation of the violence of a bordered world and its effects on populations in the Global South even as it leads us to an impasse about a path away from this world. Ai, I believe, calls for a problematic assertion of a humanitarian framework to address the "crisis" that he captures, a framework that, arguably, has already proven to be bankrupt and insufficient.[10] Before I proceed further, however, let me reiterate what makes Ai's work an important piece of artistic intervention, using these first ten minutes as a moment of illustration. His use of cinematic techniques is a good place to begin. First, as I have already mentioned, he uses the long shot, especially the overhead drone shots, to show us the scale of what we are confronting but then always moves us closer from that abstract vastness to the concrete reality of peoples' lives. Second, he uses iPhone footage to get close to his subjects and creates a sense of immediacy and urgency, especially in the sequences when the refugees arrive on the beach. Third, he pauses and stays with an image for the import of an individual's words to sink in and for her face to imprint itself on our mind. He does the same with still life images: the vastness of the sea; the blinking light of a lighthouse; a boat on the water. Finally, he establishes an unsettling image text dialectic by juxtaposing the UN refugee charter or the words of a poet with the scenes of violence, loss, and fear. The disjuncture that comes with a news ticker or crawler thread of textual associations, arguments, and proclamations create the necessary sense of (dis)comfort as our eyes fix on an image that directly echoes or contradicts the words on the screen.

Let us now consider another distinctive moment in the first ten minutes—when the single individuals line up to be filmed. Do they, at this point, become the object of our gaze or do they gain some agency by

---

[10] An hour into the film Ai tells us about the March 2016 deal between Turkey and the EU, which allows the EU to "return" refugees to Turkey. In exchange, Turkey gets six billion euro in aid and Turkish citizens receive the "privilege" of visa free travel to Europe. The economic "logic" of this arrangement is commented on. There is indirect reference to the point that the refugees also serve an instrumental role for many economies. A Turkish official says: "Europe is working hard on a treaty with Turkey. Which in my view will turn the refugees into slaves. Nothing but objects of exchange. No one really understands how to tackle the refugee problem at the root." However, the labor element of the "crisis" is not explored in any depth in the film.

staring back at us, refusing to be objectified? Is this a critique of the inevitable ways in which we, the viewers, engage in voyeurism? Is this also a critique of the dehumanizing surveillance rituals of biometric categorization that refugees must undergo and Ai's attempt to indicate that the category of the refugee is produced through such actions? Or is Ai's camera yet another technology of surveillance, participating in the production of "refugee" subjects? Eszter Zimanyi in "*Human Flow*: Thinking with and through Ai Weiwei's Defamiliarizing Gaze," addresses some of these questions:

> Ai allows the camera to linger on subjects for extended periods, prompting us to consider our own voyeurism. By doing so, the film defamiliarizes images of refugees, while alerting us to the fact that what we are witnessing is not only an ongoing humanitarian crisis but also the production of crisis itself. We watch as the "migrant" and "refugee" are formed into distinct and unequal political entities: they are figures who become knowable, surveillable, and containable through the dehumanizing routine of being examined, documented, fingerprinted, and reduced to an identification number in place of a name." (377)

While the freezing of time enables the viewer to realize that a subject is being produced, that she, in a sense, comes into being as we gaze at her, I am less convinced by Zimanyi's claim that these moments prompt us to "consider our own voyeurism." Indeed, there is little demand made on the viewer other than to absorb the story, register a face, or a voice. What might it mean for us to understand that a crisis is being "produced"? What ethical claims are being made of us at this moment?

I would suggest that Ai has a greater impact on engaging his audience when he traverses the bordered zones of our world, exposing both the violence and arbitrariness of state laws and the devastating impacts borders have on the people merely trying to survive. A series of landscapes that he uses in the first ten minutes of the film is particularly effective. When the young man who has just arrived in Lesvos announces he is from Iraq, Ai works backward from that point. We first travel to a camp in Iraq, where the two women announce that bombs were "falling like rain." The next image is of a bombed city. We then return to the individual once again as a series of refugees stand in front of a white background. What Ai accomplishes in these few minutes is to connect the ruinations of war and the eternal limbo that confronts refugees to the individual who is buffeted by these forces. Much like the effect of the drone shot, he both closes in and moves back to show us the causal chain of imperial violence.

Indeed, in general, he makes excellent use of the various landscapes that he films, whether they be arid deserts, seascapes, narrow winding roads on which trucks ply from Pakistan to Afghanistan, bombed-out buildings in areas inhabited by the Kurdish people, makeshift camps in Idomeni, Greece, apartment buildings in Gaza, or the forests of Greece through which the refugees wend their way north. Clearly, the "flow" of the title is not just an allusion to the people who are on the move. It is also about the many impediments that inhibit that flow. Indeed, the instruments of the state do everything in their ability to stop the flow. Sometimes these barriers leave little to the imagination. In Gaza, we see walls and barbed wire separating people. In another scene, a Hungarian army official gives a speech to his counterparts in the police force, saying that the role of the army was to support the police. He concludes: "It is our joint duty to secure the border." We are then witness to the barbed fence, soldiers in tanks, and armed officers walking around with muzzled dogs. At other times, the barriers verge on the absurd. At the US–Mexico border, a border guard tells the film crew with all seriousness that a wooden pole marks the point that separates Mexico from the United States.[11] In whatever form, however, barriers and borders persist. Even natural barriers play their part, as we see a group of refugees trying to cross a raging stream in northern Greece. Many speak with a sense of bemusement about these borders and barriers. One young man asks, "Border closed"? When that is confirmed, he can only exclaim, "Where do the people go?" Another family from Afghanistan asks the most basic question when they are told that Macedonia has closed its borders: "Why?"

Despite the horrors pointed out by Ai and his attention to the criminal actions of the West, he does not attempt to answer such questions. This is partly the case because the film offers little systemic critique. Indeed, the director's main "purpose is to pose the question, 'Will our global society emerge from fear, isolation, and self-interest and choose a path of openness, freedom, and a respect for humanity?" (Synopsis). Such a question

---

[11] I do, however, disagree with Dargis's more general assessment of the film in her review in the *New York Times* that "the camera shows a world in which, step by step, crisis by crisis, borders have become by turns absurd and immaterial." One might argue quite the opposite. They are very much material, even though how they are performed and enforced may be absurd.

154 K. CHOWDHURY

relies on moral abstractions and signals a dispersal of responsibility. Indeed, indicting a category such as "global society" is a disservice to the specificity of loss that he is trying to portray. And what manner of "self-interest" are we alluding to here? What exactly is being protected, for what purpose, and for whose benefit? One wonders how those refugees who posed the questions about borders would benefit from a consideration of these abstractions. It is true that there are a few speakers who mention global economic inequalities, but these statements appear at the end of the film in a section on the US–Mexico border, when two speakers mention the inequalities that are a factor in migration. There are very few political or economic explanations for the enforcement of borders. Why does the Hungarian government erect a barbed wire fence? Why do the French authorities burn down the Jungle? Why does the Israeli state subject the Palestinians to daily humiliations? What are the economic conditions that have led to this "crisis"? What is it that nativists in Europe want to protect? What, indeed, constitutes this "global society" and how "will our global society emerge" from those beliefs Ai so decries if we do not know why they exist in the first place?

It is hard to object to Ai's calls for humanitarian refugee policies and his hopes for a world in which people share resources and come together to help one another.[12] Nor does an audience watching this film doubt that refugees are human beings who should be treated with respect. Throughout the film, Ai reiterates these messages with the words of the most famous to those uttered by the anonymous refugee. Whether it is Princess Dana Firas of Jordan, who emphasizes that "[t]his humanitarian side is very important. You must always hold on to humanity" or Mohammad Fares, a former Syrian astronaut, whose words about tolerance and sharing end the film, or Rafik Ismail, a Rohingya community leader, who says, "At times we are ashamed when people call us stateless people, boat people... we too have feelings. We too are human," or the young men holding up signs in the refugee camp in Idomeni that read "RESPECT," or the protesters who cry out "Am I Not Human Too,?" we are asked to reach for our better selves. Ai tries to shame those in power by putting up the words

---

[12] Ai points out the sheer inequality that marks the way the wealthier countries in Europe and the United States have responded to the refugee crisis. Their meagre allotment of refugees, as Ai reminds us, is in stark contrast to a country like Jordan, which hosts 1.4 million refugees; a Jordanian official in the film marks the disparity: in comparison, this would be equal to an influx of 60 million people to the United States and the EU.

of the Charter of the Fundamental Rights of the European Union, 2000 on the screen—"The union is founded on the indivisible, universal values of human dignity, freedom, equality, and solidarity"—after The Jungle is destroyed by the authorities. He warns us about what is ahead. Wella Kouyo, Deputy Representative, UNHCR, Kenya mentions the problems of climate change and tells us "resources are diminishing," but doesn't tell us why this is the case. Instead, we view facts on the ticker about how "in the next few years climate change will exacerbate drought, hunger, and disease for 250 million Africans." Why is this inevitable, and who is responsible for this state of affairs?

Ai makes a concerted effort to have refugees recount their own stories and describe the rampant discrimination that they face in "host" countries such as Turkey, and to establish the fact that they do not have recourse to any system of rights. Most of them have had little success filing an asylum claim. Dr. Hanan Ashrawi, head of the PLO department of culture and information reminds us that "being a refugee is much more than a political status. It is the most pervasive kind of cruelty that can be exercised against a human being." However, there is very little attention to the ways in which this cruelty can be traced back to the politics of white nationalism, imperialism, or the vast inequalities forged by capitalism. Ioannis Mouzalas, the Migration minister in Greece is one of the few who point to the option for choosing between two Europes, one a tolerant non-racist one, based on human rights and another a xenophobic one that fails to live up to its principles.[13] But even in this instance, he seems to hold on to a notion of a Europe as a force of good—"That's not the Europe we dreamt of"—one that is a chimera. Gabriela Soraya Vasquez, lawyer and human rights activist is the only speaker who attributes migration patterns to vast global inequalities and the actions of nations who have taken possession of

---

[13] One of the most striking scenes in the film is at the 40-minute mark, when the film, which until then focuses primarily on North African and Middle Eastern refugees (and a brief section on the Rohingya), switches to the arrival of refugees from sub-Saharan African countries to a port in Southern Italy. We are informed that "[m]ore than 210,000 African refugees arrived in Italy in 2015 and 2016." Several striking images include that of the men attired in the same white covering, photographed as if being booked and arrested, and then marching in rows towards ships, accompanied by armed guards. They are then given emergency blankets as they huddle together. Finally, they are put on a bus. This entire sequence replicates exactly the rituals for men being arrested and incarcerated. Dr. Hanan Ashrawi's comment punctuates this scene, when she decries the cruelty that refugees face. For an account of the traumatic journey many of the migrants make from sub-Saharan countries to Southern Europe, see Louis-Philippe Dalembert's *The Mediterranean Wall*.

global wealth. Yet, her words are immediately counterposed by Kemal Kirişci, a senior fellow at the Brookings Institute who bizarrely attributes migration to the influence of social media and because transportation has become "so much cheaper and more effective." Globalization," he says, "has had many positive outcomes, but it also has created greater inequalities."

Indeed, the film itself is a cultural product that is enmeshed in these global inequalities. As we will see in the next chapter, oppositional cultural products have to confront their imbrication in the global entertainment system. *Human Flow* is produced by Participant Media and Amazon Studios.[14] The official website for the film has a tab that lists "Take Action." One of the options for those who want to donate is to "give" through an Amazon Wishlist which will "provide resettled refugee families with items they need to start their new life." Other than pointing out the inevitable commodification of refugee lives that such forms of marketing entail, the specter of Amazon also reminds us that the production crew of *Human Flow* had a seemingly endless access to resources during the making of this film. The enormous costs of this film are mitigated via a global chain of exploitation that is partly responsible for much of displacement that is alluded to in this film. More troublingly, Ai and his crew can cross borders with ease, entering and exiting as they please, unlike the subjects who are filmed; they, on the other hand, are trapped in limbo, a countless number never to see their homelands again. And many of those who do see their homelands are often deported back to their homeland via the services operated by the Air Transport Services Group (ATSG), a company co-owned by Amazon.[15] Perhaps like the unnamed writer in *The Wrong End*

---

[14] Ai's thoughts about working with this company demonstrate his affinity for a certain kind of "freedom," one which takes precedence over acts of corporate violence: "During the development, some investors heard about our topic, knew we were in need and moved in. My experience with them? I am a very picky and critical artist. If there is any restriction or anything in dealing with the commercial side, that would be a problem for the film. There was complete freedom left to me. For me, the relationship with these companies was very, very special. They were in touch with NGOs, human rights organisations, UN people, top American decision makers" (Macnab).

[15] ATSG's "two most prominent federal customers are the Department of Defense, which uses the firm for troop transports, and the Department of Homeland Security, which has paid the company reportedly exorbitant fees over the years in order to execute so-called special high-risk charter flights for its 'ICE Air' deportation machine" (Biddle). Moreover, Amazon "has played as central a role as Palantir [a data mining company] in providing the backbone infrastructure for many of ICE's, and DHS's, key programs. Amazon has also enjoyed a cozy relationship with the federal government that has helped it secure an outsize number of government contracts" (Hao).

of the Telescope, Ai's success in communicating the horrors of displacement is always marked by a failure of representation as well.

LA JAULA DE ORO: DRAMATIZING THE REAL

The problems of representing the migrant "other" are also present in Diego Quemada-Díez's *La Jaula de Oro* (*The Golden Dream*, 2013), but they take on different forms since this film falls into the category of a docudrama or docufiction. The aesthetic and political textures of the film are complicated by this ever-present dialectic between fact and fiction. As a viewing experience, I argue, the film, by design, undermines the audience's affective identification with the characters: just when we become accustomed to the rituals of a traditional fictional narrative (e.g., the predictable conflicts between characters, the emergence of a love triangle, the overcoming of barriers, the striking montages of passing landscapes) and attach ourselves emotionally to the characters, an unsettling reality intrudes upon our equanimity and disrupts this relationship. Indeed, one could argue that these disruptions in the trajectory of the migration narrative produces a distancing or estrangement effect (Brecht's notion of *Verfremdungseffek* is a useful reference here), interrupting an aesthetic experience rooted in an implicit pact between viewer and filmmaker regarding the familiar practices of storytelling.[16] In this sense, then, *La Jaula de Oro*, although lacking the visceral real-life images of *Human Flow*, with its bombed-out buildings and refugees traveling on dinghies, can be commended for requiring the viewer to confront the realities of the violence engendered by border rules, and even more importantly, for recognizing that those rules remain in place even after the border has been crossed.

Let me attempt to explain how Quemada-Díez is able to create a cinematic experience that is both familiar and unsettling at the same time. *La Jaula de Oro* traces the journey of three Guatemalan adolescents, one of whom, Samuel (Carlos Chajon) returns to Guatemala early in the journey, and a Mexican adolescent from Chiapas as they travel through the length

---

[16] As Walter Benjamin in his description of epic theater puts it, "instead of identifying with the characters, the audience should be educated to be astonished at the circumstances under which they function." The "truly important thing," Benjamin sums up, is "to discover the conditions of life. (One might say just as well: to alienate [*verfremden*] them.) This discovery (alienation) of conditions takes place through the interruptions of happenings" (150). Sara's abduction and Chauk's murder are classic examples of these "interruptions."

158   K. CHOWDHURY

of Mexico, attempting to the reach the Northern border in order to cross over to the United States. In some ways, the film fits neatly into the migrant journey narrative as we follow the two Guatemalan teenagers Juan and Sara (played by Brandon López and Karen Martínez) and the Mexican teenager Chauk (Rodolfo Domínguez), who encounter the cruelties of the state and the rapacity of criminal groups.[17] However, Quemada-Díez's unconventional and unsettling engagement with the structural violence of border rules gives the film a different resonance. As I have already mentioned, the film has a familiar feel of a traditional migratory narrative, but unlike some of those other films, *La Jaula de Oro* is not a film about redemption or one proposing the message that grit and courage result in fulfilled dreams or that "pure" migrants persevere in the end.[18] In the world that we are presented, the social relations engendered by the border intrude persistently on the lives of migrants and position the teenagers in particular ways long before they encounter the US–Mexico border. Indeed, Quemada-Díez makes it clear that border rules follow the migrant even as they successfully cross physical barriers.

The dialectic between the landscape of dreams and the world of social realities is emphasized by the title of the film and in a sequence a few minutes into the film. From very early on we are offered cues that signal the constant erosion of the promise that migration seems to offer. The literal translation of *La Jaula de Oro*—*The Golden Cage*, for instance, is a comment on what awaits the migrant on the other side of the border. Most Spanish-speaking border crossers are probably aware of the famous corrido of the same name, written by Enrique Franco and made famous by the Norteño band Los Tigres del Norte in an album of the same title.[19] The English translation of the film title—*The Golden Dream*—on the

---

[17] Other examples of the Central American migrant film include the classic *El Norte* (1983) and, more recently, *Which Way Home* (2009), *Sin Señas Particulares* (2020), translated as *Identifying Features*, and *Amaraica* (2020).

[18] See Cary Joji Fukunaga's *Sin Nombre* (2009), where the "blameless" teenage girl, Sayra, makes it safely to the United States, unlike her compatriot, former gang member, Casper, who fails in his attempt to do so. For a useful analysis of Hollywood's representations of the border, see Chris Vognar's "When American Filmmakers Try to Cross the Border."

[19] The Mexican ballad "Jaula de Oro" is a familiar song "about the despair of those Mexicans who have actually made it into the US, but find it a 'golden cage' because America accepts illegals' [*sic*] cheap labour—all the cooks and gardeners and office-cleaners—without allowing them the proper residency papers they need to rise beyond the faceless servant class. Despite this, the US is still a magnet for the poor of Latin America" (Bradshaw). Consider these lines from the song: "*De que me sirve el dinero /Si estoy como prisionero /Dentro de esta gran nación*" (What good is money to me / If I'm like a prisoner / Within this great nation). *Jaula de Oro* is the name of a famous album and song by the *norteña* group Los Tigres Del Norte.

5 DOCUMENTING THE MIGRANT JOURNEY IN AI WEIWEI'S... 159

other hand, plays on the dream of what the North represents.[20] We see the encapsulation of these dreams in a montage in a Mexican town, where the teenagers make a brief stop, but then those dreams are shattered immediately.

Let me offer an overview of this pivotal scene. Having earned a bit of money by performing a theatrical mime, the children, prompted by Juan, choose to spend some of it donning costumes and posing for photographs in front of manufactured backgrounds. Looking at one of the sample photographs, Sara says "*estaba en mis sueños de estas manera*" (I appeared in my dreams this way). She then poses with Samuel holding a Guatemalan flag, against a background of the statue of liberty and the American flag (one wonders how many others have taken this same photograph on their journey to the North). Another photograph frames Juan pretending to be astride a horse, wearing a "cowboy" outfit, pointing a gun at the camera. His friends call out "Shane," recalling the classic Hollywood Western hero. Chauk, meanwhile, poses against a snow-covered mountain landscape in a Native head dress. This snow-filled landscape echoes a recurring motif in the film, the image of falling snow, which for Chauk represents the promised land. Yet, these celebratory simulacra of American life are quickly followed by the intrusion of reality. As the children rest in the hot afternoon sun, the police arrive, assaulting them and pushing them against the wall. When they are asked where they are from, Juan replies, Sueños de Oro (a village in Tabasco). The irony of the town name is obvious since it echoes the texture of their dreams in the previous scene. Their answer, however, is met with mocking ridicule. The police steal all their possessions, including their shoes, lock them in a prison van, take them to a detention center from where they (including the Mexican citizen, Chauk) are summarily deported to Guatemala. As they plan their return to Mexico, Samuel decides to remain behind.

I have briefly highlighted this scene to emphasize the narrative style of the film—one that emphasizes, in my view, the frequency and the jarring

---

[20] For a nuanced reading of the contradictions of the translations of the title (specifically in English and Italian-*La Gabbia Dorrata*), see Richard Curry's nuanced note (65). Quemada-Díez also comments on the inadequacies of the translated English title: "The direct and literal translation of the title in English does not mean much and I don't like it. In Spanish, for Mexicans and Central-Americans, 'La jaula de oro' is a metaphor of the US, a prison that you enter because you look for gold, money you need. It represents this paradox and the trap the US has become for many" (Valentine).

160 K. CHOWDHURY

abruptness of border violence. I will focus on four exemplary scenes in order to convey the effectiveness of this storytelling technique, one that relies on generating an unsettling dialectic between fiction and reality, exploring, at the same time, the limitations of representation that are highlighted by these scenes. However, before analyzing these scenes, it is necessary to provide a glimpse into Quemada-Díez's cinematic vision and storytelling methods, both of which offer an insight into his attempt to represent the violence of the border experience.

Although the film does not bear the stamp of Ai's eclectic cinematic style in *Human Flow*, Quemada-Díez, by his own account, is working within a tradition inspired by auteur filmmakers such as Ken Loach.[21] The film is a fictional drama that presents the journey of four adolescents from Guatemala and Mexico to the United States, but their stories are a conglomeration of hundreds of testimonies gathered from actual migrants by Quemada-Díez. The director, born in Spain, but now a citizen of Mexico, during a trip to Mazatlán, began to encounter the many migrants who travel through that region to the North.[22] In his description of the origins of this film, he explains that "through the years, I gathered over 600 testimonies from women, children and men. I was hanging out—well, going to shelters in the border, shelters along the journey in Mexico, also in the communities in Guatemala. And also I went to prisons and shelters for kids here in the United States" (Goodman, "Extended Interview"). What began as chance meetings with migrants mushroomed into a six-year search during which time Quemada-Díez created "what he calls a 'collective testimony', a narrative compiled from the shared experience of those

---

[21] According to the *Guardian*, Quemada-Díez began his film career as a clapper loader to Ken Loach on the set of his Spanish civil war film *Land and Freedom*. Quemada-Díez then became an assistant camera operator and "protégé" of Loach's while working on two more films together. He credits Loach not only with inspiring his technical approach to filming but also for his goal of making impactful films that address reality.

[22] Unlike all the artists and creators whose work I discuss in this book, Diego Quemada-Díez is a migrant who made a migrant journey in the opposite direction, that is, from the North to the Global South. Born during Franco's rule in Spain, he grew up hearing the many stories of his mother's visits to Central America and Mexico. He recounts: "[she] travelled a lot to Guatemala and Mexico in the late 70s and 80s. She visited missionary friends, followers of the Liberation Theology, many of whom were killed by the CIA or paramilitaries. She would come back from those trips and tell me stories of occupation, of massacres, of the beauty of indigenous cultures. I used to cry and feel their suffering. I wished I had made those trips, and maybe that's why I live now in Latin America and have become a Mexican national" (Valentine).

5 DOCUMENTING THE MIGRANT JOURNEY IN AI WEIWEI'S... 161

who were riding the roofs of the trains … They were often young and alone,' he explains, "taking enormous risks as they travelled across central America and towards the US border … I just felt that they were heroes … Most of those I interviewed would say to me, 'OK, I may die on this journey, but I would rather die trying than die where I come from.' They would travel with all they had in a small backpack or even a plastic bag, but it's a journey that can take you 40 to 60 days and you really don't know what you'll encounter. You may get deported, you may get assaulted, you may have no food, you may have no money because everybody takes your money, they steal your shoes" (Bradshaw). Thus, though the film script is written by the director and Gibrán Portela and Lucía Carreras, the film is a tribute to the journey of specific individuals and a glimpse at the trauma and the hopes of millions of others. "Everything that happens in the film," Quemada-Díez explains, "someone either told me about it, it happened to me or I saw it happen to someone else" (Bradshaw).

Unlike Ai, who is an integral part of the narrative, Quemada-Díez is absent from the film and the stories of the migrants take center stage. Let us consider the significance of this realistic mode of fiction filmmaking employed by the director and the ways in which this attention to veracity enhances the film's interrogation of border rules. First, however, a note on the casting strategy used to choose the non-professional actors is necessary, as this process is an integral element of the realistic mode used by the filmmaker. The three main Guatemalan characters, children who lived in the slums, were picked with the help of a local group. Over 3000 children auditioned for the role and many of them were artists themselves—street theater performers, graffiti and mural creators, and singers and musicians. The non-Spanish speaking Tzotzil character, Chauk, similarly, was found with the help of an organization in Chiapas. Here, too, the production crew auditioned 3000 Tzotzil Maya children and Rodolfo Domínguez "was discovered during castings held in a variety of remote villages scattered throughout the mountains of Chiapas" ("Director's Statement").

The many migrants who appear in the film were also chosen by an advance team that picked them before the main production crew arrived at the location. Even the train used in the film was hired by the production company. As Quemada-Díez puts it, the "train was under our control, although it is the same train the migrants ride, and there are real migrants on it. We hired all migrants as extras and gave them a salary, food, water and a safe train to travel northbound. It made it all much more efficient and safe" (Valentine). As a final preparation for shooting, the director then

162 K. CHOWDHURY

organized a month-long workshop for the children, and hired renowned acting coach, Fátima Toledo, who "replicated the acting workshop approach she applied to great effect with illiterate or semi-literate street children in the Brazilian films *Cidade de Deus/City of God* (Meirelles and Lund 2002) and *Pixote: A Lei do Mais Fraco/Pixote* (Babenco 1981) (Goodman "Extended Interview").

Quemada-Díez's attention to pre-production details is reflected both in the form and in the content of the film. His goal is clear, which is to offer a "voice to the oppressed; making films that tell stories with a clear, well-articulated but not preachy political view" (Valentine). He supports this political message by using filming methods that often directly contrast with Ai's cinematic style: by "placing the camera where a human being would be, at eye level—no dollies, no cranes; simplicity of form; filming in chronological order; working with real people from real locations; not letting the actors know the story; using the camera as an observer of events as close to life as possible; making films that are very close to life" (Valentine).[23] The idea of shooting in chronological order is also a Loachian technique. According to Quemada-Díez, "There's the idea of shooting in continuity; that the actors don't know what's coming next and you create a context for them to discover their motives without them really ever knowing. You create an experience that they feel is real, then all you have to do is film it" (McInnes).

Amplifying the docudrama elements of the film, Quemada-Díez explains that he "shot *The Golden Dream* on super16 mm (a classic BBC documentary format) with non-actors, making the journey with real migrants in real trains, so the film and acting develops organically, with a well-structured dramatic narrative, but rewriting the dialogues with the actors as I read them the scenes five minutes before filming. I tried to take the best from documentary and the best from fiction" (Valentine). Veronique Pugibet clarifies how this combination of fiction and documentary works more specifically in the film:

[T]he movie has the characteristics of fiction since it is based on a preliminary script, a pillar of the film narration. Plus, the director, inspired in the

---

[23] In an interview with the director, Peter McInnes notes: "The camera is always at the level of the human eye, he's obsessed with that. He never puts the camera where there would not be a human being. Literally there is always a human point of view: no cranes, no helicopter, no Steadicam, no dollies, no devices" (McInnes).

5 DOCUMENTING THE MIGRANT JOURNEY IN AI WEIWEI'S... 163

previously observed reality, proposed "his" interpretation of it via the interpretation of the protagonists he went guiding. Finally, the linear structure depicts step by step the phases of the trip like in a documentary. The film portrays an authentic, natural scenery: the landfills where the waste pickers of Guatemala City work, the factory in the United States. In this *cinéma vérité* shoulder mounted camera filming is often used which is suitable for the emergence of situations, providing for shots with long focuses in order to follow the characters. Plus, the Super 16 format reminds us of classic documentaries and reinforces the truthful aspect and reality. (23)

The use of the shoulder mounted camera is highlighted in the opening few minutes of the film, which is the first scene I want to discuss. In the very first shot, we see Juan walking with purpose through the alleys of an urban slum. He walks toward the camera and then away from it. As he strides across the narrow alleys, the shoulder mounted camera presents us with images that capture the world around him: armed soldiers, children playing with guns, a woman and a child, stray dogs. He reaches his room, one made of corrugated iron and cardboard. He sits on a bed, takes out his rucksack, and then sews some dollar bills on to the inside seam of his jeans. Putting on the backpack, he departs, walking rapidly through the same alley ways. Sara, meanwhile, has entered a public toilet where she cuts her hair, binds her breasts, tucks her hair under a baseball cap, and swallows an oral contraceptive pill. The third child, Samuel, who appears to be the youngest, is shown scavenging at the city dump, along with many others. We see Juan approaching him. They look at each other soundlessly and then leave together. We then we glimpse the city in a series of images.

Maria Delgado describes the sparse but effective way in which Quemada-Díez captures the city that the three children leave behind:

> The opening scene plainly demonstrates the urban poverty these teenagers are seeking to leave behind. Soldiers march with intent through the narrow graffiti-marked streets, where fragile homes are barely protected by thin slivers of corrugated aluminium and cardboard walls; locals look out forlornly from doorways or scavenge in the massive wastelands where trash is piled high. The noises of police sirens, barking dogs and crying children fuse to create a grating soundscape, and two rows of black-and-white posters on a wall show the faces of what seem to be disappeared persons, their faded faces staring out as if warning of the fate that likely awaits the film's teen protagonists.

164   K. CHOWDHURY

Nowhere is this prospect of violence more strikingly portrayed than in the scene that captures Sara's transformation. Alessandro Rocco describes the startling and unsettling intimacy conveyed in this moment: "*La cercanía y la intimidad de la mirada fílmica son inseparables de la violencia potencial que se evoca: la necesidad de la joven de negar su identidad femenina y de tomar precauciones ante el riesgo concreto de ser violada*" (Rocco 133).[24] In a seven-minute sequence, one without any dialogue, Quemada-Díez has provided us the context for their journey and made us aware that these are children who are preparing to embark on a dangerous crossing, a voyage whose prospective dangers are amplified when we see Sara's transformation and her awareness that she may well be raped during this journey. What makes this sequence particularly effective is the lack of dialog. The first words are spoken seven minutes into the film when the children are crossing the river (significantly, one of the children asks the boatman ferrying them, "which way is north?"). All that needs to be said is offered in a montage of the spaces occupied by the children in Guatemala City. There are no farewells to family members or words exchanged among the three.

The dangers which await Sara come to light in their most brutal form in the second scene I want to examine. In the middle of the film, the train is held up by robbers who line up all the passengers, take their meager possessions, and then separate the women from the men. The women are all piled into a truck, and as the robbers scrutinize the remaining passengers, one of them sees through Sara's disguise, strips off her cap, violently jerks up her T-shirt, exposing her breasts, declaring "this one is a virgin." As she is thrown into a car, she desperately calls out to Juan and Chauk. They rush to help her but are struck down with brutal ease. The scene ends with the car driving away, as the injured boys lie unconscious on the ground. The opening scene had prepared us for this very moment, but the viewer is still taken unaware, never imagining that one of the key figures—and one could argue that until this point Sara was the one who kept the group together, providing the emotional and pragmatic glue for the trio—would just disappear from the screen. Indeed, this scene is followed by moments of silence as Chauk helps Juan recover from his wounds. As they sit together, in a beaten-up rail carriage, they realize there is nothing they can do. The only words are uttered by Juan, an admission of his feeling of

---

[24] "The closeness and intimacy of the filmic gaze are inseparable from the potential violence that is evoked: the young woman's need to deny her feminine identity and to take precautions against the concrete risk of being raped" (Rocco).

helplessness: "I did not even see the direction they took her." Though devastated and defeated, they recognize the reality of the moment and decide to continue their voyage. Arguably, the literal disappearance of Sara from the film into sex trafficking and possible death leave a rupture from which the characters and the audience never recover. There is no Ai to intervene and guide our feeling of loss and despair. Sara, though a fictional character, experiences what the many testimonies have made clear to Quemada-Díez.[25]

Rocco comments on this moment of rupture as symptomatic of the film's ability to unsettle the audience:

> Además, eliminando a la protagonista de la trama, el film no solo rompe el modelo narrativo que se había impuesto de manera estable, sino que parecería no responder ya a ningún paradigma o criterio de construcción narrativa, sino a la reproducción de la realidad tal como es. Se da así un salto cualitativo relevante en la dimensión estética del film, ya que ahora ficción y discurso narrativo parecen coincidir con la representación directa y sin mediaciones de lo real. (Rocco 135)[26]

Although I concur with Rosso that Sara's abduction marks a break with the supposed rules of "narrative construction," making, what is in effect, a "qualitative leap … in the aesthetic dimension of the film," as I have argued, we have been prepared for this moment in the very first minutes of the film. Moreover, I would dispute the fact that the film "no longer" responds to any paradigm or narrative construction.

---

[25] Quemada-Díez recalls one testimony: "another woman told me, you know, 'I will take the birth control pill, because we know we're going to get raped, or we know we're going to have to have sexual relationships with immigration officers or different people on the way in order to—as a passport.' So the girl at the beginning of the film gets dressed as a boy, cuts her hair and takes the pill. So it's like she's getting ready for—in a way, for this journey that she already knows what's going to be" (Goodman "Extended"). See also Jude Joffe-Block's "Women Crossing the U.S. Border Face Sexual Assault with Little Protection." *PBS Newshour*, March 13, 2014.

[26] "In addition, by eliminating the protagonist from the plot, the film not only breaks the narrative model that had been established in a stable way, but also seems to no longer respond to any paradigm or criteria of narrative construction, but to the reproduction of reality as it is. There is thus a relevant qualitative leap in the aesthetic dimension of the film, since now fiction and narrative discourse seem to coincide with the direct and unmediated representation of reality" (23).

166   K. CHOWDHURY

Arguably, we are lulled into a bout of complacency as another predictable narrative thread develops after Sara's abduction, which is the friendship between Juan and Chauk, and the former's gradual emergence from the prison of his own prejudices. Once again, though, this narrative balance is shattered in a sequence that follows the moment when the two successfully cross the border. This is the third scene worth marking. Juan and Chauk have been abandoned by the group who had used them as drug mules to carry drugs across the border. We have been beguiled and lead into familiar territory because of the traditional cinematic techniques that are used as the boys cross the border. They have to wade through water and evade the border patrols. As they cross over, the moving search lights and the music create a feeling of tension. Then, as they arrive at their rendezvous, the boys are not offered a ride out of the desert but are left stranded without any idea of their location. As they trudge through the scorching desert sun, despite the apparent dangers that are constantly present, we enjoy a sense of relief since, at least, the boys have crossed over. As we see them traverse the desert landscape, suddenly, a single shot rings out. Chauk collapses on the desert floor, the victim of a vigilante's bullet. We briefly glimpse a sniper firing a rifle, equipped with a silencer and a telescopic sight. Juan checks on his friend and then runs away as we hear a series of shots following him. Yet, again, our equanimity has been shattered by the summary dismissal of a character from the screen.[27]

The final scene I want to discuss shows the remaining migrant, Juan, in his promised land, where, as he had put it earlier in the film "everything is much better." As this point, even the most optimistic viewer is not surprised to see that the person who had the greatest hope for a better life (who early in the film had pronounced, "but up north everything is much better"), on the other side of the border, has met with disappointment. The film concludes with a brief montage of his life in a meatpacking plant, where he is on the lowest rung of laborers, cleaning up the offal, the blood, and the waste at the end of every shift. As the boy awaits his turn to clean up the floor, we can only conclude that the result of all the trauma, the effort, and the sheer will to cross a border is so that one's labor can be exploited by those who care as little for his existence as did the gangs and the migra along the way. His living labor, like the millions before him, is

---

[27] Jonás Cuarón's *Desierto* (2015) captures this all-too-common occurrence at the US–Mexico border. Vigilante violence at the border has a long history, of course. See Ray Ybarra and Tamaryn Nelson's documentary *Rights on the Line: Vigilantes at the Border* (2006).

5 DOCUMENTING THE MIGRANT JOURNEY IN AI WEIWEI'S... 167

fungible. It is no surprise that Juan ends up in one of the most exploitative and dangerous positions available to undocumented workers in the country.[28]

He has come a full circle from a country made uninhabitable largely because of the militaristic regimes funded by the United States to the imperial center itself. His journey marks the path of this imperial network, whether it is the scenes of poverty in Guatemala City, the Mexican military following the bidding of the United States by harassing and assaulting the migrants, the maquiladora border town of Mexicali, where low-wage workers produce goods for the US market, or the killing floors of a meat-packing plant. Across the three countries traveled by the migrants, there is little "gold" in sight. Cages, on the other hand, abound. *La Jaula de Oro* makes it clear that both these metaphors coexist in the imagination of the children. As Oscar Moralde puts it, "the flowing global network of migration is beset by political strife, cultural conflict, and economic exploitation, but on a very real level it is driven by the hope and dream that something better lies on the other side" (239).

There is little doubt, then, that Quemada-Díez gets his main point across at the end of the film, which he states explicitly in one of his interviews: "I wanted to talk about how it doesn't make any sense to do this policy of militarization of the borders and the criminalization of migrants and the incarceration of migrants, which in the United States is around half a million people, whose only crime was to cross a border" (Goodman "Extended"). However, as in my discussion of *Human Flow*, it is necessary to pause and contemplate, despite the director's fealty to his political message, what may be the shortcomings and representational inadequacies of his depiction of the violence of border rules. I will focus on three points and consider how they might have a bearing on the director's attempts to throw light on the dehumanization caused by border rules.

Unlike *Human Flow*, which juxtaposes individual stories in relation to a vast global landscape of "human" movement and change, the focus in *La*

---

[28] The brutalizing conditions at meatpacking plants were further emphasized during the pandemic when these "plants were connected to 6% to 8% of all early-pandemic Covid cases and 3% to 4% of all early-pandemic Covid deaths. And year after year, meatpacking workers are among the most likely to suffer an injury where a body part is amputated. About half of the injuries involve workers losing fingers .... In 2017, the top four meatpacking companies had a combined annual revenue of $207bn. [In 2021], the biggest of those companies, Cargill, brought in *record profits*, making $4.3bn in the first nine months of this fiscal year" (Chang et al).

Jaula de Oro is on three adolescents. Their experiences naturally intersect with the other migrants with whom they take their journey, but this group of people constitutes an anonymous mass throughout the duration of the film. They are not distinguished or individualized in any way. None of the adolescents strike up a friendship or even a sustained conversation with any of the other migrants, and we do not even know the names or histories of any of the other travelers. The three children appear to exist in a purely self-enclosed space. The dynamic between them and the shifting textures of their emotional relationships take precedence over any shared collective experience. Juan's antagonism with Chauk, the "love" triangle formed by the three adolescents, Juan's subsequent recognition of Chauk's humanity, replicate, in many ways, the individualistic thrust of mainstream Hollywood narratives. Aside from a few close-ups of migrants who sit on the roof of the train, we rarely see other individuals in close-ups. Indeed, the few that are thrust into our consciousness are the faces of those who terrorize the children. "Vitamina," the gangster who imprisons Juan and Chauk, for instance, gains more screen time than any other migrant. The only other conversation of note with another character is when Juan is duped by a young boy who promises the migrants a job but then leads them into the hands of a kidnapper. While Quemada-Díez may rightly claim that his film, particularly by focusing on the journey of three children, humanizes the abstraction of a migrant's journey, the narrative risks replicating this abstraction by reinforcing the already erased humanity of many others.[29]

Eliciting the sympathy of the viewers primarily for the three main characters also comes with its own shortfalls. By including Chauk, a Tzotzil speaking Mexican in the narrative, Quemada-Díez makes a conscious effort to show the racism that exists within "ladino" identity. Juan, whose light skin distinguishes him from Chauk sets himself up as superior to the others, especially to Chauk, and as the leader of the group. Alicia Ivonne Estrada explains that "*ladino* identity, as it is understood in Guatemala [is the] negation of indigeneity." Estrada cites anthropologist Charles Hale, who expands on this racial text: "people who identify as ladino have

---

[29] I might add, though, that every single migrant who participated in the film is mentioned by name in the film's credits; in addition, the filmmakers express their gratitude for their participation: "*Agradecemos a los mas de 600 migrantes en su ruta a USA que participaron en la fimacion de la pelicula.*" ("We thank the more than 600 migrants on their way to the USA who participated in the making of the film.")

5 DOCUMENTING THE MIGRANT JOURNEY IN AI WEIWEI'S... 169

generally absorbed an ideology of racial superiority in relations to Indians: viewing themselves as closer to an ideal of progress, decency, and all things modern, in contrast to Indians, who are regrettably and almost irredeemably backward" (191). Throughout the narrative, Quemada-Díez positions Chauk as materially opposed to this ideal of progress, demonstrating the poverty of Juan's worldview, which is most closely aligned to Western notions of "all things modern." The director elaborates on this position in an interview with *cinemaerrante*: "The indigenous character represents the spiritual realm to which we all have the potential to access. He represents the teacher, the person who can help us connect with our most evolved part. Chauk's character is the soul while Juan's is the mind, individualism, materialism." And, of course, this opposition mirrors a larger conflict that underwrites Quemada-Díez's critique of the capitalist world view that determines much of the border violence that is depicted in the film, and to his credit, the director sees the alignment between the rapacity of the consumerist model and its connections to racial ideologies. "Behind the migration issue," as he puts it, "there is an issue of the fight for the territory and its resources. The film tells the story of the clash between an indigenous—and its cosmogony—and a mixed-race Guatemalan who believes in the American consumerist model" (Valentine).[30] Juan's racism is further mirrored by the Mexican authority figures, who treat Chauk with contempt and derision.

There are many instances of Chauk's supposed attachment to the "spiritual realm" and to the natural world.[31] His first appearance is when he emerges out of the jungle. He has a knowledge of the world around him and is at ease with the rhythms of the natural world. He knows where

---

[30] Quemada-Díez elaborates on these cultural oppositions: "He is transformed into someone different. He realizes that individualism is an illusion; a lie told by society, alone we can do nothing. Another interesting thing about this structure of opposing worlds is that Juan represents the rational, the mind, and Chauk, the heart, the feeling. Over the course of their journey, Juan learns to feel. I wanted people to consider the content of the Tzotzil greeting, 'K'uxi elan avo'onton?' (How is your heart?), to communicate on a more emotional level than just a mental process. I think that inside all of us there is one part that is more like Juan and another that is like Chauk" ("Director's Statement").

[31] The director provides an important context for the character: "The name Chauk comes from my Mayan friend Chak. He taught me their cosmogony; a different way of seeing things. He gave me the book "Canek" by Emilio Abreu Gómez, a poetic gem that has both idealism and romanticism and yet filled with realism. I asked myself, 'How can I try to capture and communicate the wisdom of his people, so connected to the land, with the spiritual and poetic side of existence?'" ("Director's Statement")

170   K. CHOWDHURY

to collect drinking water from a stream; he knows how to kill a rooster with merciful ease; and he can heal wounds using natural remedies. His dreamscape of snow falling from the sky, a metaphor for the promise that lies on the other side, appears throughout the film (three times in the first hour) and is the final image of the film, establishing the point that Chauk is not forgotten. There is little doubt that if Sara carries the emotional weight of the film, Chauk is its spiritual center. However, this form of representation comes at a cost, which, in end, depersonalizes Chauk and makes him a vehicle for abstract ideas rather than a fully formed human being. Alicia Ivonne Estrada argues that *La Jaula de Oro*, like its famous predecessor, *El Norte* (1984), are "well-intentioned, because they situate the Maya immigrant experience as central, [but] they continue to employ a *ladino indeginista* framework that is grounded on varied articulations of internalized colonial lenses" (178). She makes a compelling case for reading Chauk's character as embodying stereotypical features of indigeneity, one defined by the male, ladino gaze. Indeed, casting him as the mostly silent, spiritual being, one who becomes an agent for Juan's transformation is a troublingly recurrent trope in mainstream cinema. Even if the last shot of the falling snow emphasizes that he is not forgotten, the truth is that his dream died in the arid desert; the distinctiveness of his oneiric landscape has now become part of Juan's reality.

A final note of caution regarding the intersection of aesthetics and the representation of migrants' lives needs to be made, much as I attempted to formulate in the case of *Human Flow*. *La Jaula de Oro* like *Human Flow* captures scenes of immense beauty, and the ugliness of human behavior is frequently juxtaposed against close-ups in soft lighting or in silhouettes. The train itself is often captured moving across verdant countryside or passing through mountainous landscapes. One of the most beautiful moment in the film occurs immediately after the two boys have been released by the kidnappers. We see the faces of the protagonists and other individuals sitting on top of the train as it goes through some beautiful mountainous countryside. Gradually, as the train travels northward, the greenery is replaced by a desert landscape. The final long shot of this scene is of the entire train set against a golden sunset. The song "La caña brava," by Patricio Hidalgo sung by Son del Centro with its immensely powerful lyrics forms the soundtrack for this three-minute-long sequence.[32]

---

[32] "*Hermano si te has perdido / cruzando por la frontera / siembra valor con tus pasos / pa' cruzar cuando yo quiera / Caña dulce, caña brava / no moriré en tierra extraña / esta tierra / ahora es de todos / por los muchos que se han muerto / cruzando por la montaña.*"

5 DOCUMENTING THE MIGRANT JOURNEY IN AI WEIWEI'S... 171

It goes without saying that there is no special burden that films that depict the traumatic experiences of migrants' journeys across treacherous landscapes and borders must carry in terms of adhering to an aesthetics of the sparse and the "grittily" real. The spectacular effects of the drone shots over the sea or the desert in *Human Flow* or the silhouettes of migrants framed in soft lighting in *La Jaula de Oro* are not in themselves a problem; after all, both directors are justified in capturing moments of beauty that exist even in the everyday moments of terror. Perhaps the juxtaposition of this natural beauty against the fear experienced by migrants even has a salutary purpose, emphasizing their vulnerability in the midst of what can be termed the conventionally "beautiful." What, however, needs to be kept in mind is that these representations are not viewed in a vacuum; instead, they are reproduced and circulated within a global landscape regulated by capital's reach. Cultural products, be they films, literary texts, or music videos operate in a representational landscape where the rituals of viewing poverty, violence, or even beauty are controlled by a few companies. Thus a "scene" watched through the entertainment apparatus regulated by Netflix or Amazon has a valence that is accompanied by capital's scope and dominance. It is thus necessary for us to consider the following questions: Who consumes the image? What are the expectations of the viewers as they consume these images? Where and in what form is the image circulated? What "meanings" are reproduced by these images in the process of circulation? Who profits from such reproductions? Or, in the context of these two specific films, how might a film such as *La Jaula de Oro* with its limited audience, its little-known director, and its minimal distribution capabilities fare against a film such as *Human Flow*, which has the backing of Amazon Studios and is available free for Prime members? Does the sheer scope and the massive multi continental production value of *Human Flow*, and its high-profile creator influence the conversation on borders and the refugee "crisis" in a way that is impossible for a smaller production company to emulate?[33] A consideration of such questions must

---

"Brother if you get lost /crossing the border / sow value with your steps / to cross when I want / Sweet cane, wild cane / I will not die in a strange land / this land now belongs to everyone / for the many who have died / crossing the mountain."

[33] Having garnered 14 overall nominations, "the film received the awards for best picture, best original script, best first work, best actor, best new actor, best editing, best cinematography, best sound, and best musical score" (Curry 48). Although feted at film festivals and the winner of nine Arieles awards (bestowed by the Mexican Academy of Cinematographic Arts and Sciences), the film has found it difficult to acquire an audience in the United States because of distribution and funding restrictions. For a comprehensive account of the various funding sources for the film and the range of its distribution outlets, see Shaw (287).

172   K. CHOWDHURY

accompany any evaluation of aesthetics rather than a simple gesture of assent or disapproval about a filmmaker's so-called aesthetic choices.

Another factor that must be taken into account in our commentary on these films is the artist's oppositional engagement with the immediacy of the migrant "crisis." In the case of *La Jaula de Oro*, much like the timing of *Human Flow*, Quemada-Díez's research began at a time of an increasing militarization of the border and a rise in deportations by the Obama administration. Focusing on the plight on the four children was particularly appropriate since "Between October 2013 and June 2014 ... the United States had detained some fifty-two thousand undocumented and unaccompanied Central American adolescents at the border with Mexico" (Curry 52). In addition, "political pressure and financial aid from the US. Deportations" rose "exponentially since summer 2014 when Barack Obama declared the surge in Central American child migrants a humanitarian crisis. Campaigners [then said] that Mexico migration officials [were] running a secret quota system to increase the number of expulsions" (Lakhani "Mexico Tortures Migrants"). The indigenous population of Mexico and Central America, as always, bore the brunt of this harassment. We see the results of this practice played out when Chauk is summarily deported from his own country.[34]

Unlike Ai who appears to be less interested in the root causes of the migrant "crisis" and more invested in having the West recognize its moral obligations to the migrants, Quemada-Díez is explicit about both the goals of his film and the structural problems that underwrite this crisis:

> The 'civilized' world responds by putting up walls, imprisoning and criminalizing immigrants, militarizing borders. With my film I wanted to bring up the idea that the solution is not repressing immigrants but it involves the generation of circumstances that do not force people to migrate. If the rules

[34] In a recent ruling, the Supreme Court decided: "Mexican immigration agents can no longer conduct stop and search operations on buses and highways after the country's supreme court ruled that such checks are racist, discriminatory and therefore unconstitutional. The landmark ruling, handed down in *Mexico* City on Wednesday, found in favour of three young Indigenous Mexicans who were detained and abused by immigration (INM) officials in 2015 during a US-backed crackdown. The siblings—aged 15 to 24—were on a bus of seasonal farmhands in Querétaro, central *Mexico*, when apprehended by agents who targeted them because of their physical features, clothes and limited Spanish. The agents accused them of being undocumented immigrants from neighbouring Guatemala, but they were Indigenous Tzeltal Mayans from the state of Chiapas in southern Mexico, where 25% of the population speak an Indigenous language" (Lakhani).

of international trade are controlled by the US and Europe—condemning the South to import goods and never develop its own domestic production, its stability and internal peace and social policies—people will flee. ('La Jaula')

Indeed, the director is committed to showing us the border in all its specific materiality when Juan and Chauk reach the US–Mexico border, but the border is also encountered every step of the way along their journey, for, as I have maintained throughout this book, the apparatus of the border is far reaching. Even the train, *La Bestia*, on which so much of the film is shot functions as a metaphor for the exploitative circuits that the migrants must travel.[35] The train enables their journey, but it is also the instrument of their exploitation, "a fundamental part of the assembly line in an industrial structure; it carries all of the raw materials needed to feed the great machine and, in the most dehumanizing way possible, bringing cheap and utterly disposable labor. Migrants live in slave-like conditions within a system that proclaims to champion democracy and liberty" ("La Jaula de Oro"). Not only do the children encounter agents of the state and extra-state elements who prey on them during the entire journey, but they are also unaware of the violence that will accompany them even if they are to cross over. Juan, the only one who reaches the other side, who until the final crossing still believes that "I think everything we will see over there will be really awesome. Everything will be fine, and we will get to where we want" is left alone at the end of film with nothing but the prospect of backbreaking labor ahead of him.

Unquestionably, both films interrogate and condemn the dehumanization of migrant lives, shining a special light on the brutality of the border rules that make their journeys even more treacherous. What Deborah Shaw has said about *La Jaula de Oro* could also be a statement about *Human Flow*: Films, such as *La Jaula de Oro*, she argues, that "insert themselves into a human rights framework, outline structural and social oppression and human rights abuses all the while giving characters subjectivity and agency (283). There is little doubt that these films urge us to rethink the rationale of the borders that divide us, and both filmmakers are

---

[35] Óscar Martínez's *La Bestia* is one of the most striking accounts of migrants' journeys across Mexico. The book's original title *Los Migrantes que No Importan* (The Migrants Who Don't Matter) captures the true spirit of the book, an indictment of the violent systems that treat human beings as surplus, disposable labor.

174   K. CHOWDHURY

animated by a vision of a borderless world. Ai would not disagree with Quemada-Díez's artistic and political manifesto:

> We made this adventure in the hope of deconstructing those conventions that imprison us so we can reinvent our own reality. My dream is that these boundaries that separate us dissolve, allowing us to board another train. One whose destination doesn't matter, a train whose passengers all know our existence is interconnected, a train whose obstacles inspire us to celebrate our existence with respect and conscience that transcends nationalities, races, classes and beliefs. ("La Jaula de Oro")

However, what sets the two films apart is that *Human Flow* is embedded in the problematic circuits of capital and the politics of a Western centric human rights framework. It thus cannot overcome the world of borders, nations, and the cycle of war and exploitation, and it cannot open up the possibility of another economic or social paradigm outside the logic of liberal capitalism that will abolish these categories, to allow people to "board another train," so to speak. As I have argued throughout the book, borders rules are partially in place to enable resource extraction, to exploit labor, and to boost military state apparatuses. If these remain in place, the violence that forces migrants to flee will continue to exist. Abolition, then, is the only solution.

Works Cited

Ai Weiwei. "Ai Weiwei: 'I'm like a high-end refugee,'" interviewed by Aimee Dawson. *The Art Newspaper*, 27 Mar. 2018, https://www.theartnewspaper. com/interview/ai-weiwei-i-m-like-a-high-end-refugee.

Ai Weiwei—Drifting. Directed by Eva Mehl and Bettina Kolb, Deutsche Welle, 2018.

Ai Weiwei. *S.A.C.R.E.D.* 2013, Lisson Gallery, Sant'Anonin Church, Venice.

Ai Weiwei. *Sunflower Seeds.* 2010, Tate Modern, London.

Ai Weiwei, et al. *Hansel and Gretel.* 2017, Park Avenue Armory, New York.

Amaraica. Directed by Tim Sparks, Sparkstar, 2020.

Benjamin, Walter. *Illuminations.* Translated by Harry Zohn, Schocken, 1969.

Biddle, Sam. "Amazon Co-Owns Deportation Airline Implicated in Alleged Torture of Immigrants." *The Intercept,* 17 Feb. 2022, https://theintercept. com/2022/02/17/amazon-ice-deportation-flights-omni/.

Blomfield, Isobel. "Human Flow." *Human Rights Defender*, vol. 27, no. 2, October 2018, pp. 34–2. HeinOnline.

5 DOCUMENTING THE MIGRANT JOURNEY IN AI WEIWEI'S... 175

Bradshaw, Peter. "Cannes 2013: The Golden Dream—Review." *The Guardian*, 23 May 2013, https://www.theguardian.com/film/2013/may/23/golden-cage-jaula-de-oro-review.

Chang, Alvin, et al. "The pandemic exposed the human cost of the meatpacking industry's power: 'It's enormously frightening.'" *The Guardian*, 16 Nov. 2021, https://www.theguardian.com/environment/2021/nov/16/meatpacking-industry-covid-outbreaks-workers.

"Chinese artist Ai Weiwei held for 'economic crimes.'" *BBC*, 7 Apr. 2011, https://www.bbc.com/news/world-asia-pacific-12994785.

Curry, Richard. "The Migration Genre in *La jaula de oro*: Voids and Virtues." *Studies in Latin American Popular Culture*, vol. 36, 2018, pp. 47–68.

Dalembert, Jean-Louis. *The Mediterranean Wall: A Novel*. Translated by Marjolijn de Jager. Schaffner Press, 2021.

Desierto. Directed by Jonás Cuarón, Esperanto Kino, 2016.

Rights on the Line: Vigilantes at the Border. Directed by Ray Ybarra and Tamaryn Nelson, Witness, 2006.

Dargis, Manohla. "Watching a Crisis, With No Calm in Sight: The artist Ai Weiwei travels to 23 countries to track refugees." *New York Times*, 13 Oct. 2017, pp. 1. *ProQuest*, https://login.ezproxy.stthomas.edu/login?url=https://www.proquest.com/historical-newspapers/watching-crisis-with-no-calm-sight/docview/2463554311/se-2?accountid=14756.

Delgado, Maria. "The Golden Dream." *Sight & Sound*, vol. 24, no. 7, July 2014, pp. 64–65.

European Union, *On Standards for the Qualification of Third Country Nationals or Stateless Persons as Beneficiaries of International Protection, for a Uniform Status for Refugees or for Persons Eligible for Subsidiary Protection, and for the Content of the Protection Granted*, Article 15, 13 Dec. 2011, https://eur-lex.europa.eu/legal-content/EN/TXT/?uri=celex%3A32011L0095, accessed on 26 Mar. 2023.

El Norte. Directed by Gregory Nava, American Playhouse, 1984.

Estrada, Alicia Ivonne. "Decolonizing Maya Border Crossings in *El Norte* and *La Jaula de Oro*." *The Latin American Road Movie*, edited by Verónica Garibotto and Jorge Pérez. Palgrave Macmillan, 2016.

Fernandez, Manny. "'You Have to Pay with Your Body': The Hidden Nightmare of Sexual Violence on the Border." *New York Times*, 3 Mar. 2019, https://www.nytimes.com/2019/03/03/us/border-rapes-migrant-women.html.

Goodman, Adam. "A Long Series of Uncertainties: Trials and Tribulations along the Migrant Trail from Central America to the Unites States." *The Nation*, 3 Sept. 2014, https://www.thenation.com/article/archive/long-series-uncertainties/.

Goodman, Amy. "Extended interview with Director Diego Quemada-Diéz on 'La Jaula de Oro' and migration to the U.S." *Democracy Now*, 15 Sept. 2015, https://www.democracynow.org/2015/9/15/la_jaula_de_oro_new_feature.

Hao, Karen. "Amazon is the Invisible Backbone of ICE's Immigration Crackdown." *MIT Technology Review*, 22 Oct. 2018, https://www.technologyreview.com/2018/10/22/139639/amazon-is-the-invisible-backbone-behind-ices-immigration-crackdown/.

Human Flow. Directed by Ai Weiwei, produced by Andrew Cohen, et al., Ro*Co Films, 2017. Alexander Street, https://video.alexanderstreet.com/watch/human-flow.

"Human Flow Final Press Notes." Human Flow, http://www.humanflow.com/press-kit/.

Joffe-Block, Jude. "Women crossing the U.S. border face sexual assault with little protection." *PBS Newshour*, 31 Mar. 2014, https://www.pbs.org/newshour/nation/facing-risk-rape-migrant-women-prepare-birth-control.

La Jaula de Oro [The Golden Dream]. Directed by Diego Quemada-Díez, Animal de Luz Films, 2013.

"'La jaula de oro': interview with director Diego Quemada-Díez." *Cinemaerrante*. 29 Jan. 2016, https://cinemaerrante.wordpress.com/2016/01/29/la-jaula-de-oro-interview-with-director-diego-quemada-diez/.

Lakhani, Nina. "Mexico's migrant checks on buses and highways ruled racist and illegal." *The Guardian*, 22 May 2022, https://www.theguardian.com/world/2022/may/22/mexico-migrant-checks-racist-illegal-supreme-court.

———. "Mexico tortures migrants—and citizens—in effort to slow Central American surge." *The Guardian*, 4 Apr. 2016, https://www.theguardian.com/world/2016/apr/04/mexico-torture-migrants-citizens-central-america.

Lakshmi, Rama. "Chinese Artist Ai Weiwei poses as a drowned Syrian refugee toddler." *The Washington Post*, 30 Jan. 2016, https://www.washingtonpost.com/news/worldviews/wp/2016/01/30/chinese-artist-ai-weiwei-poses-as-a-drowned-syrian-refugee-toddler/.

Macnab, Geoffrey. "Ai Weiwei: 'My 'Human Flow' Profits Will Go to Refugee NGOs.'" *ScreenDaily*, 2 Sept. 2017, https://www.screendaily.com/features/ai-weiwei-my-human-flow-profits-will-go-to-refugee-ngos/5121909.article.

Martinez, Oscar. *The Beast: Riding the Rails and Dodging Narcos on the Migrant Trail*. Translated by Daniela Maria Ugaz and John Washington, Verso, 2014.

McInnes, Paul. "The Golden Dream: I wanted to convey brotherhood beyond races, beyond nationalities." *The Guardian*, 20 Jun. 2014, https://www.theguardian.com/film/2014/jun/21/diego-quemada-diez-the-golden-dream.

Moralde, Oscar. "The Outsiders: Pathways of Migratory Experience in Latin American Films." *Latin American Perspectives*, vol. 41, no. 3. May 2014, pp. 237–39.

"One Third of Gaza Strip Population in Need of Psychological and Social Support." *UN News: Global Perspective Human Stories*, 4 Sept. 2022, https://news.un.org/en/story/2022/09/1125712

Parater, Lauren. "7 Videos Guaranteed to Change the Way You See Refugees." *UNHCR Innovation Service*, 26 Jun. 2015, https://www.unhcr.org/innovation/7-videos-guaranteed-to-change-the-way-you-see-refugees/.

Pugibet, Veronique. "Cine mexicano y migración: los pasos perdidos en La Jaula del oro de Quemada-Díez." Comunicación y Medios, vol. 36, 2017, pp. 20–32.

Quemada-Díez, Diego. "Director's Statement." WordPress, https://julianwhiting.files.wordpress.com/2014/10/english-filmnotes.pdf.

Rangan, Pooja. *Immediations: The Humanitarian Impulse in Documentary*. Duke University Press, 2017.

"Refugee Camp Statistics." *More or Less: BBC World Service*, 27 May 2016, https://www.bbc.co.uk/sounds/play/p03vnz88.

Rights on the Line: Vigilantes at the Border. Directed by Ray Ybarra and Tamaryn Nelson, Witness, 2006.

Rocco, Alessandro. "La Representación de la Migración de Centroamérica a Estados Unidos en el Film 'La Jaula de Oro' de Diego Quemada-Diez." *Oltreoceano- Riviste Sulle Migrazioni*, vol. 9, 2021, pp. 131-140.

Rösler, Paula. "Ai Weiwei's film 'Human Flow' on Oscar Shortlist." Deutsche Welle Inspired Minds, https://www.inspiredminds.de/en/ai-weiweis-film-human-flow-makes-oscar-shortlist/a-41713580

Russell, Catherine. "MIGRANT CINEMA: Scenes of Displacement." *Cinéaste*, vol. 43, no. 1, 2017, pp. 17–21, http://www.jstor.org/stable/26356821.

"Salah Al-Din." *European Agency for Asylum*, Jan. 2021, https://euaa.europa.eu/country-guidance-iraq-2021/salah-al-din.

Shaw, Deborah. "The right to rights and Central American/Mexican migration films: Reading *Sin nombre* (Fukunaga 2009) and *La jaula de oro/The Golden Dream* (Quemada-Díez 2013) with political theory." *Studies in Spanish & Latin American Cinemas*, vol. 18, no. 3, pp. 277–295.

Silberg, Jon. "Human Flow." *Digital Video*, vol. 25, no. 11, 2017, pp. 16–18.

Sin Nombre. Directed by Cary Joji Fukunaga, Scion Films, 2009.

Sin Señas Particulares [Identifying Features]. Directed by Fernanda Valadez, Avanti Pictures, 2020.

Son del Centro. "La Caña." Mi Jarana es Mi Fusil , Producciones Cimarrón, 2006.

Steadman, Ryan. "Ai Weiwei Receives Backlash for Mimicking Image of Drowned 3-Year-Old Refugee." *Observer*, 1 Feb. 2016, https://observer.com/2016/02/photo-of-ai-weiwei-aping-drowned-refugee-toddler-draws-praise-ire/.

Strickland, Patrick. "The U.S.-Mexico Border Has Long Been a Magnet for Far-Right Vigilantes." *Time*, 17 Feb. 2022, https://time.com/6141322/border-vigilantes-militias-us-mexico-immigrants/?utm_source=twitter&utm_

medium=social&utm_campaign=editorial&utm_term=ideas_immigration&lin
kId=152663298.

"Synopsis." *Human Flow*, http://www.humanflow.com/synopsis/.

"Syria war: UN Security Council truce vote delayed." *BBC*, 23 Feb. 2018, https://www.bbc.com/news/world-middle-east-43155105.

"Take Action." Human Flow, http://www.humanflow.com/action/.

Tassi, Rafael. "Alternativas fílmicas na imagem mais recente do olhar sobre a adolescência diaspórica em La jaula de oro." *Cinémas d'Amérique Latin*, vol. 23, 2015, https://journals.openedition.org/cinelatino/1831.

Tuckman, Jo. "Mexico's migration crackdown escalates dangers for Central Americans." *The Guardian*, 13 Oct. 2015, https://www.theguardian.com/world/2015/oct/13/mexico-central-american-migrants-journey-crackdown.

Valentine, Douglas. "A conversation with film director Diego Quemada-Díez." *Counterpunch*, 19 Dec. 2014, http://www.counterpunch.org/2014/12/19/a-conversation-with-film-director-diego-quemada-diez/.

Vognar, Chris. "When American Filmmakers Try to Cross the Border." *New York Times*, 31 Jan. 2019, https://www.nytimes.com/2019/01/31/movies/mexico-border-movies.html.

Winston, Brian. "The Tradition of the Victim in Griersonian Documentary." *The Documentary Film Reader: History, Theory, Criticism*, edited by Jonathan Kahana, pp. 763–75. Oxford University Press, 2016.

Which Way Home. Directed by Rebecca Cammisa, Documentress Films, 2009.

"'Worst Zoo in the World' Now History: Zoo Animals Brought Safely Out of Gaza." *Four Paws USA*, 24 Aug. 2016, https://www.fourpawsusa.org/campaigns-topics/topics/rapid-response-for-animals/mission-in-gaza.

Zimanyi, Eszter. "*Human Flow*: Thinking with and through Ai Weiwei's Defamiliarizing Gaze: Human Flow. Ai Weiwei, Director. Produced by Ai Weiwei, Chin-Chin Yap, and Heino Deckert, for Amazon Studios and Participant Media, USA, 2017; Color, 140 min. Available on BluRay, DVD, and Digital Streaming Platforms." *Visual Anthropology*, vol. 32, no. 3, May 2019, pp. 377–79.

CHAPTER 6

Visualizing Borders: M.I.A.'s "Borders" and Mural Art in Ciudad Juárez and El Paso

While the works of novelists and documentary and docudrama filmmakers circulate among a limited audience, other art forms have a far wider reach, offering opportunities for a potentially different discussion about oppositional art and its role in undermining the reigning logic of border rules. How might cultural texts that are viewed by millions raise different questions about representation and how might they "agitate" in complementary ways within alternative circuits of circulation? More significantly, how might "seeing" these texts both within and outside specific "national" contexts challenge ideas about bordered spaces? In this chapter, I take up these questions by considering the aesthetic reach of a music video and the politics of place that operates in the viewing of public murals.

M.I.A.'s "Borders": Pop and Politics Across the Waters

In November 2015, coinciding with the peak of migrations in the Mediterranean, the British singer Maya Arulpragasam, better known as M.I.A., launched a video for "Borders," a song from the album film project *Matahdatah*. Earlier that year, in July, she h ad released the video for "Swords," as part of *Matahdatah Scroll 01 "Broader Than a Border."* This audio-visual project, a six-minute clip, "consist[ed] of two songs, the new track 'Swords' and 'Warriors' (from 2013's *Matangi*) and an accompanying short film, directed by M.I.A., scored to both songs" (Minsker,

© The Author(s), under exclusive license to Springer Nature Switzerland AG 2023
K. Chowdhury, *Border Rules*, Politics of Citizenship and Migration, https://doi.org/10.1007/978-3-031-26216-6_6

179

"M.I.A. Releases"). She also released a video for "The New International Sound Pt. II," which featured 36,000 Chinese child fighters.[1]

Although the song and the film project were widely covered because of their timing (overlapping with a global catastrophe of hundreds of migrants dying in their attempts to cross the Mediterranean), the subjects of borders and migration were nothing new for M.I.A. Since the beginning of her career, she had been addressing topics related to nationalism, imperialism, and migration. Her very first album, *Arular* (named after her father, Arul, who was one of the founders of the Tamil resistance movement), released in 2005, dealt with issues relating to government acts of terror, independence struggles, and geopolitical inequities. Coming forth as an international artist in an age of the "War against Terror," M.I.A. positioned herself to give voice to the legitimate struggles of oppressed people, declaring "you can't separate the world into two parts like that, good and evil. America has successfully tied all these pockets of independence struggles, revolutions and extremists into one big notion of terrorism" (Ostroff). Using primarily a Roland TR-505 drum machine to beat out her tunes, M.I.A. made it evident that she had something to say that was not part of mainstream musical norms. The song "Sunshowers" from her debut album spelled out her credo:

> I'm doing my thing yo
> Quit bending all my fingo quit beating me like you're ringo
> You wanna go? you wanna win the war?
> Like P.L.O. I won't surrender. ("Sunshowers" 00:27–0:36)

Not only was the reference here to the PLO an unlikely one for a Western singer, but M.I.A.'s holding up the organization as a symbol of resistance was virtually unheard of for a "pop" singer. Lorraine Ali in a *Newsweek* feature described the artist's music in somewhat condescending terms as "equal mix house-party fun and freedom-fighter ire." M.I.A., on the other hand, expressed a more considered opinion about this "ire": "How can an artist not address politics?" she said. "The more we make it an out-of-reach subject, like it's just something for boring old men, the more we're f—ed" (qtd. in Ali).

---

[1] For more information on these releases, see "Watch MIA's audiovisual venture *Matahdatah Scroll 01 'Broader than a Border,'*" "M.I.A. Travels with Refugees in 'Borders' Video," and "M.I.A. and Surkin's Gener8ion Share 'The New International Sound Pt. II' Video."

6 VISUALIZING BORDERS: M.I.A.'S "BORDERS" AND MURAL ART IN CIUDAD... 181

This declaration of intent, forged by her own experiences as a refugee, informed M.I.A.'s musical aesthetic from the very beginning. Thus the antipathy that she expresses for borders in the video and the song of that name is not just a recent political position but a long-standing one: since the beginning of her musical career, her songs have surged with a variety of unbordered influences. Not only has her music always been a mixture of various styles (grime, dance hall, favela funk, bhangra, Tamil film music, hip hop); she has also drawn from a range of national musical traditions. In fact, since she wasn't allowed to enter the United States because of visa restrictions in 2006, her next album, *Kala* (2007—named after her mother), was recorded all over the world.[2] She traveled to India, Trinidad, and Liberia, and recorded with Aboriginal communities in Australia. Once again, she spoke for the underdogs, including the migrants who were forced to cross borders and were attempting to make a living and yet were reviled by the West, suspected of supposed terrorist sympathies and for taking the jobs of the native-born. Her runaway hit from that album "Paper Planes" begins with these lines:

> I fly like paper, get high like planes
> If you catch me at the border I got visas in my name
> If you come around here, I make 'em all day
> I get one done in a second if you wait. ("Paper Planes" 00:11–0:22)

Improvising on the charges of "illegality" made against those who seek to cross borders, she playfully taunts the anti-immigrant fearmongers. The very popular chorus "all I want to do is take your money," followed by the sound of four shots and the ringing of a cash register, mocks the stereotypes of immigrants' being violent and "taking away" the jobs of the native-born.

In between the release of *Kala* and the "Borders" video (2015), M.I.A. had achieved worldwide fame for her music and her live performances; she had been nominated for an Oscar along with A.R. Rahman for best song, "O... Saya," in the soundtrack of *Slumdog Millionaire*

---

[2] Reports on why M.I.A. was denied reentry into the United States sometimes differ, but a *Rolling Stone* retrospective on the album *Kala* states that it was due in part to the artist "match[ing] the profile of a terrorist." M.I.A. describes her treatment by the US Embassy in London thus: "Suddenly, I was this citizen of the Other World—someone completely threatening and disgusting who, you know, might blow up the Super Bowl. 'Oh no, she said the word 'P.L.O.' in a song!' So [*Kala*] became about being an outsider voice" (Rosen).

182   K. CHOWDHURY

(2008); her live performances at the Grammys (2009) and the Super Bowl (2012) had brought notoriety; and she had become a frequent target of the Western media, who belittled and criticized her political stances. After all, her detractors argued, she critiques global capital and advocates for the global dispossessed yet has prospered financially within the capitalist economy. Understanding her response to the Western media and their frequent charges that she was indulging in political posturing and/or being hypocritical is particularly important when trying to place "Borders" within the larger context of her role as an artist who, though born in London, had returned to the West as a refugee. Lynn Hirschberg's "M.I.A.'s Agitprop Pop" in the *New York Times* (2010), an account of her interview with M.I.A., is possibly the best example of a typically hostile appraisal of the apparent contradictions between M.I.A.'s lifestyle and her political convictions.

Hirschberg seizes upon every element of M.I.A.'s life—the food she eats during the interview, the clothes she wears, her choice of residence—to trivialize her political beliefs. According to Hirschberg, "It's hard to know if she believes everything she says or if she knows that a loud noise will always attract a crowd." She is, according to Hirschberg, a "child-of-Godard mix of politics, paranoia and pop" with an "antiestablishment/conspiracy-theory message." Hirschberg's profile refers to one of M.I.A.'s passionate exhortations—"I don't see how you can shut up and just enjoy success when other people who don't have the fame or the luxury to rent security guards are suffering. What the hell do they do? They just *die*"—as a "tirade," calls the artist's political statements "incoherent," and ridicules her for being "interested in niche hipster credibility." Hirschfield makes no bones about what she sees as M.I.A.'s contradictions: "she wants to balance outrageous political statements with a luxe lifestyle; to be supersuccessful yet remain controversial; for style to merge with substance." Such a dismissal is not an unusual stance from a *New York Times* columnist since "political" art—especially M.I.A.'s—that calls for violent resistance is not uncommonly deemed suspect and subject to ridicule.

The timing of Hirschberg's attempt to undermine M.I.A.'s credibility was particularly galling since M.I.A. had recently faced at least some financial consequences for her sincere attempt to bring attention to the systematic extra-judicial killing of Tamils by the Sri Lankan government in 2009. Her video "Born Free," released the same year as her interview, was an effort to bring these realities to the screen, depicting a police state in action, executing and brutalizing those who are different. It was a clear allusion to the Sri Lankan government's ruthless war against the Tamil minority, and it was banned almost right away by YouTube, ostensibly for its depiction of "graphic violence." As M.I.A. pointed out after the interview, the *New York Times* was part of a bigger structure that excised any coverage or serious discussions on the killings in Sri Lanka (Sawyer). In an interview rebuking the paper, she juxtaposes a *New York Times* article with the January 8 headline "Video of Sri Lankan Executions Appear Authentic, UN says" with an article three days later (on January 11), "The 31 Places to Go in 2010," which includes Sri Lanka on the list: "When the *New York Times* put Sri Lanka's beaches as the number one destination in a new year list of the 31 best travel ideas for 2010, six months after 300,000 people get bombed there … Tourism needs to be connected to politics. All wars are fought over land and you're advertising a piece of land as the best place to go and lay on and sunbathe. [You should] research that piece of land!" (Sawyer).

In Steve Loveridge's documentary *Matangi/Maya/M.I.A.* (2018), M.I.A. has addressed in greater detail many such inconsistencies in the Western media's coverage of her work. She also responds to the frequent accusations questioning the sincerity of her political commitments. Loveridge intentionally sets her worldwide popularity after the release of Kala (*Rolling Stone*'s album of the year) against images from her trip to Sri Lanka in 2001. Scenes of crowd adulation at various concerts are contrasted with shots of family members in Sri Lanka and recollections of the ever-present army patrols. The documentary makes a point of emphasizing the significance of this journey on her political consciousness and her growing awareness of the state's oppression of the Tamil minority. As news of further atrocities against the Tamil insurgents and specifically horrific acts of sexual violence against women are reported, M.I.A. declares that she knows all these events are going to become part of her for the rest of her life. She recounts riding on the public bus, when a group of soldiers enter the bus, stand near her, and grope her. Her mother tells her that if she opens her mouth, the soldiers will take both of them into the jungle and kill them and no one will care. Throughout the documentary, as the atrocities against the Tamil minority increase, we see other relatives remarking on an uncaring Western world. A news clips later in the documentary sums up what the Tamil people experience: "it's as if the Tamil people are invisible" (*Matangi/Maya/M.I.A*).

These short scenes portray a very different M.I.A. from the hedonist pop star described by Hirschberg and others in the media. Loveridge also includes a brief excerpt from the Bill Maher show that conveys in a particularly galling way how her political commitment was minimized and how the atrocities she highlights were ignored. As she makes the serious point that "under the guise of fighting terrorism, there is a genocide going on," Maher responds by smirking, asking M.I.A. to "tell the audience why you sound like Mike Jagger" (Maher). The clip foregrounds not only his condescending demeanor but also his dismissal of her attempt to call attention to the genocide. In the documentary, M.I.A., aptly, describes the message in his reaction to her plea for attention to the ongoing crisis: "go home, little girl. They shut me down." She also points to a 45-minute interview on CNN in which her reference to genocide is omitted (*Matangi/ Maya/M.I.A*). Even Miranda Sawyer in *The Guardian* is no less condescending: "Maya's problem is not that she's uninformed, but that she's emotional and personal and, like, you know, um, a bit inarticulate" ("M.I.A.: I'm Here for the People").[3]

I have given space both to some of the Western media's reaction to M.I.A.'s political positions and to M.I.A.'s own response to these frequent dismissals because such context is helpful in reading her video/song "Borders." Let me now offer—briefly—some additional context that shapes my analysis of it. The song was released as a digital single worldwide on Apple Music on November 27, 2015, a week after it was posted online; the music video was also released at the same time.[4] The moment was significant not just because of the crisis in the Mediterranean, but also because of the wider political ripples of the time. Consider that in June of that year Donald Trump had announced his candidacy for the presidency with an explicitly anti-immigrant speech, while David Cameron had been reelected in May with a promise that he would have a referendum for whether the United Kingdom should remain a member of the European Union. Meanwhile, on April 9 of the same year, 850 migrants and refugees drowned at sea, trying to cross the Mediterranean. Finally, on November 13, a series of attacks in Paris, though perpetrated by members

---

[3] M.I.A. has been subject to this condescension from her childhood days. She "tells a story about moving back to England when she was 10. On her first day at school, her class were working through a sum. Maya put her hand up, because she knew the answer. 'And literally the whole class turned round and laughed at me,' she says, laughing herself. The teacher patted her on the head and told her she didn't have to pretend. But she did know the answer—she just couldn't speak English. She didn't have the words to tell them" (Sawyer).

[4] To listen to the song and watch the video, see the Apple Music release. For more information on the announcement of the video release, see Monroe.

of racialized European minorities, nevertheless raised the specter of terrorism and the threat of the migrant other, providing European governments with yet another rationale for slamming the gates shut. Of course, the date of release, November 27, is also Tamil Remembrance Day, Maaveerar Naal (Heroes' Day), which marks the day of the first death of a Liberation Tiger of Tamil Ealam (LTTE) combatant.[5]

The video was shot in India and dedicated to M.I.A.'s uncle Bala, who was instrumental in helping the family emigrate to the United Kingdom. "I want to dedicate this video to my uncle Bala, my icon and role model," M.I.A. wrote in a tweet posted on the morning of the release. Her uncle, she said, was "[o]ne of the first Tamil migrants to come to the UK in the '60s who went [on] to inspire so many people as a creative, daring man ...." Thank you for helping my family come to England and taking us out of Sri Lanka and saving us" (Cox). Creating this video at a time when thousands were losing their lives in a fruitless effort to find refuge, M.I.A. marked the fact that she was one of the lucky few who had found refuge when her family was fleeing war and persecution. She recalls: "Luckily, Britain at the time opened its borders and during that slot of, you know, a few months, my uncle found my birth certificate, because I was actually born in England. Through being born here, I was able to help the rest of our family come with us" ("M.I.A.: 'How Can the West Turn People Away?'").

The subject matter of "Borders" was, in short, nothing new to her. Although born in London, she left with her family, shortly after, to settle in the northeast corner of Sri Lanka, where she lived until leaving for England at the age of nine. Her father's involvement in the Tamil resistance movement and the increasing violence in the country, including the anti-Tamil pogrom of 1983 made their leaving practically inevitable. Thus, M.I.A.'s own history, as a refugee from a war, has always afforded her a

---

[5] An article in the Sri Lankan newspaper *Daily FT* explains the history of the holiday: "The first-ever Liberation Tigers of Tamil Eelam (LTTE) member to embrace death in combat was Sathiyanathan of Kambarmalai. Sathiyanathan alias Shankar also known as Suresh died on 27 November 1982. Seven years after Shankar's death in 1989, around 600 LTTE cadres assembled at a secret venue in the Mullaitivu District jungles of Nithikaikulam on 27 November. The occasion was the newly-proclaimed Great Heroes Day or Maaveerar Naal as known in Tamil" (Jeyaraj).

Note that Maaveerar Naal is specific to the LTTE and not, and Jeyaraj stresses, not "a day of universal Tamil mourning." After the defeat of the LTTE in 2009, the Sri Lankan government banned any commemoration or memorials to the organization in 2013, including observance of Heroes' Day (Perera).

186   K. CHOWDHURY

glimpse of the realities confronting so many of the world's displaced people: "I was a refugee because of war and now I have a voice in a time when war is the most invested thing on the planet. What I thought I should do with this record [*Arular*] is make every refugee kid that came over after me have something to feel good about. Take everybody's bad bits and say, 'Actually, they're good bits. Now whatcha gonna do?'" (Kornhaber). In that spirit, rather than focusing further on narrow and self-fulfilling critiques of M.I.A.'s music and politics, I will explore questions about representation, identity, and resistance in her video, and consider how addressing those questions might add to our understanding of the border as both as a destructive, violent means of surveillance and control and as a generative space for resistance and struggle. This critical angle, I hope, offers a more productive line of inquiry.

I'll begin by examining the images, lyrics, and representations in the video. In many of the set pieces, the video positions M.I.A. amid a group of brown male bodies, on a boat, on land, and on a fence, as she addresses her audience with a series of questions:

> Borders
> What's up with that?
> Politics
> What's up with that?
> Police shots
> What's up with that?
> Identities
> What's up with that?
> Your privilege
> What's up with that?
> Broke people
> What's up with that?
> Boat people
> What's up with that?
> The realness
> What's up with that?
> The new world
> What's up with that? ("Borders" 00:43–01:07)

Juxtaposing real world political realities—"borders," "boat people," "police shots," "broke people"—that are presented as unnecessary absurdities caused by those in power with cultural signifiers of political engagement, such as "identities," "privilege," and "the realness," M.I.A. confronts her listeners with their own complicity in a world that has cast out millions of people. By addressing the listener directly, referring to "your privilege," while presenting images of hundreds of people confronting the barriers that have been put in place to keep them out, she makes it clear that her listeners have a responsibility that goes beyond liberal slogans about privilege and "realness." Indeed, her next series of questions make it abundantly clear that she is calling out the vogueish positions adopted by the privileged:

> Queen
> What's up with that?
> Killin' it
> What's up with that?
> Slayin' it
> What's up with that?
> Your goals
> What's up with that?
> Bein' bae
> What's up with that?
> Makin' money
> What's up with that?
> Breakin' internet
> What's up with that?
> Love wins
> What's up with that?
> Livin' it
> What's up with that?
> Bein' real
> What's up with that? ("Borders" 01:32–1:58)

Taking on the modish pronouncements of the day, many of which are connected to interpersonal relationships ("Being bae"), personal achievements ("killing it," "slaying it," "making money"), and the heralding of social justice movements ("Love wins"), M.I.A. moves the listener to encounter the reality of migrants' lives against the commodification of political alliances and the superficiality of self-empowerment mantras. Meanwhile, the xenophobic state and its nativist allies are only mentioned in passing, as M.I.A. in a sequence of pronouns, brings together her listeners and her own identity as a citizen of a Western nation—of that same state, which has those same allies—decrying the absurdity of wealthy nations denying refuge to the survivors of war: "Yeah fuck 'em when we say we're not with them/We solid and we don't need to kick them" ("Borders" 01:23–1:28). Turning against the narrow nationalism of the Northern states, she calls for a global collectivity to work against state interests. There is no one national identity secured through political borders; instead, she says, "This is North, South, East and Western" (01:29–1:31). Ultimately, it is this vision of a collective that will raise its fists against the "present state of things": those voices struggling to be heard; those who are not played "on the FM"; those "sitting on a stoop"— all of those voices—are the ones who must fashion a new reality (02:21–02:23, 02:25–02:26). As she puts it, "This world needs a brand new Re'dom/We'dom—the key/We'dom the key'dom to life!" (00:11–0:20).

These lyrics are set against a series of striking images that, of course, tells a story as well. The video opens with M.I.A. in medium close-up; behind her, in the distance, two lines of men are running single file almost in a military fashion, streaming along two roughly orthogonal lines toward the front edges of the frame. Throughout the video, M.I.A. depicts migrants in various sites and positions, including in informal tableau-like scenes: in one long shot, a group of men scales a tall barrier fence, and the arrangement of their ascending and descending bodies, paused in mid-climb, spells out "LIFE"; another group is captured in an overhead shot—a crowd of men lying supine in all directions across a boat's roof; another large group is seen in a long shot, all dressed in identical tan raincoats, standing together to form a human sculpture in the image of a boat; other shots depict a number of men sitting on boats that rest on the water or move toward a destination. M.I.A. herself is a part of these groups, often taking on their attire, as when she sits by the water on gray rocks covered in a gold Mylar blanket. Her other choice of clothing is also distinctive: in a few scenes, she wears a raincoat; in another, she wears military fatigues; and, most distinctively, in a scene by the water, she wears a T-shirt that reads "Fly Pirates," in a parody of the Emirates Airlines brand, imitating the white "away" kit of the soccer club Paris Saint-Germain, or PSG.

This last fashion statement predictably got her into trouble with the French club, but her gesture was not just a "fuck you" fashion statement; instead, the pirated shirt and its logos pointed to coexisting global realities: the brands that many migrants wear are knock-off ones (a "genuine" Emirates T-shirt, for example, would cost anything between $75 and

6 VISUALIZING BORDERS: M.I.A.'S "BORDERS" AND MURAL ART IN CIUDAD... 189

$100). These genuine and knock-offs shirts are made in sweatshops in the very same countries that many migrants are forced to leave. Also, M.I.A.'s shirt represents a critique of the United Arab Emirates, which has been cited as one of the worst human rights offenders by multiple human rights groups, not just for its treatment of dissenters, but also for its violation of workers' rights.[6] The country relies, for instance, on a huge pool of foreign laborers, exploited via the notorious Kafala system: "With about 90 percent of the UAE's over 9-million-strong population consisting of foreign nationals—most of whom are low-wage and semi-skilled workers from Africa, Asia, and elsewhere in the Middle East—the country's economy is heavily dependent on migrant workers" (Qadri).[7] Moreover, as M.I.A. pointed out, it was ironic that a club that had several second-generation immigrants on its roster would object to a video that depicted the urgency of the refugee crisis.[8]

It is important to note, too, that M.I.A. does not position herself as being separate from the migrants. She joins them on the boats, one more figure amid a tightly compressed group of bodies, and is seen on a rocky shore, wrapped, like the other individuals scattered there, in mylar. At one point, she is shown standing atop a pole that contains surveillance cameras, with—a bit further down—another migrant sitting astride the pole. M.I.A., then, is careful to show her connection and solidarity with recent migrants. However, she also demonstrates an awareness of her privilege as a prosperous musician and music producer. The portion of the video that includes the song ends with a shot of her on the highest portion of a border fence, balancing on one of its horizontal beams and holding onto a vertical rail. The fence is behind her, against a clouded sky at dusk, and she adopts relaxed poses, initially swaying with her arms above her head and

---

[6] For more information on the state of migrant workers in the United Arab Emirates, see the 2021 Human Rights Watch report: https://www.hrw.org/world-report/2021/country-chapters/united-arab-emirates.

[7] For an extended account of the abuses perpetuated by the Kafala system, see "Reform the Kafala System." https://www.migrant-rights.org/campaign/end-the-kafala-system/.

[8] M.I.A. explains her own logic for the Pirates T-shirt: "I consciously made a decision to make a separation between what's cool: arming these people that then become pirates, and separating that from peaceful non-armed human beings, like the migrants and the refugees. The whole project and the video was to define the difference between those two things. We constantly have to face people squashing those two things together—women, children, and real people in need, who get lumped in with armed conflict and militia groups and pirates. I think if you're talking about migrants or refugees or people generally living in war zones, unfortunately sportswear and football tops are part of the uniform" (Bassil).

190   K. CHOWDHURY

then standing casually with one ankle crossed behind the other and one arm bent behind her head. She is spotlit, stylishly dressed, and wearing oversized aviator sunglasses, which she calmly adjusts at one point as the camera pans. Though of course she hangs on to the rail and—at times—to the mesh of the fence, her relaxed pose suggests that she could be any-where—not perched dangerously high above the ground. Her figure is a sharp contrast to the others depicted beside and below her on the fence. There, clinging in shadow to the other side of the mesh, men appear almost in silhouette, most frozen in climbing poses rather than relaxed attitudes. The contrast in the positions and the lighting suggests that M.I.A. is quite aware that she enjoys privileges that recent migrants do not. She is both part of this group and protected from many of the diffi-culties they face. She is in the light, on the other side of the fence. However, she remains with those who struggle, and, given the context, the spotlight that illuminates her may in fact be a searchlight. The ending of the song is followed by silence and a black screen.

Then, a segment without sound rolls, perhaps to highlight the plight of recent migrants and their distance from the privileges that M.I.A. and many other citizens of the West enjoy. In the segment, a line of men is shown in a high-angle long shot walking first diagonally across the frame and then almost vertically up the center. They are wading single file through thigh-deep water, proceeding bare-backed and, at times, with considerable effort. After a cut, this line of men is shown in extreme long shot in the upper left of the frame, continuing to wade away from the camera, while in a long shot a different group of men, in a large cluster, are seen wading toward the camera, one with his arms in the air, either as a means of protecting the shoes he holds or in a gesture of surrender. These images highlight the difficulty of migrants' journeys, and, the silence accompanying them might, as I suggest below, draw attention to their having no voice.

Clearly, at least a couple of additional points about the representations of the migrants need to be made here: one, that all the supposed migrants in the video are men who appear to be of South Asian origin, with a stubble of short hair; and two, that none of the migrants in the video speak or sing. They remain voiceless. In his *Atlantic* piece, Spencer Kornhaber points to both these elements: "some may argue she's using people as props, aestheticizing poverty for her own gain, and mixing cul-tural signifiers in ways that could feed stereotypes about the developing world as an undifferentiated mass." Yet an alternative reading could suggest that M.I.A. plays precisely upon some of the stereotypes associated with migrants when she depicts them as an undifferentiated mass of brown bodies. Indeed, in the West, these are the representations that are the most familiar. Her depiction, then, may not be attempting to make the banal point that all of these men are individuals and thus deserving of our consideration—a pervasive message of liberalism. Instead, she may be challenging viewers to face the reality of the sheer numbers that are searching for refuge. Can our imagination only capture the gravity of a situation when faced with the individual representation of loss and suffering, as in the photograph of Alan Kurdi? Or can we recognize the current situation as a political problem that has, to a large extent, been created by the West? In an interview, she offers a comment that seems relevant here: "I didn't want to go to the easiest source of empathy, which is to show a child dying on the shore, because that's really what it took in Europe at the time to get a rise out of people, for them to actually pay attention. There was an actual turning point, and it's when they discovered that image of a kid being found on the beach. It shouldn't even get to that point" (Chen). After all, as I described in Chap. 2, if the economies in the Global South were not devastated by the forces of global capital or torn asunder by the destructive reach of neo-colonial wars, all these men depicted in the video would not be risking life and limb, facing death and degradation just to find a place to live, and citizens of Western countries might not view them as interlopers and invaders.

In fact, M.I.A. plays with the stereotype of the migrant as invader, as part of a "horde." In the video, on occasion, the boats with the migrants on board almost appear as an invading fleet, traveling together, moving toward the camera—toward the viewer. However, by placing the migrants always at the receiving end of a surveillance state, impeded by barbed wire and never far from the gaze of a camera, for instance, there is little room for doubt about the power dynamics in this relationship.

Another possible criticism of the video may be the point that there are no actual figures representing authorities, though there are plenty of border markers, such as surveillance cameras and fences. Likewise, none of the borders are identifiable, even though the barbed wire fence looks like the one separating Morocco from Ceuta and Melilla. These points, however, may be M.I.A.'s way of asserting the ever-presence of borders. Certainly, some borders may be harder to cross than others, but in her lyrics and in her images, she makes it clear that border rules, in general, are a form of violence.

192 K. CHOWDHURY

A few reactions to the video, predictably, ignore subtleties in the song and images and echo Hirschberg's condescending attitude. David Hayter's criticism of the song, for instance, rehearsed some of the responses in the past to M.I.A.'s overtly political challenges. "This is not an impassioned plea to the West," Hayter claims, "instead Maya asks an array of open questions, like a valley girl trying to sound deep on twitter." He adds, "From the most vital questions troubling the world's elite to tangential social assumptions and throw away thoughts about youth culture—Maya is spit balling into the void. M.I.A. has created one of the most powerful political singles in recent memory without making a single statement." Hayter, however, is also willing to acknowledge that "[t]his is no microwaved hot take in the face of a global tragedy, this is the sound of one woman reflecting on a highly individualized society that faces issues so complex and deep rooted that they are destined to overwhelm all but the most cohesive community .... Perhaps, sometimes, to truly step outside your self, you need to be met with indigent sarcasm: your every assumption, your crumbling world, what's up wid dat?" In the interview with *Time* magazine referenced above, M.I.A. clarifies her goals regarding the chorus of questions, reflecting with a greater degree of complexity than Hayter might ascribe to her: "I started writing that verse because I was thinking about how our references to being amazing are actually a reference to killing somebody: killing it, slaying it, dragging someone. If we are a society that can use aggressiveness as a compliment, then [why do] we look at these people coming on the boats as like, 'Oh my God, this is white genocide, they're coming to kill us!'" (Feeney)?

So far, I have attempted to resurrect M.I.A.'s images from frequent reactions in the Western press that too often trivialize her work and portray her as a self-indulgent provocateur. Of course, despite her rousing calls for political alliances, it is tempting to criticize M.I.A.'s own complicity in a global system that enables the injustices that she represents in her video. This line of criticism is a predictable one, and by the logic of this argument, any oppositional artist who achieves global success is immediately compromised since she benefits from the system she critiques. It may appear, for instance, that my criticism of Ai Weiwei's complicity with the commodity economy should similarly be applied to M.I.A. However, there is significant point of distinction to be made between the political positions of the two artists. Ai's critique of the West emerges from the standpoint of assumed, Western ethical so-called normative standards of rights and justice, and *Human Flow* has little to say about imperialism and

6 VISUALIZING BORDERS: M.I.A.'S "BORDERS" AND MURAL ART IN CIUDAD... 193

its impact on the continuing ruination of people's lives. M.I.A.'s body of work, on the contrary is, as I am attempting to establish in this chapter, a response to Western colonialism and capitalist violence. Indeed, she faces the condemnation of the Western media precisely because she calls out the shibboleths of Western democracy and capitalism. Additionally, gender plays a role in determining this critical reception; as Joshua Clover reminds us, "the burden of being consigned to appear rather than to act, and the fate of being rewarded and being blamed for appearance falls heavily on women" (98).

Avoiding the pitfall of following these tiresome and predictable paths of critical judgment, then, let us consider how her representations of borders add an important element to our understanding of the ways in which borders are viewed and seen in the popular media. The success of the song/video makes us consider how effectively an activist artist can use dominant perceptions of borders and migrants, working on and against them to create a resistance narrative that disrupts these very same perceptions. Can M.I.A. resolve the contradictions in two forms of representation —speaking for displaced people and presenting a homogenized image of them— as well as overcome the challenges in both cases of addressing a primarily Western audience? How might the aestheticization of the migrants in the video compromise the action of "speaking for" this embattled group of people? Is this tension heightened by M.I.A.'s position as the only one who speaks in the video, implicating her as yet another Western voice participating in the silencing of those who already have no voice? In many of the set pieces, for example, the migrants appear to be little more than props, serving as a backdrop for M.I.A. to speak to her audience. Finally, by juxtaposing the real (migrants climbing fences) with the surreal (migrants positioned so as to appear in the shape of a boat), does M.I.A. minimize the actual brutality of this journey? After all, even when the migrants appear on the boat, they are in calm waters with little sign of any external threats.

Since M.I.A. has so often been silenced or misread by Western commentators, let me again allow her to speak, here, to highlight her own perceptions about borders. Well before the 2015 migration crisis, she had already announced her philosophy on borders: "What can we do on a ground level except be open-minded—think over here, over there ... It's a big world, with lots of choices. Why sit in one place?" (Hirschberg). While the idea of being "open-minded" can be reduced to a banal liberal slogan, what she is calling for here is a borderscape, where ideas are not confined by territorial limits. She makes this point more explicitly elsewhere: "Well you know, in my mind, there's no countries, you know it's like; we're all one, we all live on this planet" (M.I.A., performer, *Colbert Report*). Taking on the more specific charge of ethical inconsistencies, especially in regard to her decision to screen the video on Apple TV, she claims that "the values we promote, the restrictions or borders and all of these things are also applicable to corporations, to the workforce that actually makes the technology, to us even selling this back to those people and pretending they are inclusive in this culture. My point is: are they or are they not [included]? Why *can't* I put this on Apple? It's the only platform I have because I don't have access to saying this on Fox News or saying this in the media when I don't have anything to promote" (Feeney). By linking media censorship and the multiple factors that determine the scope for personal expression, she calls into question an entire landscape of accommodation and complicity, where all are subject to the logic of capital.

In an NPR interview on December 15, 2015, she was even more explicit about Western hypocrisy regarding the different ways in which borders are erected or destroyed to suit the commercial interests of Western nations: "You don't put the borders on Apple, you don't put borders on YouTube, and you don't put borders on MTV," she says. "So to make the borders even taller when actually what the creative world is doing, or the business world is doing, is actually the opposite, then you're always going to have this problem" ("M.I.A.: 'How Can the West Turn People Away?'"). Of course, there is even a further irony here, as far as she is concerned. These same companies are responsible for crafting and disseminating dreams of success across the world. Why, then, are they surprised when people attempt to realize these dreams by traveling to the West? As she puts it, "If the West is so deliberate in promoting its brands and is using art and culture to inspire people's dreams … how can the West then turn people away?" ("M.I.A.: 'How Can the West Turn People Away?'"). Nonetheless, it goes without saying that even an oppositional artist, such as M.I.A., participates in creating this dreamscape. After all, she represents the prototypical success story of the refugee, who nurtured by the West, has fulfilled all its promise.

M.I.A., however, remains consistent in disavowing borders, especially in the context of the particular ways in which she creates her music. As mentioned earlier, she has traveled the world, collaborated with a wide variety of artists, sampled different sounds, and shot videos across the planet. Earlier in 2015, before filming the "Borders" video, she told EW about her forthcoming album, *Matahdatah*, which included the song: "it's like a journal. And the journal happens to be a really wide journey. It's about borders and it's kind of testing the human idea of that — whether it's physical borders, geographical or philosophical ones" (Nolfi). As she puts it elsewhere, "Conceptually, we just want to keep it broader than a border, whether that's geographical, psychological, physical, emotional, whatever the thing is, and just keep going" (Bassil). In the case of "Borders," this belief extended to her actual filming of the video, which was done in Southern India. Her original plan was to employ many of the Tamil refugees who live in refugee camps across the state of Tamil Nadu, but she failed to secure permission to do so.[9]

Three points become evident when we attempt to make any comments about the "Borders" video: One, that the Western media's reactions to M.I.A.'s efforts to take seriously the migrant crisis, particularly at a heightened political moment, was a predictable one. Not only is their response guided by racist and sexist efforts to dismiss an immigrant female artist's ability to comment on political matters; they are also operating within a corporate structure that retreats from any political commitments that challenge the reigning racial and nationalist logic. Second, M.I.A.'s own position as a celebrity artist who lives in the West, representing and speaking for those who are erased from the media, comes with the usual contradictions that accompany any oppositional art in a world where all art forms function as commodities. Finally, any aestheticization of the suffering and loss endured by others risks diminishing one's efforts to call attention to those problems.

Without minimizing either the contradictions of M.I.A.'s position or her possible aestheticization of migrants' suffering, I will reiterate that the timing of the video was essential and must be seen as a direct intervention in the migrant and racial politics of that year. M.I.A. had both the

---

[9] According to reports, "Nearly 100,000 Sri Lankan refugees are living in India in dozens of camps across Tamil Nadu, of which nearly 20,000 are students who live in a state of despair and uncertainty about their future" (Sivagnanam). M.I.A is well aware of their predicament: "In South India there's 132 camps with Tamil refugees and they've been there forever. The people that are in my video, that age group of kids in the camps are actually second generation, they were born and bred there—they didn't come across in the boats, it was their parents. That's how long they'd been there. But they're still restricted: They have curfew, they have to have a day pass to get out, get a job, but they're not actually citizens" (qtd. in Bassil).

authority and the following to influence a transnational audience, during a time when a vibrant oppositional politics, influenced by the Black Lives Movement in the United States, was taking shape in Europe. Similar to the point that I made in Chap. 4—that one of the insidious features of the migrant "crisis" in Europe was the deracialization of migrant bodies (even as their racial status was hypervisible in the representations that appeared in the media)—Nicholas DeGenova asserts:

> [Q]uestions of race and racism ... present themselves in a particularly acute way in the European migration context, haunted as Europe's borders are by an appalling proliferation of almost exclusively non-European/non-white migrant and refugee deaths and other forms of structural violence and generalized suffering. Consequently, it is particularly crucial that we do the critical work of reconfirming the precisely racial specificity of what is so commonly and casually euphemized across Europe as "migrant" or "of migrant background. (1768)

De Genova clarifies that "[b]anishing race as a critical analytical category" is not a mere coincidence. It "risks forsaking any adequate account of the distinctly European colonial legacies that literally produced race as a socio-political category of distinction and discrimination in the first place" (1769). The video's presentation of racialized migrants is particularly apposite in this context since it is impossible to see the migrants as dehistoricized, deracialized figures. Granted, these images in themselves are not enough to decenter the conversation about a generalized category of migrants, but M.I.A., by placing herself squarely amongst the migrants, makes it abundantly clear that her own history puts her in a position of solidarity with those on screen. Indeed, as Sinthujan Varatharajah points out, she is someone who has been subject to the very regimes that she critiques today. Consequently, when M.I.A. sits on the vessel sailing through the Indian Ocean, she isn't just "'traveling with refugees' or 'accompanying refugees on their journey,' as many reporters have described. No. She is a part of that very journey, albeit positioned in a different tense. Such autobiography with such difficult subject matter is something we only rarely encounter in pop culture."

And this autobiographical text is particularly important since migration politics have enhanced the idea of an essential, racialized, European identity. One need not seek out the multiple neo-fascist versions of this claim. Consider the words of Slavoj Žižek, after the multiple assault

6 VISUALIZING BORDERS: M.I.A.'S "BORDERS" AND MURAL ART IN CIUDAD...

reports in Cologne in January 2016: "they [immigrants] have to be educated (by others and by themselves) into their freedom" ("The Cologne Attacks"). A few months later, he made an even more specific claim about Europe as "our culture" (using the first-person pronoun) and, in contrast, referred to migrants again using the third-person "they": "Europe needs to be open to refugees, but we have to be clear they are in our culture. Certain ethical limits ... are non-negotiable. We should be more assertive toward our values .... Europe means something noble—human rights, welfare state, social programs for the poor. All of this is embodied in enlightenment of the European legacy" ("EU Must Militarize"). M.I.A. is well aware that minoritized and racialized Europeans constantly have to prove their loyalties and allegiances to this "noble" idea of Europe, one with its particular racial and cultural borders. Their ignoble presence in the imperial center must forever undergo a loyalty test, particularly when they announce their solidarity with other black and brown postcolonial subjects.

To date (November 24, 2022), the "Borders" video has been viewed 27 million times on YouTube; while this is a very small number compared to an Adele or a Taylor Swift video or even M.I.A.'s own hit "Paper Planes" (248 million views), such a number must be seen in relation to the exposure available for other artistic expressions. If one adds social media coverage, circulation of the video in other venues, and M.I.A.'s own interviews with major news outlets, it would be fair to claim that the video is a significant contribution to the borders debate. In this context, a noteworthy point is that M.I.A. does not localize the crisis; by not delineating or placing the migrants within particular geographical spaces or showing the specific reasons for their departure, she emphasizes the global reach of the migrant "crisis" and its imbrication within a larger system that sees these migrants as disposable. It bears repeating here that the migrants M.I.A. is representing are cogs in a global surplus labor army, risking their lives, facing criminalization and demonization—all so that, like Juan in *La Jaula de Oro*, they can arrive somewhere, only to be further dehumanized and exploited there.

The Politics of Space: Murals in the Sister Cities of Ciudad Juárez and El Paso

Unlike MIA's music video, which comments, to some extent, on the universality of the migrant experience, the public murals that I will now discuss depend on the politics of a specific space. Just as literary texts, films, and music videos operate within particular aesthetic and political registers, allowing for certain kinds of visibility and distribution, in the case of murals, their actual locations are an essential element of how they function and how they are read and "seen" within their distinctive contexts. This is particularly true for art forms that are part of the fabric of everyday life, located among people and places that lend them a special valence. Experiencing a mural, thus, in a commons area is very different from encountering art in a private space, with its rules of enclosure, its practices of viewing, and its rituals of access based on the privileges accorded through race and class positions. For this very reason, I am focusing on two sets on murals, set on different sides of the US–Mexico border. The murals are located in El Paso and Ciudad Juárez (formerly called El Paso del Norte), sister cities that are tied together through familial, social, economic, and political histories. Both cities have also experienced the impact of being a major hub of labor exploitation and commercial traffic over the last 100 years.[10]

One way in which the joint identities and fused histories of the two cities have been highlighted is through the creations of the many artists who have documented the stories of the people who live and work in the borderlands.[11] Many of these artists work across the borders, and their art is meant to speak to both communities. As in my consideration of other texts in this study, my analysis of these murals will emphasize the many ways in which they interrogate the multilayered impact of border

---

[10] The Guadeloupe Hidalgo Treaty of 1848, which saw the United States annexing more than half of Mexican territory, also established a US–Mexico boundary along the Rio Bravo, which divided the city then known as El Paso del Norte into two unequal parts: El Paso, Texas, and Paso del Norte, Chihuahua (renamed Ciudad Juárez in 1888).

[11] No contemporary account of the Borderlands is complete without acknowledging Gloria Anzaldúa's groundbreaking *Borderlands, La Frontera: The New Mestiza* (1987).

rules.[12] However, because the context for viewing these murals is so vital for an understanding of their significance, I will offer an analysis rooted in my personal experience of viewing these murals. Certainly, all texts are mediated, and their "meanings" become part of this process, and certainly factors like a viewers's identity, positionally, and purpose; the time of an encounter; and various other factors shape interpretation. However, because it is impossible to divorce murals from their setting and the serendipitous nature of a usual encounter, and because it is impossible to ignore my own experience, this section of my book will offer a more personal account of studying these particular cultural texts.

While border murals can be explicitly political, either advocating for social change, bringing to light an atrocity (one of the many cases of feminicidio in Juárez, for instance), or memorializing a loss, it is clear that, at some level, all border murals are political because of their rootedness in particular public spaces. Place, in short, is one of the principal political elements that distinguish these murals. As muralist Carlos Callejo (born in El Paso, but raised from age four to nine in Ciudad Juárez) puts it, murals "are not only protest or simply large paintings on walls; they are paintings binded [sic] into architecture; public art conceived in a given space; rooted in a specific human context ... the roots of murals speak about the dignity of the people, about the struggles, the needs, and the celebrations of traditions and the dignity of our culture" (Juárez 67). The two murals I examine are situated within a mile of each other, separated by an international border, yet also cojoined by linked histories and present realities.

It is worth elaborating on two of these realities, both of which are determining factors for understanding these bordered worlds and the murals that are produced there. This is not the place to offer an elaborate account

---

[12] There is a long history of mural painting within Mexican culture, stretching back to pre-Columbian times. Certainly, over the last 100 years, especially since the revolution, a diverse and world-renowned muralist tradition developed in Mexico, spearheaded by Los Tres Grandes: José Clemente Orozco, Diego Rivera, and David Alfaro Siqueiros. The public art created by the muralists highlighted the achievements of ordinary people, focusing on a politically emancipatory life rooted in socialist politics. This trajectory of celebrating and affirming the lives and labor of workers remains an integral part of the murals created by a range of contemporary Fronterizos artists. Anthony Lee's *Painting on the Left: Diego Rivera, Radical Politics, and San Francisco's Public Murals* and David Carey and Walter Little's "Reclaiming the Nation through Public Murals: Maya Resistance and the Reinterpretation of History" offer an important account of this tradition.

of the political and economic history of the region, but suffice it to say that even in the last several decades, the Bracero program (1942–1964), the implementation of the Border Industrialization Program–BIP (1965), and the North American Free Trade Agreement-NAFTA (1994) have had a massive impact on the residents of this region. The goals of all these programs were two-fold: to enrich a small coterie of financiers, bankers, and industrial and agricultural capitalists on both sides of the border, and to create a surplus army of labor of low-wage workers who could be ceaselessly exploited and replaced. Each of these labor extractive programs also operated as a way to regulate immigration to suit the needs of capital and to appease nationalists on the US side.[13] In recent decades, the Juárez-El Paso borderlands have been particularly affected by the rise of the maquiladora. Maquiladoras represent a microcosm of the imperial relations that govern the interactions between the two countries: they not only serve as a production point for extracting surplus but also operate as a form of immigration control that keeps Mexican and Central American workers in Mexico working low-wage jobs.[14]

The maquiladora economy has had a particularly devastating effect on the lives of young women in the borderlands.[15] These maquiladoras were deliberately placed in the border cities, "which contained large working-age populations, especially young women, many of whom were migrant workers already displaced from other parts of the Mexican interior, who did not have established roots in the border cities. Due to the precarity of

[13] For an excellent account of this history, see Justin Akers Chacón's *The Border Crossed Us: The Case for Opening the US-Mexico Border*. See also Oscar J. Martínez's. *Ciudad Juárez: Saga of a Legendary Border City.*

[14] "The Mexican government established the *maquiladora* industry in the 1960s—a *maquiladora* being a foreign-owned assembly plant that imports components and exports finished products duty-free—to take advantage of the border by providing cheap labor for foreign-owned industries who could then export their goods to the United States. Juárez became the collection point for deportees, for migrants hoping to enter the United States, and for migrants attracted by work in the *maquiladoras*. Private interests controlled the planning, or lack thereof, of urban growth, and the migrants and workers generally settled in *colonias* around the outskirts of the city" (Boudreaux 393).

[15] For a grim account of the gender violence, the feminicidios that have accompanied the rise of the maquiladora industry in Ciudad Juárez, see Nina Maria Lozano's *Not One More: Feminicidio on the Border*, Melissa Wright's "Necropolitics, Narcopolitics, and Femicide: Gendered Violence on the Mexico-U.S. Border" and Katherine Pantaleo's "Gendered Violence: An Analysis of the Maquiladora Murders."

employment and the devaluation of female-gendered labor, the architects of the maquiladora model structured production around the superexploitation of primarily women workers" (Chacón 77). Many of these women are placed in vulnerable situations due to substandard housing and poor transportation facilities and are subject to the predatory whims of their employers. Additionally, the state offers little or no protection for these women when they are assaulted or killed. Because the maquiladoras are operated under draconian labor rules, it is hard for women to organize without facing threats of violence; however, protestors in Juárez and across the nations have responded on frequent occasions to the continuing violence against women. One of the forms of protest has been the use of murals to memorialize the lives lost. These memorials, calling for justice for the many missing or murdered women, include full scale murals, as well as black crosses against a pink background, which can be found painted on lampposts and traffic lights.[16] The murals I will be examining, I believe, though not explicitly connected to these histories, have specific connections to these missing and murdered women.

Another element of the present realities that influence our viewing of the Juárez mural is, of course, the implementation of Title 42 since the eruption of the coronavirus pandemic. Put into effect by President Trump in 2020, this policy allowed the administration to invoke a little used provision of the US code, dating back to 1944, which allows the government

---

[16] There are several memorials, for example, for activist and artist Isabelle Cabanillas de la Torre, who was killed in the Juárez Centro on January 18, 2020. Soon after her death, "Women and allies dressed in black, with pink signage and masks, gathered at The Paso del Norte International Bridge between border cities and blocked it off for at least three hours. A few protesters even laid in fake pools of blood in hopes that performance art would help get the message across" (Caraballo). For an analysis of street art dedicated to the memory of Isabelle Cabanillas de la Torre, see Cali Mellin's "Producing Visibility and Community in Ciudad Juárez: Returning to Gloria Anzaldúa's Borderlands/La Frontera." See also Elva Fabiola Orozco's "Mapping the Trail of Violence: The Memorialization of Public Space as a Counter-Geography of Violence in Ciudad Juárez." Orozco points out that "the memorialization of Ciudad Juárez's landscape constitutes an attempt to decolonize existing gender relations that produce zones of female death by fostering spaces of care and solidarity" (132). Of course, this violence is not confined to these particular borderlands. For a memorial dedicated to those who die in the deserts of Arizona, see the "Mujer Migrante Memorial." *Mujer Migrante Memorial*, https://storymaps.arcgis.com/stories/5a0f3d3b42634812b33ae6 4b1924cd9a.

to prevent migrants from entering the country if it can be established that this action would prevent the spread of a communicable disease. Expelling hundreds of thousands of migrants, using the "Remain in Mexico" policy, endangered the lives of migrants and placed them at the mercy of forces who were out to exploit them. Of the 1.8 million migrants, who have been expelled between April 2020 and March 2022, 60 percent have been from Mexico (Gramlich). Although expulsions have decreased under President Biden, the vast majority of migrants continue to be expelled; meanwhile the status of Title 42 remains unclear. The misery caused by Title 42 hangs like an ominous shadow over the many interrelated and separated lives across the borderlines.[17]

Under the Bridge/Bajo el Puente

Since I am not a resident of these borderlands, it is necessary to affirm that, despite my knowledge of these histories, my experience of these murals can only represent a partial account of their significance. Further complicating any objective analysis of these murals is the fact that as a brown-bodied person, but as one holding the privileges of US citizenship, I am conscious both of being a person who is an object of surveillance at the border and as someone who can cross these borders with ease as a holder of the necessary documents of passage. My "position" at the border and my experience viewing these public murals in both cities became inseparable from my analysis, part of the text itself. Indeed, in the case of the Juárez mural, the "viewing experience" became inextricably linked with the original object of analysis, and it overturned how I had "imagined" my encounter with the mural would be.

---

[17] The US Centers for Disease Control and Prevention announced plans to end Title 42 on May 23, 2022, because COVID-19 cases have decreased, and vaccines are widely available. This plan was impeded, however, by a Louisiana federal judge who ruled in favor of upholding the policy, claiming that the Biden administration had not followed proper procedure in terminating Title 42. As of August 2022, expulsions of migrants under this policy were still taking place. Most recently, on November 15, 2022, US District Court Judge Emmet Sullivan blocked the use of Title 42, arguing that the order was "arbitrary and capricious in violation of the Administrative Procedure Act" (qtd. in Ward and Gerstein). The current expectation is that the use of Title 42 will end when the public health emergency connected to the pandemic concludes on May 11, 2023.

6 VISUALIZING BORDERS: M.I.A.'S "BORDERS" AND MURAL ART IN CIUDAD…   203

The 65-foot mural *Under the Bridge/Bajo el Puente*, in Juárez is the creation of Jorge Perez Mendoza, also known as Yorch, of the Colectivo Rezizte.[18] The mural, located beneath the Paso del Norte bridge entering Mexico from the United States, was completed in January 2022. It depicts the industrial workers and farmers of the borderlands, marking their labor and recognizing the spirit of resistance that has been an element of this region for the last 150 years. Apparently, the mural "is a larger format, in-color rendition of a silkscreen print [that Mendoza] made in 2012 in black and white. El Paso's Hope Border Institute, a migrant aid organization, helped sponsor the mural" (Villagran). The spatial politics of this particular location marks not just an international border, but so-called mutually "governed" territory as well: "The International Boundary and Water Commission owns the canal, but the artwork is in Mexican territory" (Villagran). However, this "mutual" interest, as is the case in many of the circumstances guiding US–Mexico relations, is slanted toward the United States since the imperial power almost always benefits from the resolution of any territorial disputes.

Other features of this space are also extremely important. This mural is located on the southern slope of the canal and is visible to those crossing

---

[18] Colectivo REZIZTE is described as "a multi-disciplinary artist collective in Ciudad Juárez, Chihuahua, Mexico. REZIZTE shows the true image, true of a city like Juárez under attack from several sides. The collective creates graffiti/street/urban/mural art interventions that help to fight to empower the people" (Mural Arts Philadelphia). David Flores, the founder of Ciudad Juárez 's Colectivo Rezizte and co-founder of Puro-Borde, offers an introduction to the work of the collective: "the first artists to develop the Rezizte collective were "transborderistas" who used art as a way to develop a fronterizo identity. 'Colectivo Rezizte was born in 2003 out of the crack that opens between two juxtaposed cultures on the northern border of Mexico […] bringing together different forms of expression and different genres to celebrate the diversity that makes us fronterizos,' says Flores. When these artists began hosting lively community events, they established themselves at the center of cultural life along the border" (White). Pérez also owns the bakery Panadería Rezizte in Juárez. He directly supports migrants by donating bread almost daily to various shelters in Juárez. Pérez has also offered the bakery as a gathering place for events such as a poetry reading by Guatemalan migrants and outdoor film screenings in the adjacent alley. In turn, some of the shelters have occasionally paid for special orders from Panadería Rezizte, in what Pérez termed 'reciprocal support,' especially during the early months of the pandemic that threatened the survival of his business. For Pérez, the mixing of protest, art and bread is as natural as the mixing of people and culture at the border" (Boudreaux).

Fig. 6.1 Yorch, Under the Bridge/Bajo el Puente, View from the Bridge, 1 May, 2022

the international bridge toward Mexico (see Fig. 6.1, Yorch, *Under the Bridge/Bajo el Puente*, View from the Bridge, May 1, 2022).[19] The view from above the mural, on the Mexican side near the bridge, is revealing. Standing above the artwork, and looking north across the canal, one sees the American border fence, with its newly erected concertina wire shining in the sun. A bit further west, the wall suddenly ends, and there is a small gap. It is here that migrants often turn themselves in to the Border Patrol on the US side. This gap also happens to be the traditional crossing point between the two cities. Both banks are patrolled by the Guardia Nacional. Between the southern slope and the northern slope, which has no drawings or markings, is a barely filled canal, with the meager remnants of the Rio Bravo, containing sewage water pooled at the bottom.

---

[19] Although I did make contact with the artists, I was unable to acquire reproduction copies of the murals. Consequently, I am using my own photographs of the murals.

Wastewater has been released into the river on both sides.[20] The area is near a series of highways on which cars speed by, and there appears to be no easy way to reach the space where the mural is painted. (I was informed by a resident of Juárez, however, that residents are able to access this space more easily than outsiders to the city.)

Having established the spatial context of this mural, let me describe the mural itself.

Viewed from the bridge, the mural depicts two main figures: in the middle ground at left, a male farmworker—a bracero—tilling a field and in the background at right, a woman in a *maquiladora* uniform, surrounded by the large gears of industrial machines. (For unimpeded views of the mural, see Omar Omelas's photos the *El Paso Times* article by Lauren Villagran, https://www.elpasotimes.com/story/news/2022/01/04/border-art-collective-unveils-rio-grande-mural-downtown-juarez/9078448002/).The field in which the farmworker toils features strong orthogonal lines and is rendered in warm pinks and browns. Dressed in blue jeans, an orange shirt, a blue bandana, and a white cowboy hat, the man is hoeing along a row at sunrise or sunset, his back to the viewer, the sky ahead of him a bright turquoise. This intense hue also appears prominently in the right half of the mural, defining the large gears behind the working woman, which stand out against the darker, cooler blues of the woman's shirt, her work station, and this segment's background. The worker faces forward—towards the bracero and the viewer—and wears modern factory gear—an orange hard hat (a hue echoing that of the

---

[20] Martha Pskowski reports that "[s]ince mid-August [2021], millions of gallons a day of wastewater have flowed down the river along the length of El Paso-Juárez .... The Frontera Force wastewater main transports sewage from West El Paso for treatment at the John T. Hickerson Water Reclamation Facility. When the pipeline and its backup ruptured in August, El Paso Water determined a diversion into the Rio Grande was the best way to avoid human contact with the sewage" ("Sewage Discharge"). Local artist, Janette Terrazas places this contamination within a larger context: "The racist policies in the border between México and USA have eroded from our collective memory the notion that the Rio Grande is a living organism. If we re-signify our concept of the river as one of our main sources of life and not as a territorial boundary between the two countries, perhaps many things could start to change."" The problem of pollution in the Rio Bravo," she adds, "affects the health of the populations along the border on both sides and its effects flow into the Gulf of Mexico. Hundreds of plastics are threatening human life and species in this area" (Terrazas). Most recently, on November 21, 2022 "Blockages in a sewer line caused an estimated 250,000 gallons of wastewater to spill into the Rio Grande flood plain near the University of Texas at El Paso early this week" (Pskowki, "El Paso Water").

bracero's work shirt)—safety goggles, and a clip-on security/identification badge. She is wielding a hand tool like an inline screwdriver as well as manipulating small parts. The blue base hues of her shirt and the lighter tones defining its folds resemble those in the blue jeans of the bracero.

Curving across the frame, a stylized, blue-gray bridge bisects the mural diagonally, separating the two figures. The two ends of the bridge morph in the center to join as arms—two hands clasping at the wrists: one palm up, the other palm down. Each hand is a mirror image of the other and is identical in color—a warm hue with pale pink highlights—the same soft colors used to delineate the furrows in the field at the left. The "two" arms of the bridge are sketched in similar hues, tones, and lines, although on the left (the American) side, an extra element emerges, darker and described with more angular lines, perhaps a stylized depiction of the border wall—or simply the supports of the bridge.

The curved bridge divides the two segments of the image, but its placement, angle, and gentle curve also unify the composition, balancing it and allowing the two regions to interpenetrate. The image of the field and bracero, for instance, stretches past the center of the mural, its lines leading to and blending with those of the bridge, while the colors and images associated with the drawing of the factory worker extend, if thinly, entirely across the work.

Such interpenetration, along with the facing figures and the many colors echoes between the two segments, links the two halves of the image, the two workers, the two regions. The mural highlights the fact that despite the artificial separations, there is no "*otro lado.*" Interestingly, too, each worker is depicted as having several hands, a detail which of course conveys motion/ activity over time (particularly as a viewer walks across the bridge), but may also emphasize the repetitive nature of the work, the ceaseless motion required, the many, many hours of labor endured, the extreme forms of exploitation that the workers must live through as they toil in the fields and the factories. The multiple hands may also serve as a collective represented by the single individual. In other words, the multiple hands may be seen as visible symbols of the super-exploitation experienced by workers; yet the hands may also signify solidarity and the hope for resistance across the boundaries of time and space.

It is worth mentioning another significant detail about the mural in its context. At its extreme right, an indigenous woman is depicted with her child, her right arm raised with fists clenched. At first glance, there seems to be no clear separation of this figure from the "Bajo el Puente" mural. The image shares the same blue background, and the line of the woman's shoulders continues the line of the bridge's railing. The figure seems to blend naturally into the Yorch mural as another subject. However, she is part of a *separate* mural. Similarly, another mural adjoins the *Bajo el Puente* mural on the left, featuring different colors but incorporating a curve that mirrors the arc of the adjoining bridge in the "Bajo el Puente" mural. This mural represents the green stems and one white bloom of a columnar cactus. A significant point about the seamless blending of these images with the "Bajo" mural is that it directly opposses the Western notion of individualized pieces of art that must be seen in their singular glory. Indeed, weaving the indigenous woman and the cactus blossom into the mural can be seen as intentional acts on the part of the creators and viewers. Needless to say, it is appropriate that a work celebrating a borderless world reflects that political goal in its own creative form.

This mural, according to Mendoza, "is a symbol of the history of the El Paso-Juárez border." 'We are this unity, between El Paso and Juárez," he says (Villagran). Mendoza refers to the mural as marking "bygone patterns of migration … of *mexicanos* who crossed as Braceros to work the fields in the U.S., and of *mexicanas* who migrated to Juárez in search of opportunity in the city's ubiquitous factories" (Villagran). Mendoza distinguishes between the unity created and lived by the people rather than one manufactured by state policies: "The mural speaks to the unity of the border but (the unity) is due to the people here, families, people that work, study, that go back and forth. It's not about international policies." Even though Mendoza himself doesn't "go to the United States," he acknowledges that "there has been so much that has come to me from there. There is so much that is generated by this cross-border life, so much that jumps (across both sides), whether it's information, exhibitions or materials" (Boudreaux).

However, this mural is not just a celebration of the unity of place and people or "bygone practices." It is also an urgent and timely artistic call to arms, protesting the "contamination of the river that the U.S. and Mexico share. He and other artists belonging to the Rezizte border art collective painted the mural over a week, despite the stomach-turning stench of raw sewage running in the canal" (Villagran). "The reality is that this sewage here in the river means that things are not OK," Mendoza said, "referring to El Paso's untreated wastewater spilling into the Rio Grande since August. "People literally have to be covered in excrement to be able to cross over, and it's just sad" (qtd. in Boudreaux). Since August 2021, "El Paso Water has been dumping millions of gallons a day of wastewater into the river known as the Rio Grande in the U.S. and Río Bravo in Mexico, after a wastewater main ruptured. El Paso Water connected the new wastewater pipeline in December and the sewage discharge is supposed to end after a testing phase in January" (Villagran).

Having established the spatial context for this mural, let me now relate my experience of "viewing" this mural. Such an experience, I think, is vital to meaning-making and goes along with a more traditional "reading" of a text. My first glimpse of this mural was when I was crossing the international bridge. It is significant that, because of the security wiring that covers the entire walkway, it is impossible to see the mural with any degree of clarity from the bridge. Thus, it seems important to view the mural from the vantage point of the canal. As an outsider, I had no inside knowledge about the best way to reach the exact spot where the mural was located. Approaching the area from the Juárez side, I had to cross a busy highway and then make my way to the edge of the slope on which the mural was painted. Since the mural is completely obscured if one stands facing the border fence, it is necessary to descend to the canal. A guardrail is placed all around the top of the slope to prevent pedestrians from accessing the canal. I decided to clamber down the slope to view the mural from the side of the canal. There wasn't a soul in sight, though I must have been clearly visible to those crossing the bridge. As I took out my phone to take some pictures of the main murals and several others that were on the south slope, I saw that my phone had a message which said that it was not operating at the moment—that I should try back in 15 minutes. I put away the phone in order to examine the mural more closely; at that moment, I saw a white *Guardia Nacional* pick-up with flashing lights driving rapidly in my direction. Two officers were in the cab, and two other heavily armed officers stood in the bed of the truck. They stopped and called me over. A conversation ensued in Spanish. They asked for my name, my place of origin, and the reasons for my being at this spot. I tried to explain in my limited Spanish that I was interested in the mural and wanted to photograph it. They seemed bemused by that explanation. "Para qué?" was the repeated question. Based on my partial comprehension of what they were saying, they seemed to suggest that I was trespassing and that it was illegal for me to be where I was. I apologized and they, very fortunately, did not prolong the interrogation, asking me to leave. As they drove away, I clambered back up the slope.

I think the contours of this incident are important to reflect on. My first thought was that it is ironic that this important piece of art that celebrated the unity of the two cities should be located at this desolate spot, next to a canal with sewage flowing by, with a heavily guarded border fence patrolled by the armed might of the state, whose emissaries see little point in anyone viewing this particular piece of art. Indeed, the fact that viewing it should be seen as a transgression seemed highly ironic. However, on reflection, I realized that the location of this art is intricately linked to the art piece itself. Indeed, how appropriate it is that this mural should be exactly where it is. This is not a government-sanctioned mural, located downtown, made famous because it offers a banal message of unity. Indeed, everything about the location of the mural was completely synchronous with its message. This mural is about ordinary workers who are confronted by state sanctioned borders and profit seekers on both sides. The people depicted on the mural represents the workers who grow the food and make the products that Americans use. The labor of these workers is produced on the land of people who have been displaced and dispossessed. The owners of capital and nation states have no scruples benefiting from the labor of the frontier workers, and they will put up whatever barriers necessary—physical or otherwise—to exploit labor on both sides. Despite all these oppressive circumstances, the people of both cities refuse to be separated, to be divided against each other. It also became evident to me that perhaps this mural is best seen by those crossing back and forth on the bridge above as they prepare to encounter the border ahead of them. They may be reminded as they attempt to cross that this border constitutes an arbitrary separation, one determined by caprice, chance, and capital.

Sister Cities/Ciudades Hermanas

Less than a mile from the *Bajo el Puente* mural is the El Segundo Barrio in El Paso, the entry point to the United States. This neighborhood has a rich and storied history, serving as a border location where many of the residents recognize few distinctions between the United States and Mexico.[21] Over the last 100 years and more, the famous and the not so

---

[21] The El Segundo Barrio and its adjoining neighborhood Barrio Duranguito have a storied past: "When the Mexican Revolution started, in 1910, the people dislocated from south of the river gave these neighborhoods the character of a barrio. In many ways, the area is as historic for Mexico as it is for the United States. Mexican revolutionary Francisco Madero, for example, kept an office here during the revolution, not long before his brief tenure as Mexico's president. Pancho Villa's ghost is everywhere too. Villa spent his exile in Duranguito before returning to Mexico to take over the famed División del Norte. He hoarded guns and gold in houses around the neighborhood" (Hooks).

famous went back and forth across the river, and the neighborhood attained a distinctive character that still survives. Today, it remains a primarily Latine neighborhood, adjoining both a wealthy downtown area to the north and the international border on the south. Walking south on El Paso Street toward East Father Rahm Avenue and the international border, it becomes apparent that this is a neighborhood that has maintained its independence from land developers. Although there are a few signs of gentrification, by and large, the neighborhood is a collection of homes, stores, restaurants, and small businesses, catering to residents from both sides of the border. There is a singular lack of chain stores or restaurants. If the shoppers were to walk a few blocks north toward downtown, the prices for food items and essentials would double. However, because of this proximity to downtown and because of an unstated but obvious attempt to de-Mexicanize the neighborhood, some 15 years back, a group of businessmen and city politicians, using the power of eminent domain, tried to colonize the neighborhood, attempting to force hundreds of residents to leave their homes. The neighborhood would have become what is a familiar sight in many US cities: a combination of condos, lofts, and mixed-use developments. Avoiding this fate, one that would have expanded already existing structural inequities, the residents of El Segundo Barrio fought back, and, today, there is not a Starbucks in sight in the Barrio.[22]

The texture of this spirit of resistance and community solidarity permeates the neighborhood, and arguably the many murals play a significant role in marking the distinctive and continuing history of this

[22] El Plan, as it was then known, was supported by politicians and businessmen. Beto O'Rourke, then an emerging politician, was one of the voices calling for this reinvention of the neighborhood. According to reports, "The redevelopment plan was drawn up behind closed doors over two years by the Paso del Norte Group, a civic organization of wealthy oligarchs, industrialists, real estate developers, and politicos from both sides of the border" (Welcome). For a sample of the "visionary" hopes of these "leaders," consider this statement: "Wouldn't it be fun if there was this neat urban center with lots to do downtown? That's what we'd like to see for El Paso," says Kathryn Dodson, the city's economic development director. "It would be great for El Pasoans to go to a Starbucks downtown" (qtd. in Welcome). See also Alena Semuels's "El Paso's Learning That Not Everyone Hates Sprawl" in *The Atlantic* (January 2016).

6 VISUALIZING BORDERS: M.I.A.'S "BORDERS" AND MURAL ART IN CIUDAD… 211

community.[23] What makes the neighborhood particularly unique, as I have already mentioned, is its proximity to the international bridges that connect it to Ciudad Juárez. As frequent border crossers and new migrants cross over from Mexico on the Paso del Norte international bridge, they are greeted with the "Bienvenidos" sign on El Paso Street. The rituals and structures of the military state apparatus that accompanied the crossing—the border guards, the checkpoints, the questions, the walls, and the barbed wires—are replaced with familiar street signs, a familiar language, and the sound of familiar songs. Pay phones—a rare sight these days—line the street, and private taxis await some of those who continue their journey from this point. Certainly, this arrival is not available for everyone, and undoubtedly not for those turning themselves in to the border authorities or those risking an unauthorized crossing.

Its sister city, Ciudad Juárez, El Paso, and especially El Segundo Barrio has a long and storied history of mural art.[24] Eduardo García points out: "Community service centers, churches, and schools situated in the *Segundo*

[23] One of the ways in which murals in this neighborhood and the spirit of resistance are celebrated is the Borderland Jam street art festival. Myker Yrrabali, a muralist and tattoo artist from El Paso, who has been involved with the annual event sees these occasions as a way to resist the division imposed by outside forces: "This is *our* land, this is *our* home …. Many people here have family across the border. Many come back and forth for work or school or both. It is our sister city and they are trying to block the view of her beautiful face. We want our work to say loudly, 'you can't keep us out, and you can't keep us in!'" When asked about the contentious border wall, Yrrabali seems undaunted. "We hope it's paintable because both sides will shout till it crumbles. It does not belong in our landscape. This land is beautiful, the world is beautiful, and it is greedy to want to corral it in and tear families apart, and prevent learning and appreciating other cultures" (White). The Borderland Jam Graffiti Art Show returned to El Paso after five years in February 2022, over President Day's weekend. Over 100 artists from Europe and the United States accompanied local artists to paint murals in the South El Paso neighborhood. See the *El Paso Times* article "Photos: The Borderland Jam graffiti art show returns to El Paso after five years" to view the various murals.

[24] Eduardo García comments that "[m]uralism in the city of El Paso, Texas has historically been linked to societal issues affecting the members of its *barrios*. From the early examples of murals linked to social institutions providing services to the members of the community to the lineage of Chicano and transnational sensibilities instilled through Bowie High School art programs in post-Civil Rights El Paso, it is evident these traditions have a long-standing importance to the community" (García). For an analysis of how a mural became a point of contention for the Anglo community in El Paso, see Martin Paredes's "What A 1994 Mural Controversy Says About Who Speaks For El Paso." El Paso's distinctive history of mural-making was also featured in a 2021 *New York Times* piece, "Art Without Borders."

For a detailed history of mural art in El Paso, see Miguel Juárez's *Colors on Desert Walls: The Murals of El Paso.*

Barrio have long been relevant to its history of cross-culture demographics. These facilities have not only served the downtown district of El Paso through social action; they have also formed part of the community's identity and its access to public art" ("El Paso Segundo"). Nora Rivera draws our attention to a longer tradition that connects contemporary mural painting to its aesthetic and political antecedents:

> Chicanx murals are part of a robust multimodal tradition of co-composing knowledge rooted in the ancient Mesoamerican practice of the *tlacuilo* (painter, writer, historian), also called *tlahcuilo* or *tlahcuiloque. Tlacuilos* recorded history and culture in pictographic codices made of animal skin called *amoxtli*, which European colonizers refused to validate as the first books conceived in the Western Hemisphere. Like *amoxtli*, Chicanx murals chronicle the history and the stories of a culture and provide a rhetorical outlet that in each interpretation grants readers an active role in the process of meaning making." (120)

García's and Rivera's comments indicate that these contemporary murals are not just autonomous pieces of art but acquire a co-constituted meaning because of their presence in a community with a distinctive history. The murals, in other words, are a living and evolving presence, and rather than offering a uniform or fixed meaning, they are actively decoded and reconstituted based on the viewers' own particular experiences within the community.

This point becomes salient when we consider the mural, "Sister Cities/ Ciudades Hermanas," a 2015 creation of LxsDos on the wall on East Rahm Street, where it meets El Paso Street (see Fig. 6.2, LxsDos, "SisterCities/Ciudades Hermanas," May 3, 2022). LxsDos is a duo that consists of partners Ramon and Christian Cardenas. "Sister Cities" is "wheat pasted" on the wall and can be seen as one walks north on El Paso Street. It is one of the first murals, in fact, that one sees after crossing the bridge into El Paso. This is one of the busiest locations in the neighborhood, and the intersection is usually buzzing with people. Salespeople shout out the prices of their wares and call out to prospective customers. Piles of clothing rest on tables as people search for good deals. A soundtrack accompanies these activities, either of popular songs or announcements over loudspeakers publicizing competitions, events, and sales at the nearest store. Creating art in this environment is clearly a dynamic process. Muralist Lupe Casillas-Lowenberg describes this creative process thus: "it is emotion, spatial and spiritual action involving an audience or

Fig. 6.2 LxsDos, "Sister Cities/Ciudades Hermanas," 3 May 2022

community. What is important is the relationship between the two, the interaction of each other at every phase of the piece" (qtd. in Juárez 39).

At the most basic level, the mural announces the fact that the two cities are inseparable. The sisters are embodied as one. Their hair fuses as do their bodies. Their eyes are directly facing the artificial boundary erected

Fig. 6.3 LxsDos, "Sister Cities/Ciudades Hermanas," Lattice Detail, 3 May 2002

by the states, one that the sisters' presence explicitly contradicts. The lattice work that clothes them conveys both realities of the border: On the one hand, it evokes chain links, and the fence that separates many families, and yet the lattice work also serves as a unifying theme. It is both enclosure and link, a chain that imprisons, and a chain that binds together. The lattice work is dotted with images of cacti, flowers, and faces (see Fig. 6.3, "Sister Cities/Ciudades Hermanas," Lattice Detail, May 3, 2002). According to the artists, these faces, some wearing masks, are of community members. The river, likewise, that flows through the middle of the mural is not a symbol of separation. Indeed, it appears to emerge from the sisters and their unity, even if it is drained of its life by commercial interests. The businesses on both sides of the river are not distinctively apart. Aside from a sign "Richards Printing," the businesses on the US side may as well be in Mexico. There is an eatery advertising a classic Mexican dish, Menudo; the sign for "La Bota" has the artists' signature, Los Dos on it, which may not just refer to the artists but to the sisters—the two of them, both of them (together). The signs on the Juárez side reflect the realities and contradictions of cross border commercial traffic. Indeed, the *Dentista* and the *Cambio* are the first stops for many when they cross over. The dentist charges far less in Mexico (prices can be at least 70 percent less in Mexico), and it is not uncommon for residents of Texas to cross the border to the other side merely for dental work. Ramon Cardenas reminds us that the mural signifies "how the two cities rely on each other. And that's important for us to show" (White). "We see our work as an intersection between Mexican muralism and street art," says Cardenas. "It's about re-appropriating public spaces with images that are relatable to us as a community, and in which we are protagonists" (White).

One of these images is that of the jaguar that sheds light on the two sisters. The jaguar, recalling Rivera's comment, is part of a long tradition, heralding the ways in which this image functions in Mesoamerican art.[25] Significantly, one of the attributes of the jaguar is that the animal crosses over between worlds. The sisters are also blessed by the jaguar's spirit of strength and protective power. Many of the faces within the lattice work are wearing jaguar masks, "a mask worn by warriors in pre-Hispanic cultures, to update an ancient symbol of power" (Martinez). Juxtaposing the Mesoamerican image of strength at the top of the mural with the modern cities and its people and shops at the bottom of the mural connects the past and the present. If one task of the muralist is to remind the people who have been dispossessed and marginalized and told over the years that their pasts and their histories are inferior or are to be disregarded in the face of an immensely superior Western culture, then the artist's addition of the jaguar is an affirmation that an equally rich past remains with them. It is significant that the sisters, too, are not depicted in a style that represents a particular moment in history; more significantly, they symbolize a collective since their bodies are made of the landscape and the people of the borderlands.

As I mentioned in my introduction to this section, the role of gender in representing a certain reality of these borderlands is a significant factor in "reading" this mural. Christian Cardenas reminds us that "'Sister Cities' is a straight-up political comment on the borderland. It's about how these two cities have had to back each other up. And it's important to have them be women, have symbols that are feminine because Juarez has been

---

[25] See Nicholas Saunders's edited collection, *Icons of Power: Feline Symbolism in the Americas* (1998).

216   K. CHOWDHURY

suffering for years. I mean, as a woman who grew up in Juarez, it's been really hard to see how a political boundary can change how women are treated or how safe you are when walking down a street" (Martinez). Just as the representation of the maquiladora worker in the Juárez mural pays homage to the labor of the hundreds of thousands who have toiled in these factories, the image of the two sisters not only represents the cities themselves, but also comments on the special burden that the exploitative landscape of the borderland has inflicted on women. After all, many of the murdered women in the borderlands are workers who have migrated in order to seek employment. According to Ramon Cardenas, "The women [in the mural] are used as a metaphor for the connection between the border communities. The characters illustrated inside the sister's chain fence pattern shirt represent the people who have been at the mercy and directly affected by capitalist trade agreements and interests, which have a very notable impact on our communities. At the bottom, both landscapes converge at the center with a dried up river in between. It talks about our commonalities, like being illuminated by the same sun, but also about our struggles" (White).[26]

As I mentioned in my comments on the "experience" of seeing *Bajo el Puente* at its site, the El Segundo Barrio location, similarly, is a vital element in how people encounter "Two Sisters." This mural is located in the midst of the bustling ordinariness of everyday life. Thousands see this mural every day, many of whom are border crossers themselves. Without casting a long interpretive shadow on how this image may be seen by others, it is important to mention that this image interrogates commonly held notions of art and its purpose. Unlike state sanctioned murals that have become points of interests for tourists, the murals in El Segundo barrio are as much a part of the natural landscape of this neighborhood, as are the signs for sales or the services advertising cell phone plans. The

---

[26] Another well-regarded artist Jesús "Cimi" Alvarado, captures this element of binationality even while acknowledging both the labor of border women and their vulnerability. Not far from the Segundo Barrio, his Pachuca Blood mural is located in the underpass bridges connecting Mexico to the United States in the Lincoln Park area. Alvarado captures the Chicana woman, known as the Pachuca, with the two flags of the United States and Mexico. Describing the significance of this mural, García points out: "The Pachuca stands tall and with fierce determination on her face, reaffirming her proud yet liminal placement in between two countries. Alvarado dedicated this mural to the women affected by the violence of the late 2000s throughout Ciudad Juárez, the border city plagued in recent years by cartel drug wars, government corruption, and silenced femicide" (García).

6 VISUALIZING BORDERS: M.I.A.'S "BORDERS" AND MURAL ART IN CIUDAD... 217

working-class residents of this barrio do not have the time to visit or are rarely welcomed into the formal spaces of museum, yet they are constantly consuming art in the midst of their daily work life. Ramon Cardenas stresses the significance of this art for the people, art that depicts their own lives. Explaining the import of their art project Make Shift, Cardenas affirms that it is

> work about normal people: workers, photographers, journalists, migrants, musicians, street vendors. It's for people of the community. When they see these bigger than life works, it's our hope they feel empowered. A lot of the murals that they're used to seeing aren't relatable to them ... It's also an homage. An homage to artisans and farmworkers, and it's what we're trying to do with Make Shift. The term itself is a play on words. People making do with what they have. Being ingenious. (Maritinez)

Indeed, the spirit of these principles can be directly applied to the *Bajo el Puento* mural across the border.

In her pathbreaking work *Borderlands, La Frontera: The New Mestiza*, Gloria Anzaldúa refers to the US–Mexico border as "*una herida abierta* [an open wound] where the Third World grates against the first and bleeds. And before a scab forms it hemorrhages again, the lifeblood of the two worlds merging to form a third country—a border culture" (3). Anzaldúa also speaks about the indomitable spirit of resistance that informs the borderlands. "I see oposición e insurrección" in the borderlands, she writes, affirming that "someone in me takes into our own hands, and eventually, takes dominion over serpents—over my own body, my sexual activity, my soul, my mind, my weaknesses and strengths. Mine. Ours" (51). Anzaldúa's words capture the spirit of the art on the walls of Juárez/ El Paso. Making art in the shadow of militaristic states has particular significance since it not only directly confronts the many barriers and walls that loom over these adjoining neighborhoods, but also unapologetically declares that the people of these borderlands will not be separated by states that care little about their lives other than the surplus that can be extracted from them. The spirit of resistance is alive not just because the artists want to affirm it but because they see it in the textures of peoples' everyday lives. Through their everyday actions, their art, and their crossings, people from both cities enact a refusal of border rules—rules that are in place to enable economic extraction and to further the power of the state.[27]

Although Yorch and the LxsDos muralists appear to occupy different artistic terrain from M.I.A., all of their creations reflect a spirit of solidarity with those who are on the receiving end of border rules. Moreover, both art forms, the murals and the music video, enjoy a far greater public reach than novels or mainstream films, partly because of their immediate visual impact and partly because of their wide availability, and thus can become part of a broad public conversation. Both, too, offer the possibility for radical alliances across borders. As such, they radiate a political energy and embody hope for change.

In spite of these similarities, there are of course many, many differences between M.I.A.'s video and the murals. An obvious one relates to location: a music video clearly has the potential to reach a transnational audience, informing a poetics of resistance wherever the violence of border rules destroys the lives of "others." Murals in the borderlands, on the other hand, acquire their significance, including their ability to bring people together, because of their location within a specific space. Another difference between the texts relates to the degree to which they or their art might be seen as politically compromised. As I have demonstrated in this chapter, while M.I.A. is embedded in the world of capitalist commodity relations, a fact that problematizes her acts of solidarity with the dispossessed and oppressed, the muralists are very much of their community, and their work emerges from and is dedicated to their community. Despite these differences, however, the artists in both cases make use of visually charged, accessible art forms, challenge the norms of border rules, and point the way toward abolition.

Works Cited

Agresta, Michael. "How a Public Art Project in El Paso and Ciudad Juárez is Spurring Cross-Border Conversations." *Texas Monthly*, 13 Nov. 2019, https://www.texasmonthly.com/arts-entertainment/border-tuner-art-el-paso-juarez-rafael-lozano-hemmer/.

---

[27] The lives of ordinary people in this region counter the popular representations of Juárez as the epicenter of crime and terroristic activities. For an oppositional reading of such representations, see Carlos Gallego's "'Juarez, the Beast': States of Fantasy and the Transnational City in *Sicario*," a film in which Juárez is depicted "as a menacing entity encompassing everything that is threatening about the US-Mexico border" (66–67).

Ali, Lorraine. "Music: A Refugee Gone M.I.A." *Newsweek*, 27 Mar. 2005, https://www.newsweek.com/music-refugee-gone-mia-114505.

Alvarez, Priscilla. "Federal judge blocks Biden administration from lifting Title 42 for now." *CNN*, 20 May 2022, https://www.cnn.com/2022/05/20/politics/title-42-biden-us-mexico-border/index.html.

Alvarez, Robert. "Reconceptualizing the Space of the Mexico–US Borderline." *A Companion to Border Studies*, edited by Thomas M. Wilson and Hastings Donnan, Blackwell Publishing Ltd., 2012, pp. 538–556.

Anzaldúa, Gloria. *Borderlands, La Frontera: The New Mestiza*, 4th ed., Aunt Lute Books, 2012.

Baca, Annette. "Puro Borde murals show the colors of hope in the border cities." *Borderzine: Reporting Across Fronteras*, 17 May 2012, https://borderzine.com/2012/05/puro-borde-murals-show-the-colors-of-hope-in-the-border-cities/.

Bassil, Ryan. "M.I.A. Talks About the 'Borders' Video and Why She's Getting Legal Threats for a Soccer Jersey." *Vice*, 12 Jan. 2016, https://www.vice.com/en/article/64y57q/mia-interview-2016.

Boudreaux, Corrie. "Juárez artist, baker depicts border life in murals and pan." *El Paso Matters*, 10 Jan. 2022, https://elpasomatters.org/2022/01/10/juarez-artist-baker-depicts-border-life-in-murals-and-pan/.

———. "Public Memorialization and the Grievability of Victims in Ciudad Juárez." *Borders and the Politics of Mourning*, special issue of *Social Research*, vol. 83, no. 2, Summer 2016, pp. 391–417.

Boudreaux, Corrie. "Public Memorialization and the Grievability of Victims in Ciudad Juarez." *Borders and the Politics of Mourning*, special issue of *Social Research*, vol. 83, no. 2, 2016, pp. 391–417.

Caraballo, Ecleen Luzmila. "'Ni Una Más': Hundreds Demand Justice for Isabel Cabanillas and Countless Other Femicide Victims." *Remezcla*, 20 Jan. 2020, https://remezcla.com/culture/isabel-cabanillas-femicides-mexico-juarez-protest/.

Chacón, Justin Akers. *The Border Crossed Us: The Case for Opening the US-Mexico Border*. Haymarket, 2021.

Chavez Leyva, Yolanda. "Lxs Dos: The Power of Fronterizx Art." *Fierce Fronteriza*, 28 June 2017, https://www.fiercefronteriza.com/fierce-fronteriza-blog/lxs-dos-the-power-of-fronterizx-art.

Chen, Min. "Catch Me at the Border: M.I.A.'s negotiation between art and politics culminates in her video for 'Borders.'" *Proxy Music*, 21 Nov. 2018, https://proxymusic.club/2018/11/21/mia-borders-video/.

Clover, Joshua. *Roadrunner*. Duke University Press, 2021.

"Colectivo Rezizte." *Mural Arts Philadelphia*, https://www.muralarts.org/artist/colectivo-rezizte/.

220   K. CHOWDHURY

Conlon, Deirdre and Nancy Hemstra. "Detention Economies: Commodifying Migrant Social Death." *Migration and Mortality: Social Death, Dispossession, and Survival in the Americas*, edited by Jamie Longazel and Miranda Cady Hallett, Temple University Press, 2021.

Cox, Jamieson. "M.I.A. embarks on a refugee's journey in her new 'Borders' video." *The Verge*, 27 Nov. 2015, https://www.theverge.com/2015/11/27/9807064/mia-borders-music-video-matahdatah-album-refugee-crisis.

De Genova, Nicholas. "The 'migrant crisis' as racial crisis: do *Black Lives Matter* in Europe?" *Ethnic and Racial Studies*, vol. 41, no. 10, 2018, pp. 1765–1782, https://doi.org/10.1080/01419870.2017.1361543.

Dunn, Timothy. *Blockading the Border and Human Rights: The El Paso Operation that Remade Immigration Enforcement*. University of Texas Press, 2010.

"'EU must militarize chaotic immigration, identify states behind Middle East crisis'—Zizek to RT." *RT*, 22 Apr. 2016, https://www.rt.com/news/340562-eu-refugee-policy-chaos-militarization/.

Feeney, Nolan. "Why M.I.A. Made a Video About the Migrant Crisis and Put It on Apple Music." *Time*, 24 Dec. 2015, https://time.com/4160294/mia-borders-apple-music-migrant-crisis-interview/.

Gallego, Carlos. "'Juarez, the Beast': States of Fantasy and the Transnational City in *Sicario*." *Arizona Quarterly: A Journal of American Literature, Culture, and Theory*, vol. 74, no. 1, Spring 2018, pp. 45–72.

García, Eduardo. "El Paso Segundo Barrio Muralism: Barrio History, Memory, and Identity in Community Artwork." *Chamisa: A Journal of Literary, Performance, and Visual Arts of the Greater Southwest*, vol. 1, no. 1, 2021.

González Rodríguez, Sergio. *The Femicide Machine*. Translated by Michael Parker-Stainback, Semiotext(e). 2012.

Goodman, David, and Edgar Sandoval. "Abbott Threatens to Declare an 'Invasion' as Migrant Numbers Climb." *New York Times*, 30 Apr. 2022, https://www.nytimes.com/2022/04/30/us/texas-border-abbott.html.

Gramlich, John. "Key Facts About Title 42." *Pew Research Center*, 27 Apr. 2022, https://www.pewresearch.org/fact-tank/2022/04/27/key-facts-about-title-42-the-pandemic-policy-that-has-reshaped-immigration-enforcement-at-u-s-mexico-border/

Hayter, David. "M.I.A.—'Borders' Review." *411Mania*, 28 Nov. 2015.

Hirschberg, Lynn. "M.I.A.'s Agitprop Pop." *New York Times*, 25 May 2010, https://www.nytimes.com/2010/05/30/magazine/30mia-t.html.

Hooks, Christopher. "The Battle for El Paso's South Side." *Texas Monthly*, October 2017, https://www.texasmonthly.com/news-politics/battle-el-pasos-south-side/.

Jeyaraj, D.B.S. "The LTTE's 'Great Heroes Day.'" *Daily FT*, 1 Dec. 2021, https://www.ft.lk/columns/The-LTTE-s-Great-Heroes-Day/4-726794.

Juárez, Miguel. *Colors on Desert Walls: The Murals of El Paso*. Texas Western Press, 1997.

Kornhaber, Spencer. "M.I.A.'s Critique of Wokeness." *The Atlantic*, 5 Oct. 2018, https://www.theatlantic.com/entertainment/archive/2018/10/mia-maya-matangi-documentary-interview/571750/.

———. "The Rapper of Refugees: What M.I.A.'s 'Borders' Video Really About." *The Atlantic*, 30 Nov. 2015, https://www.theatlantic.com/entertainment/archive/2015/11/mia-borders-video-refugees-migration-appropriation/418017/.

Lee, Anthony. *Painting on the Left: Diego Rivera, Radical Politics, and San Francisco's Public Murals*. University of California Press, 1999.

Little, Walter E., and David Carey Jr. "Reclaiming the Nation through Public Murals: Maya Resistance and the Reinterpretation of History." *Radical History Review*, vol. 106, Winter 2010, pp. 5–26.

LxsDos (Ramon and Christian Cardenas). *Ciudades Hermanas/Sister Cities*. El Paso, 2015.

Lozano, Nina Maria. *Not One More!: Feminicidio on the Border*. Ohio State Press, 2019.

Lugo, Alejandro. *Fragmented Lives, Assembled Parts*. University of Texas Press, 2008.

Maher, Bill. "Episode #7.13." *Real Time with Bill Maher*, directed by Hal Grant, Bill Maher Productions, 22 May 2009.

Matangi/Maya/M.I.A. Directed by Steve Loveridge, Cinereach, 2018.

Martinez, Freddy. "On the Streets of El Paso and Juárez, "Sister Cities" Art Project Pays Tribute to Border Communities." *Remezcla*, 7 July 2016, https://remezcla.com/features/culture/interview-los-dos/.

Martinez, Marta. "Central American women find safety and strength in mural painting." *UNHCR*, 18 Jan. 2019, https://www.unhcr.org/en-us/news/stories/2019/1/5c41fa414/central-american-women-find-safety-strength-mural-painting.html.

Martínez, Oscar J. *Border Boomtown: Ciudad Juárez since 1848*. University of Texas Press, 1978.

———. *Ciudad Juárez: Saga of a Legendary Border City*. University of Arizona Press, 2010.

Mellin, Cali. "Producing Visibility and Community in Ciudad Juárez: Returning to Gloria Anzaldúa's *Borderlands/La Frontera*." English Master's Essays, 30, University of St. Thomas, 2020, https://ir.stthomas.edu/cas_engl_mat/30/.

Mendoza, Jorge Peres (Yorch). *Under the Bridge/Bajo el Puente*, Ciudad Juárez, January 2022.

M.I.A. "Borders." *AIM*, Interscope, 2015.

———. "Borders." *Apple Music*, 27 Nov. 2015, https://music.apple.com/us/post/1062992861.

———. "Paper Planes." *Kala*, Interscope, 2008.

———. Performer. "M.I.A." *Colbert Report*, 2013.

222   K. CHOWDHURY

————. "Sunshowers." *Arular*, XL Recordings, 2004.
"M.I.A.: 'How Can the West Turn People Away?'" *NPR*, 15 Dec. 2015, https://www.npr.org/2015/12/15/459114242/m-i-a-how-can-the-west-turn-people-away.
"MIA reveals audiovisual project 'Matahdatah Scroll 01 Broader Than a Border' via Apple Music." *NME*, 13 July 2015, https://www.nme.com/news/music/mia-39-1216318.
Minsker, Evan. "M.I.A. and Surkin's Gener8ion Share 'The New International Sound Pt. II' Video." *Pitchfork*, 15 June 2015, https://pitchfork.com/news/59974-mia-and-surkins-gener8ion-share-the-new-international-sound-pt-ii-video/.
————. "MIA Releases Audiovisual Project 'Matahdatah Scroll 01 Broader Than a Border' via Apple Music." *Pitchfork*, 13 July 2015, https://pitchfork.com/news/59908-mia-releases-audiovisual-project-matahdatah-scroll-01-broader-than-a-border/.
Monroe, Jazz. "M.I.A. Travels with Refugees in 'Borders' Video." *Pitchfork*, 27 Nov. 2015, https://pitchfork.com/news/62287-mia-travels-with-refugees-in-borders-video/.
"Mujer Migrante Memorial." *Mujer Migrante Memorial*, 5 May 2021, https://storymaps.arcgis.com/stories/5a0f3d3b42634812b33ae64b1924cd9a.
Nolfi, Joey. "M.I.A. tackles NFL in 'Boom ADD.'" *Entertainment Weekly*, 25 Feb. 2016, https://ew.com/article/2016/02/25/mia-nfl-boom-add/.
Omelas, Omar. "Under the Bridge/Bajo El Puente." *El Paso Times*, 4 Jan. 2022, https://www.elpasotimes.com/story/news/2022/01/04/border-art-collective-unveils-rio-grande-mural-downtownjuarez/9078448002/.
Orozco, Elva Fabiola. "Mapping the Trail of Violence: The Memorialization of Public Space as a Counter-Geography of Violence in Ciudad Juárez." *Journal of Latin American Geography*, vol.18, no. 3, October 2019, pp. 132–157.
Ortiz, Victor. *El Paso: Local Frontiers at a Global Crossroads*. University of Minnesota Press, 2004.
Ostroff, Joshua. "Tiger, Tiger, Burning Bright: Tamil Pop Provocatrice M.I.A. Wages War on the Dancefloor." *Eyeweekly*, 27 Jan. 2005,
Pantaleo, Katherine. "Gendered Violence: An Analysis of the Maquiladora Murders." *International Criminal Justice Review*, vol. 20, no. 4, December 2010, pp. 349–365.
Paredes, Martin. "What A 1994 Mural Controversy Says About Who Speaks For El Paso." *El Paso News*, 24 Jan. 2022, https://elpasonews.org/2022/01/24/what-a-1994-mural-controversy-says-about-who-speaks-for-el-paso/.
Perera, Melani Manel. "Paying tribute to Tamil Tigers banned in Sri Lanka." *Asia News*, 26 Nov. 2013, https://www.asianews.it/news-en/Paying-tribute-to-Tamil-Tigers-banned-in-Sri-Lanka-29648.html.

"Photos: The Borderland Jam graffiti art show returns to El Paso after five years." *El Paso Times*, 22 Feb. 2022, https://www.elpasotimes.com/picture-gallery/entertainment/2022/02/20/photos-borderland-jam-graffiti-art-show-returns-el-paso/6866830001/.

Pskowski, Martha. "Sewage discharge in the Rio Grande: One of the biggest border stories of 2021 will continue in 2022." *El Paso Times*, 30 Dec. 2021, https://www.elpasotimes.com/story/news/2021/12/29/sewage-rio-grande-pollution-water-border-2021-2022/9029724002/.

———. "Spring cleaning at the Rio Grande: River cleanup complete following sewage disaster." *El Paso Times*, 6 May 2022, https://www.elpasotimes.com/story/news/2022/05/06/rio-grande-cleanup-complete-sewage-irrigation-season/9679314002/.

———. "El Paso Water reports another wastewater spill near Rio Grande." *El Paso Times*, 23 Nov. 2022, https://www.elpasotimes.com/story/news/local/el-paso/2022/11/22/el-paso-water-reports-another-wastewater-spill-near-rio-grande/69670868007/

Qadri, Mustafa. "The UAE's Kafala System: Harmless or Human Trafficking?" *Carnegie Endowment for International Peace*, 7 July 2020, https://carnegieendowment.org/2020/07/07/uae-s-kafala-system-harmless-or-human-trafficking-pub-82188.

"Reform the Kafala System." Migrant-Rights.org. https://www.migrant-rights.org/campaign/end-the-kafala-system/.

Rivera, Nora K. "Chicanx Murals: Decolonizing Place and (Re)Writing the Terms of Composition." *College Composition and Communication*, vol. 72, no. 1, September 2020, pp. 118–149.

Rojo, Luis. *Uniting Families and Celebrating a Third Nation: Bridging the Wall, a True Binational Park for the Borderland of Juarez—El Paso.* ProQuest Dissertations Publishing, 2021.

Rosen, Jody. "How M.I.A. Made 'Kala.'" *Rolling Stone*, 19 Mar. 2013, https://www.rollingstone.com/music/music-news/how-m-i-a-made-kala-96345/.

Sadowski-Smith, Claudia, editor. *Globalization on the Line: Culture, Capital, and Citizenship at US Borders.* Palgrave, 2002.

Saunders, Nicholas, editor. *Icons of Power: Feline Symbolism in the Americas.* Routledge, 1998.

Sawyer, Miranda. "MIA: 'I'm here for the people.'" *The Guardian*, 13 Jun. 2010, https://www.theguardian.com/music/2010/jun/13/mia-feature-miranda-sawyer.

Semuels, Alana. "El Paso Is Learning That Not Everyone Hates Sprawl." *The Atlantic*, 28 Jan. 2016, https://www.theatlantic.com/business/archive/2016/01/el-paso-urban-walkable-americans/431661/.

Spechler, Diana. "Art Without Borders." *New York Times*, 8 Apr. 2021, https://www.nytimes.com/2021/04/08/opinion/el-paso-art-murals.html.

Sivagnanam, Sujatha. "Why Sri Lankan Tamil refugees in India attempted mass suicide." *Al Jazeera*, 21 Sep. 2021, https://www.aljazeera.com/news/2021/9/21/sri-lanka-tamil-refugees-india-suicide-tamil-nadu-camp.

Terrazas, Janette. "Rio_Arduino." *Janette Terrazas, (México, 1985)—Contemporary Textiles*, 16 May 2021, https://janette-terrazas.matd.work/2021/05/16/rio_arduino-2/.

Thomas, Mary. "Bricozaje: Between Contested Terrains and Aesthetic Borderlands." *Archives of American Art*, vol. 61, no. 1, Spring 2022, pp. 44–63.

"United Arab Emirates." *Human Rights Watch*, n.d., https://www.hrw.org/world-report/2019/country-chapters/united-arab-emirates.

Varatharajah, Sinthujan. "MIA's Borders: For refugees by refugees." *Sri Lanka and Diasporas*, 28 Nov. 2015, https://slkdiaspo.hypotheses.org/4979.

Villagran, Lauren. "Border art collective unveils Rio Grande mural depicting migration history in El Paso, Juárez." *El Paso Times*, 4 Jan. 2022, https://www.elpasotimes.com/story/news/2022/01/04/border-art-collective-unveils-rio-grande-mural-downtown-juarez/9078448002/.

Ward, Myah and Josh Gerstein. "Judge Blocks Title 42 Limits at Border." *Politico*, 15 Nov. 2022, https://www.politico.com/news/2022/11/15/immigration-judge-blocks-title-42-limits-00067083.

"Watch M.I.A.'s audiovisual venture Matahdatah Scroll 01 Broader than a Border." *The Guardian*, 13 July 2015, https://www.theguardian.com/music/2015/jul/13/watch-mia-audio-visual-venture-matahdatah-scroll-01-broader-than-a-border.

Welsome, Eileen. "Eminent Disaster: A cabal of politicians and profiteers targets an El Paso barrio." *Texas Observer*, 4 May 2007. https://www.texasobserver.org/2483-eminent-disaster-a-cabal-of-politicians-and-profiteers-targets-an-el-paso-barrio/

White, Avery, and Holly Devon. "The Chicano Artists Transcending the US-Mexico Border." *Vice*, 3 July 2017, https://www.vice.com/en/article/payvxk/the-chicano-artists-transcending-the-us-mexico-border.

Wright, Melissa. "Necropolitics, Narcopolitics, and Femicide: Gendered Violence on the Mexico-U.S. Border." *Signs*, vol. 36, no. 3, March 2011, pp. 707–731.

Žižek, Slavoj. "The Cologne attacks were an obscene version of carnival." *New Statesman*, 13 Jan. 2016, https://www.newstatesman.com/world/2016/01/slavoj-zizek-cologne-attacks.

CHAPTER 7

A Borderless World: Abolition Democracy and the Politics of Refusal

We got a right, know the situation
We're the children of globalization
No borders, only true connection
Light the fuse of the insurrection
This generation has no nation
Grass roots pressure the only solution
—Asian Dub Foundation (2003)

My claim throughout this book has been that border rules constitute a social relation, one that determines access to wealth and resources and shapes hierarchies of power based on historically specific ruling strategies located in the continuing yet shifting politics of empire, race, gender, and settler colonialism. If my discussion of border rules and the continuing conflicts emerging from these rules make any conclusion self-evident, it is that for the immediate future, the nation state will remain in a state of perpetual crisis, and one way that rulers will handle this crisis is by strengthening border rules. It is precisely this reality that informs the overriding argument for my study. I contend that the one solution to the current situation that I have described throughout my study is the abolition of borders. In this chapter, I want to draw from a specific political genealogy to support this claim, suggesting also that the road forward is not one that can be neatly charted.

© The Author(s), under exclusive license to Springer Nature
Switzerland AG 2023
K. Chowdhury, *Border Rules*, Politics of Citizenship and Migration,
https://doi.org/10.1007/978-3-031-26216-6_7

225

Abolition and Solidarities Across Borders

In a letter drafted by Marx and sent by the International Working Men's Association to Abraham Lincoln in January 1865, congratulations were passed on to the "American people upon [Lincoln's] re-election by a large majority." The letter goes on to affirm that from the beginning of the war "working men of Europe felt instinctively that the star-spangled banner carried the destiny of their class." Emphasizing both the class consciousness of the "working classes of Europe" and their solidarity with the enslaved across the Atlantic, Marx alludes to the fact that, despite "the hardships imposed upon them by the cotton crisis," the workers "opposed enthusiastically the pro-slavery intervention of their betters [*sic*]- and, from most parts of Europe, contributed their quota of blood to the good cause" ("Address of the International Working Men's Association"). The words in this letter capture the spirit of abolition and link it to the "reconstruction of a social world," one, in which workers across an ocean are united, despite national boundaries and ruling class interests that attempt to separate them. It is, of course, no surprise that Marx, who, along with Engels in *The Communist Manifesto* declared, "The working men have no country. We cannot take from them what they have not got," should draw attention to forms of solidarity across borders. Marx and Engels also stated in the *Manifesto* that "as the antagonism between classes within the nation vanishes, the hostility of one nation to another will come to an end" ("Manifesto"). The abolition of exploitative property relations, in effect, would destroy the need for a nation state and its attendant rules designed to keep those property relations in place.

The spirit of my concluding comments is based on a similar belief. As I have stressed throughout the book, any true justice for migrants or any attempt to formulate more humane border policies—even a relatively radical attempt, such as making a case for open borders—ultimately can only lead to surface modifications in immigrant or refugee programs and a temporary improvement in the living and working conditions for most people who are affected by border rules. As long as the overriding logic of capital accumulation and dominance through racialized systems of exploitation remain in place, reforms will accomplish little. However, I also want to add that I am not suggesting an either-or political program, eschewing all reform efforts until the horizon of a borderless world can be reached.[1] Reforms represent important steps in the progress toward this horizon; however, in this case as in others, the nature of the processes by which we reach our goals unquestionably matters; reforms themselves must not circumvent or forestall the prospects for more radical changes or inhibit revolutionary possibilities.[2]

If rights and advocacy groups can maintain pressure on nations and international organizations to institute reforms that can lead to more humane border policies, then that work must certainly continue. If perilous, potentially fatal journeys can be eliminated, if detention centers can be closed, if migrants can be granted refuge, and if migrants can be accorded the same rights as citizens in host nations, those changes would of course be cause for celebration. However, as I have tried to demonstrate in this study, such changes do not alter the relationships rooted in exploitative, extractive practices that are at the heart of border rules, relationships which play a crucial part in determining who has access to property, power, and privilege. An easing of border rules will not change this fundamental social arrangement. Thus, a genuine transformation of border rules can only be accomplished by the elimination of borders. For this to happen, nothing less than a global revolution in social relations is necessary.

[1] In this context, I find the words of the labor leader Elizabeth Gurley Flynn both salutary and inspiring: "What is a labour victory? I maintain that it is a twofold thing. Workers must gain economic advantage, but they must also gain revolutionary spirit, in order to achieve a complete victory. For workers to gain a few cents more a day, a few minutes less a day, and go back to work with the same psychology, the same attitude toward society is to achieve a temporary gain and not a lasting victory. For workers to go back with a class-conscious spirit, with an organized and determined attitude toward society means that even if they have made no economic gain they have the possibility of gaining in the future" ("The Truth about the Paterson Strike").

[2] For a comprehensive example of the discussion on the importance of the nature of reforms, see Robert Klemko and John Sullivan's article on the "never-ending" cycle of police reform. Covering three decades of racial profiling and police brutality in America, "The Push to Remake Policing Takes Decades, Only to Begin Again" goes into depth about how attempts to reform police departments across the country have continually failed. Referencing the failure of "early warning systems" meant to identify officers at risk of using excessive force, County of Los Angeles, Inspector General Max Huntsman states "The Los Angeles Sheriff's Department is an illuminating example of why any reform effort can be destroyed if it's not part of a universal reform effort with real teeth" (Klemko and Sullivan). Another useful source on the subject of reforms is André Gorz's *Strategy for Labor: A Radical Proposal*.

Such a call will inevitably lead to a slew of objections and accusations of utopian world- making that will be deemed unsuitable for our present moment. Since the predictable outrage from the nationalist wings and a catalog of their objections are familiar to all, I will instead consider the skepticism regarding a borderless world from a voice on the Left—Étienne Balibar, in *Politics and the Other Scene* (2012):

> [A] "borderless world" ... would run the risk of being a mere arena for the unfettered domination of the private centres of power which monopolize capital, communications and, perhaps also, arms. It is a question, rather, of what democratic control is to be exerted on the controllers of borders—that is to say, on states and supra-national institutions themselves. This depends entirely on whether those on the different sides of the border eventually discover common interests and a common language (common ideals). But it depends also on the question of *who* will meet in those unliveable places that are the different borders. Now, in order to meet, one most often needs interpreters, mediators. Disheartening as their experience is today, it seems to me that those who defend the right of asylum precisely rank among those mediators. (85)

In his formulation of a possible borderless world, Balibar assumes that such a world will continue the regime of "private centers of power." The diffusion of centralized and privatized forms of power, on the contrary, is precisely what abolition would entail. Moreover, a No Borders-politics rests on the basis that "*democratic* control" [my emphasis] over the "controllers of borders" and "states and supra-national institutions" is not a viable option, so long as the militarized state and finance capital hold full sway over the means of production and the movement of people, limiting the possibility of true democracy. Finally, the trajectory of change that Balibar suggests depends, in his words, on people discovering "common interests and a common language" on "different sides of the border." There are, in fact, no dearth of solidarity movements across borders that have already recognized their common bonds.[3] It is the ruling class interests that create "different sides of the border" that must be challenged, along with the prejudicial and otherwise divisive ideologies that the ruling class stimulates.

---

[3] See Robin Alexander's *International Solidarity in Action: The relationship between the United Electrical Workers (UE) and Frente Auténtico del Trabajo (FAT)* (2022) for one example of such cross-border solidarities.

In short, if we can agree that borders exist to create and reproduce certain immanent needs for a capitalist system, then it becomes evident that a mere attention to policy, such as the "right of asylum" can only accomplish so much. After all, even if more humane border policies were put in place and greater "democratic" control over border policies were achieved, the ideology of "secure" borders would not be eliminated. This notion plays on the anxiety and fear that have been fostered for generations in Western citizens that any "humane" border policy will end up "flooding" wealthy countries with refugees from poorer ones. The ruling class counts on reproducing the narrative that the "way of life," both from the culturalist perspective (for imperial nations, generally a white supremacist stance) and from the economic "security" perspective that the "security" people "enjoy" will end up being compromised if more "permissive" policies are put in place. Liberals and conservatives are aligned on this ideology. Their main disagreement regarding refugees, for instance, is about the numbers that will be granted asylum, not the principle of limiting refugees. Notice the minor real distinctions (rather than the rhetorical ones) between Trump's and Biden's border policies.[4]

However, border politics, as much else in capitalist systems, are beset by contradictions. Nations maintain a fragile balance between allowing borders, on the one hand, to regulate and discipline labor, while at the same time keeping them open so that capital can move freely. This arrangement is a tenuous one because so-called trade wars about tariffs and regulations are both about nations' leaders jockeying for position in the global commodity system and about impressing their own citizens with their commitment to the "national" cause. In reality, some of the most hard-line nationalist leaders and politicians, such as Bolsonaro, Erdogan, Modi, Netanyahu, Orban, Putin, and Trump, are also the ones most likely to promote the movement of global capital and the demolition of national welfare programs. Operating according to the rules of the neoliberal playbook, government officials remove regulations so that the capitalist class benefits across national borders; meanwhile, the state methodically undercuts national safety nets. Such contradictions by themselves, however, are not enough to overturn a system. If that were the case, capitalism would have collapsed by now. Nonetheless, these cracks and contradictions, as I have demonstrated throughout the book, reveal the ideological elements accompanying border rules. Narratives about nations and borders and

---

[4] See Henry Gass's "Immigration: Why Biden's Policy Looks a Lot Like Trump's."

230   K. CHOWDHURY

what they represent become a way of cementing divisions based on race, class, and religion. In recent years, these divisions have been amplified by regimes across the globe even as systemic contradictions have multiplied. Nandita Sharma refers to this phenomenon as the "territorialization of people's consciousness," or the idea that notions of ownership over space have become hardened (51).

Keeping these points in mind, in this concluding chapter, I will focus on three points of discussion: First, I will explore the ideas of some of the advocates and proponents of No Borders movements, elaborating on both the benefits and limitations of these movements, especially as they pertain to notions of "refusal." Second, I will draw from current and increasingly popular calls for abolition democracy that may inform a No Borders politics, focusing particularly on the foundational insights of W.E.B. Du Bois. Finally, I will articulate what an abolitionist refusal of border rules might look like and point to some potentialities that hint at future flourishing.

THE NO BORDERS MOVEMENTS AND THE IDEA OF REFUSAL

Writing in 1995, during the midst of the Balkan crisis, Giorgio Agamben notes that as a result of the "inexorable decline of the nation state and the general corrosion of the traditional legal-political categories, the refugee is perhaps the only imaginable figure of the people of our day" ("We Refugees" 114). Because, he argues, the refugee breaks up "the identity between man and citizen, nativity and nationality, the refugee throws into crisis the original fiction of sovereignty" (117). Agamben suggests that rather than placing the refugee within that amorphous container, the "Rights of Man," which would position the refugee within the category of the "right to asylum," the refugee should be "considered a border concept that radically calls into question the principles of the nation state" (117). Taking the case of Jerusalem, which is the capital of two different states, Agamben argues for an eviction of the nation state, replaced by political communities, where the "guiding concept would no longer be the *ius* of the citizen, but rather the *refugium* of the individual" (118). Such an idea would then turn the "Europe of nations" into an aterritorial or extraterritorial space in which all the residents of the European states (citizens and non-citizens) would be in a position of exodus and refuge, and the status of the European would mean the citizen's being-in-exodus (obviously also immobile)" (118). During the peak in the arrival of refugees in Europe some twenty years later, Agamben's hopes for Europe to be turned into "an aterritorial or extraterritorial space" were promptly extinguished, as the European nations began feuding over their response to this arrival. Moreover, rather than the national citizen coming to identify their condition as "the refugee that he is," and the "ius of the citizen" being replaced by the "refugium of the individual," nationalism and the rituals of citizenship and belonging have risen to new heights since that moment. Agamben, of course, might conclude that this response, in fact, confirms his belief in the "inexorable decline of the nation state," as increased assertions of nationalism might indicate a fundamental insecurity in the structure of the state.

However, announcing or forecasting the decline of the nation state or constructing idealist categories such as "the refugium of the individual" fails to address an obvious point: the nation state remains both the key barrier against and the primary facilitator for providing refuge. It not only participates in the exclusive rituals of citizenship and rights (which, by the way, also create multiple ways to discipline its population) but also provides the ballast for an unstable global trading system whose logic requires national borders for the regulation of labor and the movement of commodities and currencies. Furthermore, as I have attempted to demonstrate in this book, the magnitude of the so-called refugee crisis has worsened over the last several years since the most vulnerable nations have had the remaining shreds of their sovereignty compromised, while, not coincidentally, imperial nations and their satellites have strengthened their border rules. We are in a moment where the logic of neoliberal accumulation generates inevitable conflicts, and damages both livelihoods and the environments that sustain them, wreaking havoc on the most defenseless communities on the planet. The border rules of wealthy nations also ensure that the majority of the planet's migrants find refuge only in the Global South, thus compounding the problems in what are already fraught economies.

I will now briefly explore two important texts to clarify some of the arguments that animate a No Borders movement and that resonate closely with the theme of this book: refusal.[5] The first text, "'We are all foreigners': No Borders as a practical political project" by Bridget Anderson, Nandita Sharma and Cynthia Wright (2012), demonstrates how the calls

---

[5] There are a range of such movements across the globe, with varying degrees of commitment to a borderless world. Some examples are "Abolish Frontex," the "No Borders Network," "No One is Illegal," and "Pueblos Sin Fronteras."

for No Borders "are made on the basis of interrelated ethical, political, social and economic grounds. The authors' challenging of nation-states' sovereign right to control people's mobility signals a new sort of liberatory project, one with new ideas of 'society' and one aimed at creating new social actors not identified with nationalist projects" (74).The second text, Natasha King's *No Borders: The Politics of Immigration Control and Resistance* (2016) offers a glance at a range of resistance efforts located primarily in Athens and the Calais "Jungle," at ways of living that are "other to the system," including "anti-deportation campaigns, detention visitor projects, language clubs, No Borders camps and detention prison blockades" (7). King also illustrates how these activist movements are "connected to the ways people create other communities more generally, from squatting and occupying land, to holding free parties" (7).

Anderson and others effectively put in crisis the notion of "citizenship-rights" as a possible solution for structures of oppression that target migrants, arguing, correctly, in my opinion, that such an approach is "unable to take on board forms of politics that involve the *refusal* of citizenship, including for example by colonised people. Additionally, attempts to move beyond the citizenship designated by border controls and capitalist social relations, relationships borne of—and still dependent on—practices of expropriation and exploitation, do not tackle the problem of *exclusion*" (81). The writers are clear that "the signal demand of No Borders is for every person to have the freedom to move *and*, in this era of massive dispossession and displacement, the concomitant freedom to not be moved (i.e., to stay)" (82). An attention to capitalist social relations is not incidental to this call but lies at the root of the analysis: "a No Borders politics clarifies the centrality of border controls to capitalist social relations, relationships born of—and still dependent on—practices of expropriation and exploitation" (82). As a radical reimagining, then, a No Borders politics "is part of a global reshaping of economies and societies in a way that is not compatible with capitalism, nationalism, or the mode of state-controlled belonging that is citizenship" (84). In short, a "radical No Borders politics acknowledges that it *is* part of revolutionary change" (84). Pointing to a range of practices that can be placed within the category of anti-borders activism, the authors indicate that, ultimately, a "No Borders politics can be seen as part of a broader, reinvigorated struggle for the commons" (85) It is this reinvigorated, radical notion of "common rights" or the "rights of persons" that will enable this revolutionary end.

Likewise, in *No Borders: The Politics of Immigration Control and Resistance*, Natasha King identifies refusal as a "form of resistance," but, drawing from David Graeber's *Direct Action: An Ethnography*, poses this resistance as "a kind that also involves opposing the border indirectly; taking action in ways that effectively turn away from the state and seek to live a life as if it wasn't there" (19). Although King seems committed to the autonomy-of-migration theoretical path, she argues that a No Borders politics is not defined simply as an anti-state autonomous movement.[6] Certainly, some of the actions of people turning away from the state and its dictates that are cited by King may seem to replicate autonomous practices, but she also points out that "at times when life becomes unsustainable because of the border regime, people have to come together to make demands on the state" (21). Thus, a "no border politics is not only autonomous practices, nor only visible practices, but a constant negotiation of these two things" (21). Freedom to migrate is a central element of this movement, but this struggle "can be read in a way that resonates with a variety of different ideologies, from anarchist to left perspectives to perspectives that have no ideological basis at all" (22).

I am somewhat drawn to King's notion of refusal as an act of disobedience and disavowal, if only because it potentially exceeds what can be termed the passivity of that act. She argues that "there's something more ambiguous or undecided about refusal. It's a rejection, but one that hints at the possibility of something else or something incomplete" (25). For King, refusal, again, is not merely a turning away from current conditions, but includes an effort to "create a *different reality*" (27). King attempts to place the No Borders movement between the autonomy-of-migration theoretical school and the acts-of-citizenship approach, the latter path focusing on issues of representation and rights while pressuring the state to transform as a result of accepting the demands placed upon it. As she puts it, "We seek another way of being to the state, while also having to navigate our position within it" (49). However, King does not try to reconcile the two approaches, identifying this tension as a "fundamental dilemma at the core of a no borders politics" (50). This leads to a

---

[6] The autonomy of migration approach can be traced back to the Italian *Autonomia* or *operaismo* of the 1960s and 1970s. The theoretical framework of the autonomy of migration method highlights the movements of peoples as an assertion of their autonomy. For a more substantial description of this approach, see Cobarrubius et al.'s "An Interview with Sandro Mezzadra."

234   K. CHOWDHURY

somewhat nebulous claim that "a no borders politics largely slips out of any existing political ideology" (149). It is hard to avoid the conclusion that such a "politics" can be everything and nothing at the same time. For King, change will ultimately emerge because of a "multitude of micro-refusals that are connected to each other rhizomatically and in their connections will render the state more and more redundant" (151). Displaying a hint of postmodern skepticism and pessimism, King takes a stand against "mass movements," suggesting in an anarchist vein that such movements will inevitably "bring about a new kind of domination" (151). The quest for radical egalitarianism, in her view, must be a constant process of becoming. The noun "process" and the gerund "becoming" may seem to suggest, for King, movement and change, but her analysis lacks force, specificity, and sufficient emphasis on the foundations of oppression and exploitation. King has little to say about the modes of production and how they will be appropriated or used during this "process of becoming" or how micro-refusals can deal with the totality of global accumulation. Too often, refusal appears to be the end rather than a tactical means for accomplishing a revolutionary future.

ABOLITION DEMOCRACY AND NO BORDERS

Countering King's affirmation of a politics of disavowal and refusal are the practices and principles of Abolition Democracy.[7] Though most often connected with the politics of resistance to the carceral economics of the United States, this political program offers many pathways to activists across the world. Indeed, its principles are rooted in the spirit of internationalism and in notions of planetary transformation that reject an attachment to specific locations and regions.

In order to reflect on the current potentiality of Abolition Democracy, we must briefly trace the main points of abolition democracy as articulated by W. E. B. Du Bois, most famously, in *Black Reconstruction in America: An Essay Toward a History of the Part Which Black Folk Played in the Attempt to Reconstruct Democracy in America, 1860–1880*. Before we consider these points, however, it's important to recall the context for Du Bois's thinking. He was writing at a time of revolutionary hope, in the early to mid-1930s, when the potential for workers' solidarity was high, and he was

---

[7] Angela Davis, drawing from Du Bois, defines Abolition Democracy as the "comprehensive abolition of slavery." For this to happen, "new democratic institutions would have to be created" (*Abolition Democracy* 73, 95).

immersed in Marx's thought and moving toward a more defined Marxist analysis, so it is no surprise that he paid special attention in this text to the intersections between capital, class, race, and the politics of white supremacy.[8] An analysis of these intersections was also influencing ongoing global struggles against imperialism, colonialism, and fascism. Alongside the emergence of fascist movements, the rise of popular fronts in France and Spain were significant historical moments, posing the possibility of a viable transnational resistance against fascism. This spirit of resistance was also highlighted by the Seventh Congress of the Comintern, held the same year as the publication of *Black Reconstruction*. The Congress made a strong anti-fascist declaration, calling for a united working-class resistance to fascist policies, which were viewed as perfectly aligned with the interests of imperial capital.

It is in this revolutionary context that Du Bois considers the historical task of abolition. Du Bois stresses that the abolition of slavery was only the first step toward a new democracy. For real transformation to occur, he argues, the apparatus of racial capitalism and the mechanisms that have generated and reproduced white supremacy must be demolished. In his analysis, Du Bois scrupulously identifies the dialectical movement between capital and white supremacy. In his view, each works through and within the other: White supremacy allows capitalism in the United States to produce value in particular ways. Likewise, the exploitative systems of capitalism ensure that racial structures are maintained. The result is a system, he concludes, that keeps in place an exploitable pool of both black and white labor.

Reconstruction offered the first real possibility of revolutionary change. Abolition Democracy, in Du Bois's mind, contrasted most directly with the notion of the American Assumption, a belief that "wealth is mainly the result of its owner's effort and that any average worker can by thrift

---

[8] Du Bois was teaching a seminar on Marx while writing *Black Reconstruction* and in 1933 in a speech "On Being Ashamed" had declared that "production for private profit was immoral; collective ownership of the means of production was necessary." However, this stance was not entirely a new one: as early as 1920, writing in the essay "Of Work and Wealth," Du Bois argued: "The freeing of the black slaves freed America. Today we are challenging another ownership, —the ownership of materials which go to make the goods we need … we are demanding general consent as to what materials shall be privately owned and as to how materials shall be used. We are rapidly approaching the day when we shall repudiate all private property in raw materials and tools and demand that distribution hinge, not on the power of those who monopolize the materials, but on the needs of the mass of men" (48–49).

become a capitalist" (*BR*,183). In contrast to this affirmation of ruling class ideology, Du Bois demonstrated how, during the Civil War, an enslaved population had written themselves into history through their own actions—not in order to accumulate private wealth but to democratize social relations. By declaring a general strike—withdrawing their labor from the exploitative grip of the plantation economy, and constituting over 10 percent of the Union Army—they ensured the defeat of the South. For abolition to work, he argued, the state would have needed to redistribute property and wealth after the war, but this did not happen since ruling class interests remained paramount. Indeed, a multiracial dictatorship of the proletariat—in Du Bois's view, the only realistic path to redistribution and to a change in exploitative relations—was never really on the cards (*BR* 185).

The hopes for Abolition Democracy, to some measure, lay in this ideal of cross-racial solidarities united in the class struggle against both the Southern plantation oligarchy and the Northern capitalists. For these solidarities to form, though, Du Bois suggests that an interventionist state was needed: the state must "expropriate the expropriators." During Reconstruction, this expropriation was partly the role of the Freedmen's Bureau. Du Bois describes the work of the Freedmen's Bureau as a possible enunciation of Abolition Democracy, even if put in place by a state that was already beginning to compromise with the wishes of the Southern planter class and the Northern industrialists. But, as the failure of Reconstruction demonstrated so fully, Du Bois comments, the state is ultimately the instrument of the propertied classes. In short, he notes, unless there is a dictatorship of the proletariat to enable this moment of transition, this form of state intervention is doomed to fail.

In the immediate years after the war, Du Bois explains, the Northern ruling class went along with the agenda of Reconstruction since they saw the Southern plantation system as an impediment to the expansion they sought. It was in their best interests to have a waged labor force that extended their domination to the South. Moreover, they needed free black people as consumers for a rapidly expanding economy. They were, for the moment, Du Bois concludes, willing to let some of the methods for instituting Abolition Democracy (voting rights, free public education, distribution of rations, etc.) remain in place. The only realistic version of Abolition Democracy, then, became a modified and deradicalized form that suited the interests of Northern capital. As Du Bois concludes:

"industrialists after the war expected the South to seize upon the opportunity to make increased profit by a more intelligent exploitation of labor than was possible under the slave system. They looked upon free Negro labor as a source of profit" (185). The unsurprising paradox that Du Bois highlights is that the North fought for suffrage so that they could exploit black labor.

Ultimately, any potential for the radical possibilities of Abolition Democracy, according to Du Bois, was sabotaged because Northern capital saw in Reconstruction two terrifying possibilities: one, black and white workers, through a redistribution of property and wealth, gaining strength and the power to make their own demands on Northern owners of capital; two, a real prospect for industrial workers, Southern poor whites, and the formerly enslaved to unite in a common cause. A compromise with the Southern plantation owners then takes place, where the latter concede a few economic advantages to the North in exchange for complete civil, political, and economic control of the freed population.

I have provided a somewhat detailed account of Du Bois's analysis of the potential for and obstacles to Abolition Democracy during Reconstruction because they help us to contextualize the challenges facing the politics of abolition in the present moment. It is also helpful to remember that the spirit of abolition has had many iterations in the last 150 years and has met with varying degrees of success. Its basic principles were reproduced in movements from the Philadelphia Dock strikes of 1913 to the agitation by the Alabama sharecroppers Union in the 1930s to the statement produced by the Combahee River Collective in 1977 to the current Poor Peoples' Campaign, which directly calls for the building of a Third Reconstruction.[9] Abolition, although now commonly connected to an abolition of the prison industrial complex, can be seen in many other contexts as well—Abolition Ecology, Abolition Geography, and the abolition of borders, to mention a few.[10]

Keeping the above contextualization in mind, I would like to identity some of the principles of contemporary forms of Abolition Democracy

---

[9] See the Rev. William J. Barber and Jonathan Wilson-Hartgrove's *Third Reconstruction: How a Moral Movement is Overcoming the Politics of Division and Fear*.

[10] See Nik Heynen and Megan Ybarra's "On Abolition Ecology and Making 'Freedom a Place,'" Ruth Wilson Gilmore's *Abolition Geography: Essays Towards Liberation*, and Gracie Mae Bradley and Luke de Noronha's *Against Borders: The Case for Abolition*.

and suggest a complementary relationship with a No Borders movement. Indeed, Abolition Democracy would not be a realistic goal without the elimination of borders, and the notion of creating new democratic institutions—a point insisted upon by Du Bois—offers a pathway that is not always evident in No Borders politics. The challenge also is to take a movement, such as Abolition Democracy, that has its roots within a particular socio-historical context and to apply it to other regions. Without flattening the regional particularities, I would suggest that the following points may be relevant for a larger transnational attempt to build a politics informed by an abolitionist refusal of border rules.

An Abolitionist Refusal of Border Rules

The problem of the nation state: It is abundantly clear that there is no abolition of the border without the concomitant abolition of the nation state in its present incarnation. King's attempt to put her faith in a no border politics that negotiates between rights-based struggles and an autonomous approach unwittingly shines a light on this problem since any meaningful act of resistance against the state will be contested and met with violence. Thus, while the struggles against border rules can be multifaceted, there is ultimately little hope that capital will concede any ground in asserting its predominance through the mechanism of the state. It is no surprise, then, that in the context of contemporary calls for abolition, Angela Davis, Ruth Wilson Gilmore, and others are less interested than Du Bois was in having the state play any kind of role in advocating for the principles of abolition.

However, Du Bois's analysis of the role of the state in the immediate aftermath of the war remains salutary as we consider how we may interact with the state while moving toward abolition. Du Bois recognized that in the immediate moment after the war, the Freedmen's Bureau, despite being an organ of the state, buoyed the prospects for democracy. This is not the place to evaluate the work of the Bureau, but when its work was terminated and the protection of the federal forces was withdrawn, it only increased the misery and the terror in the South for the newly freed people.[11] However, Du Bois also offers us a historical lesson about the role of a state in a capitalist society. The Freedmen's Bureau failed precisely because it was achieving a degree of success in enabling free people to gain some measure of autonomy. We must go forward with an awareness that state power will likely attempt to quash any movement that threatens its current configuration. As in the period of Reconstruction, the state now remains an essential spoke in the wheel of capital accumulation. The capitalist state will only go so far in granting rights and as a support to capital, will continue to uphold its interests. It is no wonder, then, that abolitionists today see little hope in the idea of a benevolent, rights-granting state.

We cannot, however, wish away the state; any revolutionary process includes a period of transition, and an attention to the dialectics of transitions must include the question of the state and its role in a future revolutionary society. I believe that for a No Borders movement, the state cannot be entirely dismissed at the outset. Clearly, the Freedmen's Bureau provides a model that could include the state using its resources to expropriate vast reserves of wealth, initiate a redistribution of land and wealth, and enact policies granting free access to education, housing, health care, and the other necessities of life. But, as Du Bois also points out, the Bureau can only do so much if the racist state apparatus stays in place. Then, and in the present, the vital third step, as Angela Davis affirms in her description of Abolition Democracy, is not just about a "negative process of tearing down, but ... also about building up, about creating new institutions." As she puts it, "a host of democratic institutions are needed to fully achieve abolition" (73).

---

[11] In the essay "Of the Dawn of Freedom," included in *The Souls of Black Folk*, Du Bois evaluates the work of the Freedmen's Bureau thus: "It set going a system of free labor; it established the black peasant proprietor; it secured the recognition of black freemen before courts of law; it founded the free public school in the South. On the other hand, it failed to establish good will between ex-masters and freedmen; to guard its work wholly from paternalistic methods that discouraged self-reliance; to make Negroes landholders in any considerable numbers. Its successes were the result of hard work, supplemented by the aid of philanthropists and the eager striving of black men. Its failures were the result of bad local agents, inherent difficulties of the work, and national neglect" (29).

Ultimately, the state, unless appropriated by the new democratic public, will remain an impediment to the building of a "host of democratic institutions." Du Bois realized that even the most favorable interpretation of the Freedmen's Bureau's work was that it constituted an attempt to democratize American capitalism, not to abolish it. If Abolition Democracy and the No Borders movement are to fulfill their ultimate destiny, they must abolish capitalism as the reigning economic logic through a mass movement that creates democracy through an eventual abolition of the capitalist state.

The central role of prison abolition: An important element of Abolition Democracy is its prominent role in resisting the carceral state apparatus.[12] The prison system is an essential part of border rules, distinguishing who belongs to and is excluded from national communities, which sections of the population are subject to exploitation, and how different arms of the police state accumulate profit and mete out punishment. In this instance, once again, Du Bois's analysis of post-slavery society serves as a useful precedent for demonstrating why the prison system involves a great deal more than just punishment and confinement. As Du Bois elucidates, in a so-called free society, it was necessary for free black men to be turned into criminals, put under supervision of a penal system, so that their labor could be exploited. Davis, similarly, explains, "convict leasing was a totalitarian effort to control black labor in the post-Emancipation era and it serves as a *symbolic reminder* to black people that slavery had not been fully disestablished" (11). In the present, the Prison Industrial Complex (PIC) serves as a form of capital extraction, as a way to diminish black and brown social wealth, and—most significantly—as a node in the interrelated systems of oppression, manifested in the apparatuses of health care, housing, and so on. Ruth Wilson Gilmore names these interconnections in a useful way, advocating an analysis that always names the specific determinations and keeps in mind the social totality:

> The particular also implies entire historical geographies in constant churn. For some examples, think: gentrification. Auto or steel manufacturing. Coal

---

[12] See Anna Hales's "Beyond Borders: How Principles of Prison Abolition Can Shape the Future of Immigration Reform" for a reading of abolition theory that "encourages us to envision [that] there is something beyond immigration enforcement" (1440).

mining. Gold mining. Conflict minerals. Fracking. New shipping technologies. Robotics. Commodity chains. Finance capital. The challenge is to keep the entirety of carceral geographies—rather than only their prison or even law-enforcement aspects—connected, but without collapsing or reducing various aspects into one another. (478)

The "entirety of carceral geographies" enumerated by Gilmore is clearly not confined to a particular nation state but radiates across the globe.[13] The PIC is present in countries across the world; it may take different forms in Egypt, India, Brazil, or the Philippines, but, as in the United States, it remains a system linked to structural brutalities and exploitative practices across the social spectrum.[14]

A striking example of the relationship between the PIC and border rules is the growing emphasis on detention economies. Echoing some of my claims in Chap. 2 about migrants existing on the cusps of exploitation, expulsion, and forced abandonment and death, Deirdre Conlon and Nancy Hemstra alert us to the persistence of "detention economies," a salient element of the PIC in an age of hardening borders. "[I]mmigration detention," they argue, is a "key institutional mechanism that contributes to migrants' social death in the United States and elsewhere" (101). These mechanisms consist of "the extensive array of infrastructure—including operations and management, transport, communications, food, and medical care systems—that makes up the detention system and the range of private- *and* public-sector involved in these systems" (101). These economies, in their view, "generate losses that produce and amplify migrant

---

[13] For an account of these global connections, see Angela Davis's interview with Avery Gordon, where she points out that as "capital moves with ease across national borders, legitimised by recent trade and investment agreements such as NAFTA, GATT and MAI, corporations close shop in the United States and transfer manufacturing operations to nations providing cheap labour pools. In fleeing organised labour in the US to avoid paying higher wages and benefits, they leave entire communities in shambles, consigning huge numbers of people to joblessness, leaving them prey to the drug trade, destroying the economic base of these communities and thus affecting the education system, social welfare—and turning the people who live in those communities into perfect candidates for prison" ("Globalism and the Prison Industrial Complex").

[14] See Faiz Ullah's "Tihar Jail's Increased Use of Prison-Private Partnership is a Cause for Worry" as one example of these practices.

social death while they also ensure gains for both private and public sectors. Central to this process is the commodification of migrant life in detention" (101). Social death entails "a series of losses—loss of identity, loss of social connectedness, loss associated with the body's disintegration" and thus these groups may be seen as "having limited utility: unable or unwilling to conform to the neoliberal norms of market competitiveness and profit seeking and associated mechanisms of neoliberal governmentality"; however, this exclusion does not locate them outside the "circuits of economic value" (102). Detention economies ensure that "losses that produce and accelerate migrants' social death and gains are linked to the commodification of migrant lives" (102). These economies are a vital element of border rules, and the ongoing criminalization and commodification of migrants, as we see, are an inextricable component of the PIC. If border-related detention economies are part of the PIC, then abolition of the PIC and the elimination of borders are inextricably linked.[15]

Intersecting Alliances: Although Du Bois focuses mostly on the dialectical relationships between race and class and demonstrates how racialized systems are produced in conjunction with class rule, his analysis of Abolition Democracy makes it abundantly clear that a new democratic public life should include the entire spectrum of the underclass. However, he is relatively inattentive to the significant role of women in the abolitionist movement in determining the principles of Abolition Democracy. Activists and revolutionaries, from Sojourner Truth and Harriet Tubman to Claudia Jones and Assata Shakur, make it clear that women have always played a vital role in the struggles for abolition. In fact, Herbert Aptheker reminds us that one of the revolutionary aspects of the abolitionist movement to end US chattel slavery was the centrality of women in that undertaking. He suggests this was the "first great social movement in US history in which women fully participated in every capacity: as organisers, propagandists, petitioners, lecturers, authors, editors, executives, and especially rank- and-filers" (77).[16] Also, as I've made plain, the disruption of and ultimate dismantling of mechanisms of border rules must include an

[15] See Angela Davis's *Are Prisons Obsolete?* for an account of some of these links.

[16] Black suffrage, as Derecka Purnell reminds us, is not the only right that black people fought for. "Many of our abolitionist ancestors," she points out, "alongside people of all races, fought and died for so much more, including self-determination, an end to capitalism, the return of Indigenous land, the redistribution of land for newly freed Black people, and for autonomous regions where communities could test their independence" (121).

attention to the differences engendered by the systemic violence based on gender and sexuality. The foundational logic of heterosexist patriarchy is a vital part of border rules, dependent as they are on the role of the state as the site and the means for the social reproduction of capitalist relations. Moreover, the super-exploitation of women's labor under capitalism is enabled by border rules: consider, for instance, the sweatshops and maquiladoras across the world that produce value because of laws that are designed to trap women within specific national boundaries. Abolishing borders without the abolition of heteropatriarchy and paternalism in all its guises is no victory at all. In this instance, once again, the advocates of contemporary Abolition Democracy have a long tradition of "intersectionality" to draw from.

Even in the last several decades, consider Claudia Jones' statement in 1949 that "the growth of militancy among Negro women has profound meaning, both for the Negro liberation movement and for the emerging anti-fascist and anti-imperialist coalition" (3) or the work of groups such as the Combahee River Collective (1977) that have been particularly attentive to the intersectional elements of the struggle. As this collective puts it in their founding statement, "We believe that sexual politics under patriarchy is as pervasive in Black women's lives as are the politics of race and class. We also often find it difficult to separate race from class from sex oppression which is neither solely racial nor solely sexual, e.g. the history of rape of Black women by white men as a weapon of political repression" (19). What gives this attention to intersectionality (before Kimberlé Crenshaw theorized the concept in a legal context) a specifically radical cast was summarized by Barbara Smith, one of the founders of the Collective, in a 2017 interview, when she clarified that the "reason Combahee's Black feminism is so powerful is because it's anticapitalist. One would expect black feminism to be anti-racist and opposed to sexism. Anticapitalism is what gives it the sharpness, the edge, the thoroughness, the revolutionary potential" (69). A few years later, the publication of *This Bridge Called My Back: Writings by Radical Women of Color* (1981), edited by Cherríe Moraga and Gloria Anzaldúa, made a similar point, reiterated more than 30 years later by Moraga in a new edition published in 2015: "We are 'third world' consciousness within the first world. We are women under capitalist patriarchy" (xix).

And, of course, this spirit of anticapitalism and an attention to capitalist patriarchy are reflected in other elements of contemporary abolitionist intersectionality. While Du Bois, for instance, had little to say about the specific injustices prompted by the continuing project of settler colonialism, no talk of Abolition Democracy today should exclude an attention to this history.[17] Moreover, abolition, as Derecka Purnell puts it, must be considered "alongside other paradigms, such as feminism, decolonization, and internationalism" (9). Purnell's recognition of internationalism is particularly pertinent since most adherents of Abolition Democracy are committed internationalists, and this world historical understanding and an attention to the particularity of settler colonialism are appropriate for the politics of the No Borders movement. A No Borders politics is unsustainable—and illogical—if confined to the borders of a single nation; it must have planetary reach. However, in the movement toward a borderless future, nations must also embrace the paradox of a liberatory nationalism, as Fanon once described it: "National consciousness, which is not nationalism, is the only thing that will give us an international dimension" (179). As we well know, it is not merely capitalism that makes this struggle a global one; patriarchy and white supremacy have a global reach, and abolition cannot just be "alongside" internationalism but must be at its core an international movement.[18]

Futurity: It goes without saying that Abolition Democracy offers a roadmap for a future egalitarian society—one that comes into being because of collective, revolutionary action. Ruth Wilson Gilmore's comments on this matter, drawing directly from Du Bois's analysis of Abolition Democracy, are apposite: "since slavery ending one day doesn't tell you anything about the next day—Du Bois set out to show what the next day, and days thereafter, looked like during the revolutionary period of radical Reconstruction. So abolition is a theory of change, it's a theory of social life. It's about making things" ("Prisons and Class Warfare"). In the

---

[17] See Glen Coulthard's *Red Skin, White Masks: Rejecting the Colonial Politics of Recognition* for an excellent account of settler-colonialism, which he defines as a relationship "characterized by a particular form of domination; that is, it a relationship where power—in this case, interrelated discursive and non-discursive facets of economic, gendered, racial, and state power—has been structured into a relatively secure or sedimented set of hierarchical social relations that continue to facilitate the dispossession of indigenous peoples of their lands and self-determining authority (6–7).

[18] It's worth recalling that in the 1930s, when Du Bois was writing *Black Reconstruction*, a large number of diasporic intellectuals and activists were committed members of the Third International, which had as one of its guiding principles the self-determination of colonized peoples and nations.

Du Bois himself was a steadfast internationalist, and in *Black Reconstruction*, he was quick to point out the global implications of the failure of Abolition Democracy. The "rise in America in 1876 [of] a new capitalism and a new enslavement of labor," he explains, ultimately led to the "exploitation of white, yellow, brown and black labor, in lesser lands" (634).

present context of Abolition Geography and a No Borders politics, abolition means, according to Gilmore, that we challenge "the normative presumption that territory and liberation are at once alienable and exclusive—that they should be partitionable by sales, documents, and walls" ("Prisons and Class Warfare"). Gilmore exhorts us to enact change by "repeating ourselves—trying as C. L. R. James wrote about the run-up to revolutions, trying every little thing, going and going again—we will, because we do, change ourselves and the external world. Even under extreme constraint" (238). At some level, one of the most damaging effects of capitalism and white supremacy is that even those of us who are against them in principle, have interiorized their ideologies. Thus, Abolition Democracy is not just about changing institutions, but it is also a call to transform ourselves through collective actions. The task of undoing social relations that are based on hierarchies, on separation and segregation, on the rituals of private property is not an easy one, and it must be accompanied by a groundswell of organization and defiance.

This is why the path toward an abolitionist refusal can never be reduced to a set of frozen principles and end goals that must be accomplished in some mechanical manner. As the struggle progresses and the forces of reaction fight back with all means at their disposal, every movement must adjust, adapt, and renew itself. Davis reminds us that real democratic institutions must be built even as oppressive structures are abolished. Indeed, despite the massive barriers in our paths and the power of the military industrial complex to repel any challenges to the system, we must take heart at the potential that is before us. There are a range of movements across the world that already hint at the promise that lies in the everyday struggles of ordinary people.[19] Davis's words are, once again, appropriate: "In order to work toward a better future, we need to believe that future is possible."

It is this spirit, animating many resistance movements, that I encourage as I bring this book to a close. Some might argue that concluding a book, as I do here, with a suggestion that the only real solution for a borderless future is to work for a global transformation in social relations could leave

---

[19] One such example The City Plaza Collective's takeover of the City Plaza Hotel in Exarcheia, Athens in 2016 created a squatter community, organizing housing for migrants. This collective provided some of the best housing for migrants, did so in the middle of the city, and along the way demonstrated that migrants and locals could coexist and act together to be a center for the struggle against neoliberal forces. For more information about the City Plaza, see *The Best Hotel in Europe* and Vicki Squire's "Welcome to City Plaza, Athens: a new approach to housing refugees."

readers feeling hopeless. At the moment, such a future with the abolition of capitalist social relations and all its attendant ills, including the nation state, seems highly improbable, and even the most optimistic of readers will admit that an overhaul of this nature, if it were to happen, would lie in the distant future. But envisioning such change, as I have suggested above, does not prevent our engaging in less ambitious acts of resistance and refusal that themselves can prove constructive. And surely, as Harsha Walia entreats us in *Undoing Border Imperialism*, dreaming of a different future is in itself a revolutionary act: "I think the notion of dreaming in a time where we are told that it is foolish, futile or not useful is one of the most revolutionary things we can do. To have our lives determined by our dreams of a free world—instead of reactions to a state-imposed reality—is one of the most powerful tools of decolonization" (229). Indeed, one could argue that migrants themselves, who face death and danger during their journeys and who lead protests in detention centers and in the cities in which they are often trapped with little recourse to justice, are the greatest bearers of hope.

Karina Alma, for instance, in "Miskitu Labor and Immigrant Struggles" reminds us that migration is a form of civil disobedience, where people refuse to accept the social death that has been written into law. Despite the treacherous conditions that migrants confront, and despite the many fatalities that occur on these journeys, "the institutional effort to keep migrants within a bare-life existence has been challenged by the migrants' effort to make their migration visible and vocal, a breathing and living collective body" (251). As Du Bois said in another context, those in the midst of desperate circumstances "must live and eat and strive, and still hold unfaltering commerce with the stars" (*Dusk to Dawn* 7). Undertaking a journey that may result in death is, in some ways, the ultimate act of resistance, a leap toward liberation, despite enormous odds. To mark this yearning as purely an act of desperation is to minimize the agency of those who confront numerous barriers and endure incredible loss when they attempt to cross over. Their actions and the sacrifices of those that enable their journeys represent the most direct refusal of border rules and may herald their eventual abolition. Migrants and their allies persist in holding "unfaltering commerce with the stars": on a wall in Montevideo, Uruguay, a mural inspires with its expressions of solidarity between those who attempt these perilous journeys and those who share their collective hope for a different world: "*Bienvenidxs migrantes-La Patria Es El Mundo Entero*" (Centro Social Cordón Norte). Such solidarity represents the path to a borderless future: "Welcome Migrants-The Homeland is the Whole World."

Works Cited

Agamben, Giorgio. "We Refugees." *Symposium: A Quarterly Journal in Modern Literatures*, vol. 49, no. 2, 1999, pp. 114–119.

Alma, Karina. "Miskitu Labor and Immigrant Struggles." *Migration and Mortality: Social Death, Dispossession, and Survival in the Americas*, edited by Jamie Longazel and Miranda Cady Hallett, Temple University Press, 2021.

Anderson, Bridget, et al. "Editorial: Why No Borders?" *Refuge*, vol. 26, no. 2, 2009, pp. 5–18.

———. "'We are all foreigners': No Borders as a practical political project." *Citizenship, Migrant Activism, and the Politics of Movement*, edited by Peter Nyers and Kim Rygiel, Routledge, 2012, pp. 73–91.

Aptheker, Herbert. *Abolition: A Revolutionary Movement*. Twayne Publishers, 1989.

Asian Dub Foundation. "Fortress Europe." *Enemy of the Enemy*, FFRR Records, 2003.

Balibar, Étienne. *Politics and the Other Scene*, Verso, 2012.

Barber, William J., II, and Jonathan Wilson-Hartgrove. *The Third Reconstruction: How a Moral Movement is Overcoming the Politics of Division and Fear*. Beacon Press, 2016.

Bradley, Gracie Mae, and Luke de Noronha. *Against Borders: The Case for Abolition*. Verso, 2022.

Centro Social Cordón Norte. "Si lo borran se pinta de nuevo. Cordón sin xenofobia." *Facebook*, https://www.facebook.com/centro.social.cordon.norte/photos/a.397740407359706/1415651062235297/.

Cobarrubias, Sebastian, et al. "An Interview with Sandro Mezzadra." *Environment and Planning D: Society and Space*, vol. 29, 2011, pp. 584–598.

Conlon, Deirdre, and Nancy Hiemstra. "Detention Economies: Commodifying Migrant Social Death." *Migration and Mortality: Social Death, Dispossession, and Survival in the Americas*, edited by Jamie Longazel and Miranda Cady Hallett, Temple University Press, 2021.

Coulthard, Glen Sean. *Red Skin, White Masks: Rejecting the Colonial Politics of Recognition*. University of Minnesota Press, 2014.

Davis, Angela Y. *Are Prisons Obsolete?* Seven Stories Press, 2003.

———. *Abolition Democracy: Beyond Empire, Prisons and Torture*. Seven Stories Press, 2005.

———. "Globalism and the Prison Industrial Complex: An Interview with Angela Davis Conducted by Avery Gordon." *transversal texts*. Oct. 2014, https://transversal.at/transversal/1014/davis/en

Du Bois, W.E.B. *Black Reconstruction in America: An Essay Toward a History of the Part Which Black Folk Played in the Attempt to Reconstruct Democracy in America, 1860—1880*. Harcourt, Brace, and Company, 1935. Free Press, 1998.

———. *Darkwater: Voices from Within the Veil*. Oxford University Press, 2007.

———. *Dusk to Dawn.* Oxford University Press, 2014.

———. *The Souls of Black Folk.* Oxford University Press, 1903.

———. "On Being Ashamed of Oneself: An Essay on Race Pride." *The Crisis*, vol. 40, no. 9, 1933, pp. 199–200.

Fanon, Frantz. *The Wretched of the Earth.* Translated by Richard Philcox, Grove Atlantic, 2007.

Flynn, Elizabeth Gurley. "The Truth About the Paterson Strike." *Iowa State University Archives of Women's Political Communication*, https://awpc.cattcenter.iastate.edu/2020/10/15/the-truth-about-the-paterson-strike-january-31-1914/.

Gass, Henry. "Why Biden's immigration policy looks a lot like Trump's." *Christian Science Monitor*, 7 Feb. 2022, https://www.csmonitor.com/USA/Politics/2022/0207/Why-Biden-s-immigration-policy-looks-a-lot-like-Trump-s.

Gilmore, Ruth Wilson. *Abolition Geography: Essays Towards Liberation*, edited by Brenna Bhandar and Alberto Toscano. Verso, 2022.

———. "Prisons and Class Warfare." Interview with Clément Petitjean. 2 Aug. 2018. https://www.versobooks.com/blogs/3954-prisons-and-class-warfare-an-interview-with-ruth-wilson-gilmore.

Gorz, André. *Strategy for Labor: A Radical Proposal.* Beacon, 1967.

Graeber, David. *Direct Action: An Ethnography.* AK Press, 2009.

Hales, Anna. "Beyond Borders: How Principles of Prison Abolition Can Shape the Future of Immigration Reform." *UC Irvine Law Review*, vol. 11, no. 5, 2021, pp. 1415–1440.

Heynen, Nik, and Megan Ybarra. "Abolition Ecology and Making "Freedom as a Place."" *Antipode*, vol. 53, no. 1, Jan. 2021, pp. 21–35.

Jones, Claudia. "An End to the Neglect of the Problems of the Negro Woman!" *Political Affairs*, June 1949, pp. 3–19.

King, Natasha. *No Borders: The Politics of Immigration Control and Resistance.* Pluto, 2016.

Klemko, Robert, and John Sullivan. "The push to remake policing takes decades, only to begin again." *Washington Post*, 10 June 2021, https://www.washingtonpost.com/investigations/interactive/2021/police-reform-failure/.

Lewis, David Levering. *W.E.B. Du Bois: The Fight for Equality and the American Century, 1919–1963.* Henry Holt, 2000.

Marx, Karl. "Address of the International Working Men's Association to Abraham Lincoln, President of the United States of America." *Marxists Internet Archive*, https://www.marxists.org/archive/marx/iwma/documents/1864/lincoln-letter.htm.

Marx, Karl and Friedrich Engels. "Manifesto of the Communist Party." Translated by Samuel Moore, *Marxists Internet Archive*, https://www.marxists.org/archive/marx/works/download/pdf/Manifesto.pdf.

Moraga, Cherríe, and Gloria Anzaldúa. *This Bridge Called My Back: Writings By Radical Women of Color,* 4th ed., SUNY Press, 2015.

Purnell, Derecka. *Becoming Abolitionists: Police, Protests, and the Pursuit of Freedom.* Penguin Random House, 2021.

Quinn, Lester. "Whose democracy in which state?: Abolition democracy from Angela Davis to W. E. B. Du Bois." "Freedom Dreaming Symposium" and Special Issue on Black Lives Matter, special issue of *Social Sciences Quarterly,* vol. 102, no. 7, Dec. 2021, pp. 3051–3169.

Salter, Mark. "Places everyone! Studying the performativity of the border." "Interventions on Rethinking the Border," edited by Corey Johnson, et al. *Political Geography,* vol. 30, no. 2, 2011, pp. 61–69.

Sharma, Nandita Rani. *Home Economics: Nationalism and the Making of 'Migrant Workers' in Canada.* University of Toronto Press, 2006.

Smith, Barbara. *How We Get Free: Black Feminism and the Combahee River Collective,* edited by Keeanga-Yamahtta Taylor. Haymarket, 2017.

Squire, Vicki. "Welcome to City Plaza, Athens: a new approach to housing refugees." *The Conversation,* 16 Aug. 2016, https://theconversation.com/welcome-to-city-plaza-athens-a-new-approach-to-housing-refugees-63904.

"39 Months City Plaza: The End of an Era, The Beginning of a New One." *The Best Hotel in Europe,* https://best-hotel-in-europe.eu.

Ullah, Faiz. "Tihar Jail's Increased Use of Prison-Private Partnerships is a Cause for Worry." *Scroll.in,* 18 Sept. 2014, https://scroll.in/article/679669/tihar-jails-increased-use-of-prison-private-partnerships-is-a-cause-for-worry.

Walia, Harsha. *Undoing Border Imperialism.* AK Press, 2013.

Index[1]

A

Abolish Frontex, 231n5
Abolition, 3, 5, 17, 21, 114, 127, 131, 174, 218, 225–230, 234n7, 235–240, 240n12, 242–246
Abolition Democracy, 21, 225–246, 234n7, 244n18
Activist(s)
  activism, 107, 232
Adotey, Edem, 84, 85, 89
Afghanistan, 2n3, 28, 43, 47, 73, 82, 109, 110, 112, 122n13, 153
Agamben, Giorgio, 230, 231
Ai Weiwei, 17, 141–174, 142n1, 192
Alameddine, Rabih, 16, 17, 116–127, 117n9, 136, 137
Amazon, 156, 156n15, 171
  Amazon Studios, 156, 171
Anzaldúa, Gloria, 133, 198n11, 201n16, 217, 243

Apple, 184, 194
Arulpragasam, Mathangi
  "Maya," 19, 179
  See also M.I.A
Asian Dub Foundation, 2n3
Asylum, 2, 2n3, 6, 9–11, 28, 34, 61, 62, 98, 108, 113, 120, 122n14, 125, 126n16, 127, 147n7, 149n8, 155, 228–230

B

"Bajo el Puente/Under the Bridge," 20, 202–209
Balibar, Étienne, 82, 83, 86, 228
Betts, Alexander, 74–76, 97
Biden, Joe, 11n13, 28, 202, 202n17, 229, 229n4
Black Lives Matter, 111n6
Black Reconstruction, 234

---

[1] Note: Page numbers followed by 'n' refer to notes.

© The Author(s), under exclusive license to Springer Nature Switzerland AG 2023
K. Chowdhury, *Border Rules*, Politics of Citizenship and Migration,
https://doi.org/10.1007/978-3-031-26216-6

251

252 INDEX

Black Reconstruction in America: An Essay Toward a History of the Part Which Black Folk Played in the Attempt to Reconstruct Democracy in America, 1860–1880, 234
Bolsonaro, Jair, 44, 229
Border abolition, 5, 92, 141
Border Industrialization Program (BIP), 200
"Borders," 1–22, 179–218
Borderscapes, 84–88, 115, 125, 130, 193
Bracero Program, 49, 200
Branson, Richard, 27, 29–31, 35, 36, 147
Brexit, 9, 32, 33
Bush, George W., 43, 121, 122

C

Capital, 1, 3, 4, 7, 12, 14, 15, 17, 22, 27, 33–36, 41n15, 43–53, 50n24, 55–64, 57n31, 58n32, 71, 73, 75–78, 81n15, 83, 87, 89, 90, 92, 96–100, 107, 108, 110, 115, 129, 137, 147, 171, 174, 182, 191, 194, 200, 209, 228–230, 235–241, 241n13
  accumulation, 1, 3, 4, 14, 16, 31, 48, 52–54, 71, 97, 98, 107, 226, 239
Capital, 1, 81n15
Capitalism, 13n16, 41n15, 50n24, 52, 53, 56–58, 57n31, 58n32, 64, 74, 80, 84n16, 87, 93n21, 98n23, 99–101, 115, 131n19, 155, 174, 193, 229, 232, 235, 240, 242n16, 243–245, 244n18
Caracol Industrial Plant, 77, 78
Cardenas, Christian, 20, 212, 215
  See also LxsDos
Cardenas, Ramon, 215–217
  See also LxsDos

Chacón, Justin Akers, 16, 98–101, 200n13, 201
Chicanx, 212
China, 46, 46n22, 50n25, 54, 141
Christianity, 120
Ciudad Juárez, 19, 20, 64, 198–218, 198n10, 200n15, 201n16, 203n18, 216n26
Cohen, Andy, 142
Colectivo REZIZTE, 203, 203n18
Collier, Paul, 74–76, 97
Colonialism, 235
Communist Manifesto, 226
Conlon, Deirdre, 241
Corporations, 35, 76, 78, 194, 241n13
COVID-19, 11n14, 46n21, 126n16, 202n17
Crisis, 2n3, 12–14, 13n16, 27, 46, 47, 63, 64, 73–76, 108, 109, 109n3, 111n6, 113, 130, 131n19, 133, 142, 145, 148, 151, 151n10, 152, 153n11, 154, 154n12, 171, 172, 184, 189, 193, 195–197, 225, 226, 230–232

D

Davis, Angela, 21, 234n7, 238–240, 241n13, 242n15, 245
Defamiliarization, 136, 145, 146
De Genova, Nicholas, 60, 62n34, 111n6, 196
Democracy, 12, 55, 74, 110, 173, 193, 228, 230, 234, 235, 238, 240
Detention Economies, 241
Development politics, 4, 55, 59, 77, 78
Discrimination, 78, 90, 120, 155, 196
Displacement, 13, 13n16, 17, 43, 54, 111, 115, 126, 133, 143, 148, 156, 157, 232

INDEX 253

Dispossession, 50, 54, 57, 63, 81, 128, 232, 244n17
Du Bois, W.E.B., 21, 80, 81, 230, 234–240, 234n7, 235n8, 239n11, 242–244, 244n18, 246

E
El Paso, 19, 20, 179–218
Engels, Friedrich, 226
European Union (EU), 8, 37, 100, 155, 184
Exploitation, 5, 12, 14, 20, 30, 33, 45, 45n19, 47, 49, 50n24, 56, 60–62, 62n34, 72, 75–79, 95, 96, 98, 99, 99n24, 99n25, 101, 107, 110–112, 115, 129, 132, 136, 156, 167, 173, 174, 198, 206, 226, 232, 234, 237, 240, 241, 244n18

F
Fascism, 235
"Failed state," 72–82
Femicide, 216n26
    on the U.S.-Mexico border, 200n15
Feminism, 243, 244
"Fortress Europe," 2n3, 94, 113
Frontex, 11

G
Gaza Strip, 146n6
Gender and sexuality, 243
    gender violence, 200n15
Genocide, 184, 192
Gentrification, 210, 240
Gilmore, Ruth Wilson, 21, 237n10, 238, 240, 241, 244, 245
Globalization, 64, 94, 95, 98, 156
Global North, 29, 32
Global raciality, 71, 79–82

Global South, 4, 8, 12, 15, 30, 34, 35, 37, 43, 45, 49, 50, 54, 54n30, 55, 57–59, 61, 72, 74, 79, 108, 110–112, 151, 160n22, 191, 231
Guatemala, 27, 28, 54, 54n30, 74, 157–161, 160n22, 163, 168, 172n34

H
Haiti, 28, 28n2, 29, 59, 74–79
Harris, Kamala, 27–29, 31, 35, 36
Hemstra, Nancy, 241
Herrera, Yuri, 127
Honeypot state, 75
Hope Border Institute, 203
Human Flow, 17, 18, 141–174, 146n5, 192
Human rights
    abuses, 173
    discourse, 3, 55

I
Immigration and Customs Enforcement (ICE), 10, 39, 61, 91, 101, 156n15
Imperialism, 14, 16, 27–64, 71, 73, 155, 180, 192, 235
Indigenous peoples, 51n26, 244n17
Internally displaced persons (IDP), 50
Iraq, 2n3, 28, 41, 43, 73, 82, 109, 109n2, 110, 149, 150, 152
Israel, 8, 13, 42, 42n17, 44

J
James, C. L. R., 245

K
Kafala system, 189, 189n7
King, Martin Luther, Jr., 42–44

254 INDEX

King, Natasha, 233, 234, 238
Kurdi, Aylan, 121, 144n4, 191

L
Labor discipline, 3, 48
Ladino identity, 168
La Jaula de Oro/The Golden Dream,
 17, 18, 141–174, 197
Lesbos, 16, 17, 116–118, 117n10,
 122, 124
Liberation Tigers of Tamil Eelam
 (LTTE), 185, 185n5
Loach, Ken, 160, 160n21
Loveridge, Steve, 183
LxsDos, 20, 212
 See also Cardenas, Christian;
 Cardenas, Ramon

M
Maquiladoras, 47, 63, 200, 200n14,
 201, 243
Marx, Karl, 1, 1n1, 34, 35, 48, 51–54,
 59, 80, 81, 81n15, 226,
 235, 235n8
Matangi/Maya/M.I.A., 179, 183, 184
Mbembe, Achille, 55, 56
Mediterranean Sea, 41
Mendoza, Jorge Perez, 20, 203, 207
 See also Yorch
Mexico, 2, 5, 8, 10, 18, 93, 99, 100,
 136, 153, 158–160, 160n22,
 172, 172n34, 173n35, 198n10,
 199n12, 200, 200n15, 202–204,
 203n18, 205n20, 207, 209,
 209n21, 211, 214, 215,
 216n26
M.I.A., 19, 179–218, 180n1, 181n2,
 184n3, 189n8
 See also Arulpragasam,
 Mathangi "Maya"

Migrants, 1–7, 9–14, 9n9, 9n11,
 12n15, 16, 18, 19, 28–32, 34,
 36, 42, 49, 50n25, 51, 55, 56,
 60, 62–64, 71, 73–75, 77–80, 83,
 86, 88, 89, 97–99, 99n26, 101,
 107–114, 111n6, 116, 120, 121,
 127, 141–174, 155n13, 158n17,
 160n22, 168n29, 173n35, 180,
 181, 184, 185, 187–191, 189n6,
 189n8, 193, 195–197, 200,
 200n14, 202–204, 202n17,
 203n18, 211, 217, 226, 227,
 231, 232, 241, 242, 245n19, 246
Migrants Protection Protocol
 (MPP), 10
Migration, 8, 10, 13n16, 17, 18, 28,
 29, 49–51, 50n25, 59n33, 60,
 74, 75, 79, 95–97, 101,
 111–114, 127n18, 134, 142,
 154–158, 167, 169, 172, 179,
 180, 193, 196, 207, 233,
 233n6, 246
Militarization of the U.S.-Mexico
 Border, 9
Modi, Narender, 44, 51n27, 229
Mural art, 19, 179–218,
 203n18, 211n24
Myanmar, 4, 13, 44, 45, 100, 109

N
NAFTA, 200
Nationalism, 7, 9, 44, 83, 155, 180,
 188, 231, 232, 244
9/11, 84
 post-9/11, 35, 121
No Borders Network, 231n5
No Borders politics, 228, 230,
 232–234, 238, 244, 245
Non-governmental organization
 (NGO), 8, 12, 17, 76, 84, 84n16,
 112, 116, 117, 122, 156n14

Non-refoulement, 122n14
No One is Illegal, 231n5
North American Free Trade
    Agreement (NAFTA)
North Atlantic Treaty Organization
    (NATO), 40

O

Obama, Barack, 10, 73, 172
Ocasio-Cortez, Alexandria, 28
Oppression, 44, 80, 115, 119, 173,
    183, 232, 234, 240
Orban, Viktor, 10n12, 229

P

Palestine, 8, 40, 47
El Plan, 210n22
Postcolonial, 45, 46, 57, 58, 63, 80,
    85, 111, 111n6, 197
Primitive accumulation, 4, 15, 47–64,
    52n28, 57n31
Prison abolition, 240
Prison industrial complex (PIC),
    237, 240–242
Protest, 107, 126n16, 141–157, 199,
    201, 203n18, 246
Public Law 613, 39, 40n10
Pueblos Sin Fronteras, 231n5
Purnell, Derecka, 242n16, 244

Q

Quemada-Díez, Diego, 17, 18,
    141–174, 159n20, 160n21,
    160n22, 165n25, 169n30

R

Race, 12, 14, 16, 17, 27–64, 72–82,
    80n14, 101, 111–113, 111n6,
    115, 120, 122n14, 137, 150,

174, 196, 198, 225, 230, 235,
    242, 242n16, 243
discrimination, 78, 196
Raciality, 71, 79–82
Refoulement, 122n14
Refugee(s)
    camps, 2n3, 56, 62, 62n34,
        117n10, 122, 125, 126n16,
        142, 147n7, 148, 154,
        195, 195n9
    crisis, 2n3, 13, 47, 63, 75,
        97, 108, 109, 148, 171, 189,
        230, 231
Refusal, 5, 5n6, 21, 48, 92, 110,
    111n6, 114, 131, 132, 137,
    217, 225–246
Religion, 80, 120, 122n14, 137,
    150, 230
Rio Grande, 205n20, 207
Rohingya, 4, 44, 109, 154,
    155n13

S

Sanyal, Kalyan, 55–59, 58n32, 62
Saudi Arabia, 33, 75, 79
El Segundo Barrio, 20, 209–211,
    209n21, 216, 216n26
*Señales que precederán al fin del
    mundo/Signs Preceding the
    End of the World*, 16,
    17, 107–137
Sexual violence, 3n4, 183
Sharma, Nandita, 230, 231
"Sister Cities/Ciudades
    Hermanas," 209–218
Social death, 58, 241, 242, 246
Sri Lanka, 33, 183, 185
Surplus population, 15, 35,
    47–64, 110
Syria, 2n3, 9, 43, 47, 73, 119,
    126, 150
war in Syria, 9

256 INDEX

T

Taliban, 73, 109, 109n5, 126n16
Tamils
    oppression in Sri Lanka, 183
Terrorism, 41, 84, 180, 184, 185
Title 42, 11n13, 28, 201,
    202, 202n17
Trump, Donald, 33, 73, 184,
    201, 229
2010 earthquake in Haiti, 77
Tzotzil Maya, 161

U

United Arab Emirates, 189,
    189n6
United Kingdom, 59, 184, 185
United Nations (UN), 108, 146n6,
    151, 156n14, 183
United Nations High Commissioner
    for Refugees (UNHCR), 14n17,
    27n1, 50, 108n1, 116n8, 124,
    147n7, 155
United Nations Refugee Convention
    (1951), 150
United States, 2, 8–10, 11n13, 11n14,
    12n15, 28, 29, 29n3, 33, 34n7,
    36, 37, 39–44, 41n15, 42n17,
    47, 49, 60, 61, 73, 75, 78, 81,
    82, 91, 93, 93n21, 94, 98–100,
    98n23, 99n25, 111, 127,
    127n18, 136, 150, 153, 154n12,
    158, 158n18, 158n19, 159n20,

160, 161, 163, 167, 168n29,
    171n33, 172, 172n34, 173, 181,
    181n2, 196, 198n10, 200–204,
    200n14, 205n20, 207, 209,
    209n21, 210, 211n23, 214,
    216n26, 234, 235, 241,
    241n13, 242
U.S.-Mexico border, 8–14, 9n9, 17,
    20, 28, 30, 47, 48, 77, 78, 92,
    93n20, 98, 99, 127n18, 153,
    154, 158, 166n27, 173, 198,
    217, 218n27
Uyghurs, 13

W

Walia, Harsha, 16, 73, 96–101, 246
War against Terror, 180
The Wrong End of the Telescope, 16, 17,
    107–137, 145, 156

X

Xi Jinping, 44

Y

Yorch, 20, 203, 204
    See also Mendoza, Jorge Perez

Z

Zimanyi, Eszter, 144, 152

Printed in the United States
by Baker & Taylor Publisher Services